Diaspora, Development and Distress

Diaspora, Development and Distress

Indians in the Persian Gulf

Edited by
Ajaya Kumar Sahoo

RAWAT PUBLICATIONS
Jaipur • New Delhi • Bangalore • Hyderabad • Guwahati • Kolkata

ISBN 978-81-316-0687-2

Published by
Prem Rawat for **Rawat Publications**
Satyam Apts, Sector 3, Jawahar Nagar, Jaipur 302 004 (India)
Phone: 0141 265 1748 / 7006 Fax: 0141 265 1748
E-mail: info@rawatbooks.com
Website: www.rawatbooks.com

New Delhi Office
4858/24, Ansari Road, Daryaganj, New Delhi 110 002
Phone: 011 2326 3290

Also at *Bangalore, Hyderabad, Guwahati* and *Kolkata*

Typeset by Rawat Computers, Jaipur

Printed at Chaman Enterprises, New Delhi

Contents

Part II: Diaspora and Connections

Part III: Development and Change

Part IV: Migration and Distress

List of Tables

List of Abbreviations

BBC	British Broadcasting Corporation
BC	Backward Castes
BMET	Bureau of Manpower, Employment and Training
BOP	Balance of Payments
BPL	Below Poverty Line
CDS	Centre for Development Studies
CEDAW	Committee on the Elimination of Discrimination Against Women
CHR	Commission on Human Rights
CPI	Communist Party of India
ECNR	Emigration Check Not Required
ECR	Emigration Check Required
GCC	Gulf Cooperation Council
GDP	Gross Domestic Product
GNI	Gross National Income
GOI	Government of India
GOSI	General Organization for Social Insurance
GTWCA	Gulf Telangana Welfare and Cultural Association
HRW	Human Rights Watch

ICCPR	International Covenant on Civil and Political Rights
ICESCR	International Covenant on Economic, Social and Cultural Rights
ICM	India Centre for Migration
ICOE	Indian Council of Overseas Employment
ICWF	Indian Community Welfare Fund
ILO	International Labour Organization
IMDS	International Migration and Diaspora Studies
IOM	International Organization for Migration
ICT	Information and Communication Technology
IT	Information Technology
IWRC	Indian Workers Resource Centres
KALA	Kuwait Arts Lovers Association
KMCC	Kerala Muslim Cultural Centre
KMS	Kerala Migration Survey
KOC	Kuwait Oil Company
KSA	Kingdom of Saudi Arabia
KTMCC	Kuwait Town Malayalee Christian Congregation
LMRA	Labour Market Regulation Authority
MENA	Middle East and North Africa
MFA	Migrant Forum in Asia
MGPSY	Mahatma Gandhi Pravasi Suraksha Yojana
MNE	Ministry of National Economy
MOA	Memorandum of Agreement
MOIA	Ministry of Overseas Indian Affairs
MOU	Memorandum of Understanding
MPI	Migration Policy Institute
MRCs	Migrant Resource Centres
MSC	Migrant Services Centre
NECK	National Evangelical Church of Kuwait
NGO	Nongovernmental Organization
NRI	Non-Resident Indian
NRK	Non-Resident Keralite
NSDP	Net State Domestic Product
NSS	National Sample Survey

OMCAP	Overseas Manpower Company Andhra Pradesh Ltd.
OWRC	Overseas Workers Resource Centre
PBBY	Pravasi Bharatiya Bima Yojana
PGE	Protector General of Emigrants
PIO	Persons of Indian Origin
PLIF	Pension and Life-insurance Fund
POE	Protector of Emigrants
RBI	Reserve Bank of India
RMI	Return Emigrants
RNS	Relief Net Service
SC	Syrian Christian
SNDP	Sree Narayana Dharma Paripalana Yogam
ST	Scheduled Tribe
UAE	United Arab Emirates
UGC	University Grants Commission
UN	United Nations
UNCTAD	United Nations Conference on Trade and Development
UNDESA	United Nations Department of Economic and Social Affairs
UNDP	United Nations Development Programme
UNFPA	United Nations Population Fund
UNODC	United Nations Office on Drugs and Crimes
WHO	World Health Organization
WTO	World Trade Organization

Acknowledgements

This volume is the culmination of the International Conference titled 'Development or Distress: 21st Century Indian Immigrants in the Persian Gulf', which was held at the University of Hyderabad during 11–12 March 2013. I would like to acknowledge and thank all the contributors of this volume who have cooperated in sending their revised papers on time without which this volume would not have been possible. I also thank Professor Binod Khadria and Professor S. Irudaya Rajan for giving permission to reprint their chapters in this volume.

I would like to thank Professor Ramakrishna Ramaswamy, the Vice Chancellor; Professor E. Haribabu, the Pro-Vice Chancellor and Professor Aloka Parasher Sen, the Dean, School of Social Sciences of the University of Hyderabad for their encouragement and support in organizing the conference. I would also like to thank all the administrative staffs of the University of Hyderabad for their cooperation in making this conference successful.

I thank my colleague Dr Amit Mishra for his friendly support throughout. Without the cooperation of the students (MPhil and Ph.D. students) of the Centre, this conference would have been difficult to organize. Special thanks go to all the students of the Centre.

I would like to thank the following funding agencies that supported this conference financially: Centre for the Study of Indian Diaspora (UGC Area Studies Programme), University of Hyderabad; Indian Council of Social Science Research (ICSSR), New Delhi; and the University with Potential for Excellence (UPE Phase II) of University of Hyderabad.

I would like to thank Mr Pranit Rawat of Rawat Publications for his guidance and support in bringing out the volume in time.

Ajaya Kumar Sahoo

Contributors

Binod Khadria is Professor of Economics at the Zakir Husain Centre for Educational Studies, School of Social Sciences, Jawaharlal Nehru University, New Delhi, and Director of the International Migration and Diaspora Studies (IMDS) Project. His published works include the widely acclaimed *The Migration of Knowledge Workers: Second-generation Effects of India's Brain Drain* (Sage, 1999), and several research papers published by the ILO, OECD, IRD-France, Institute of Developing Economies – Japan External Trade Organization (IDE–JETRO), Harvard International Review, Global Commission on International Migration (GCIM), etc. Professor Khadria has been a Fulbright and a Times Fellow, and a visiting professor at leading universities in various countries. He sits on the Steering Committees and Advisory Boards of both national and international bodies and is a member of the editorial boards of several international journals and encyclopaedias. With *India Migration Report 2009: Past, Present and the Future Outlook*, he launched the IMR series, followed by *India Migration Report 2010–2011: The Americas*, published in 2012 by Cambridge University Press, New York.

S. Irudaya Rajan is Chair Professor, Ministry of Overseas Indian Affairs Research Unit on International Migration at the Centre for Development Studies (CDS), Thiruvananthapuram. He has coordinated six migration surveys in Kerala since 1998 (with Professor K.C. Zachariah) and the Goa Migration Survey 2008, and have been instrumental in organizing the Gujarat, Punjab and Tamil Nadu migration surveys, and also published extensively in national and international journals on social, economic and demographic implications on international migration. He is editor of the annual series, 'India Migration Report', and also Editor-in-Chief of the international journal *Migration and Development* (Routledge).

D. Narayana is Professor at the Centre for Development Studies, Thiruvananthapuram, Kerala. His research interests include decentralization, migration, marginalized social groups, population and health.

Basant Potnuru is a Research Officer and Head Projects In-charge at India Centre for Migration (ICM), New Delhi. His areas of research interest are Gulf migration, gender issues on international migration and migration and health. Prior to joining ICM, he was a faculty of Economics at the Department of Management, Invertis University, Bareilly, Uttar Pradesh.

Vishishta Sam is a Research Assistant at India Centre for Migration (ICM), New Delhi, and is currently working on the UN Women and Gulf Migration Project. Prior to joining ICM, she completed an internship at UN Women South Asia Sub Regional Office with the Ending Violence against Women Unit and worked as a student consultant with Voluntary Service Overseas (VSO), UK. She has been associated with NGOs/development Think Tanks over the past 5–6 years and several internship stints with organizations such as Human Rights Law Network, Centre for Civil Society, Centre for Public Policy Research and Institute for Human Development.

Marie Percot is anthropologist. She is affiliated with the Institut Interdisciplinaire d'Anthropologie du Contemporain (French National Council for Scientific Research/EHESS, Paris). Her main research fields are anthropology of labour and anthropology of migration. She has carried long-term research on female migration from India, more particularly on migration of nurses to Gulf countries. Lately, she has started to work in Bangladesh on environmentally led migration. Among her last publications in English is *Dynamics of Indian Migration: Historical and Currents Perspectives*, co-edited with S. Irudaya Rajan (Routledge, 2011).

Ginu Zacharia Oommen is a Junior Fellow at the Nehru Memorial Museum and Library (NMML), Teen Murti House, New Delhi, and

Associate Fellow at MIGRINTER, Universite de Poitiers, France. Earlier, he was a Hermes Post-Doctoral Fellow at MIGRINTER, Universite of Poitiers, France, and an Associate Fellow at the Fondation Maison des Sciences de l'Homme (FMSH), Paris. He was Research Fellow at the Indian Council of World Affairs, New Delhi, and Visiting Faculty at the Gulf Studies Programme, School of International Studies, Jawaharlal Nehru University (JNU), New Delhi.

Sandhya Rao Mehta is presently in the Department of English Language and Literature at Sultan Qaboos University, Oman. She has a PhD in the literature of the Indian diaspora and is presently working on projects revolving around the Indian diaspora in Oman. She has also worked on English Language Teaching (ELT) and has co-edited an anthology entitled *Language Studies: Stretching the Boundaries* published by Cambridge Scholars Press. She has presented papers as well as published research on oral narratives of Indian women in Oman and the contribution of the Indian community in the changing landscape of the city of Muscat.

Anisur Rahman is currently Associate Professor cum Deputy Director, Academic Staff College, Jamia Millia Islamia, New Delhi. Before joining Jamia, he has also worked at Institute of Applied Manpower Research, Planning Commission, Government of India. His areas of interest and specialization include migration and diaspora; issues of minorities and staff development and higher education. He has published five books: *Indian Migration to the Gulf: A Socio-Economic Analysis* (2001); *Contesting Homogeneity in the Gulf Society* (2008); *Human Rights and Social Security: Perspective, Issues and Challenges* (edited, 2011), *Discoursing Minority: In-Text and Co-Text* (co-edited, 2014) and *West Asia in Transition* (edited, *forthcoming*). He also has about 30 research papers to his credit. He has been visiting fellow at Maison des Sciences de l'Homme (MSH), Paris, France.

Ajmal Khan is a PhD candidate at the Tata Institute of Social Sciences, Mumbai. He is particularly interested in the Muslim question in India and their overall developments. He is also interested in the question of marginalities of dalits, tribals and women. He was awarded TISS-Max Plank Institute Fellowship and also contributes to the alternative media forums in English and Malayalam on contemporary issues.

Naresh Kumar is currently Assistant Professor in Centre for Diaspora Studies, Central University of Gujarat, Gandhinagar. He did his MA, MPhil and PhD from Centre for the Study of Regional Development

(CSRD), Jawaharlal Nehru University (JNU), New Delhi. His areas of research interest are internal/international migration, Indian diaspora, demography, regional development, regional geography and research tools and techniques. He has attended various national/international conferences in India and abroad. He has published several papers in journals related to his research area. He is a member of various national and international organizations/agencies such as the Population Association of America (PAA), International Union of Scientific Study of Population (IUSSP), Asian Population Association (APA), GOPIO, Royal Geographical Society (RGB) London, IIPS (International Institute of Population Sciences), ISLE and IASP.

Habibul Haque Khondker is a Professor at the Department of Humanities and Social Sciences of Zayed University, Abu Dhabi. Previously he taught at the National University of Singapore. Khondker studied in University of Pittsburgh, Carleton University, Ottawa, and University of Dhaka, Bangladesh. Khondker held visiting professorship at the United Nations University, Tokyo. His current research is on governance of labour migration in the UAE and expatriates. Khondker has co-authored *Globalization: East and West* (Sage, 2010) with Bryan Turner; and co-edited *21st Century Globalization: Perspectives from the Gulf* (2010) with J.N. Pieterse and *Asia and Europe in Globalization* (Brill, 2006) with Goran Therborn.

Mehraj Jahan received her PhD from the University of Pittsburgh, USA. She is an Adjunct Professor at Zayed University. Previously, Dr Jahan taught at the National University of Singapore. Her current research is on women's education in Bangladesh and female migration in the United Arab Emirates. She has been a coordinator of NAW, an NGO dedicated to securing rights and well-being of women in Bangladesh. In her early career, Dr Jahan worked for the UNICEF, Bangladesh. She is also involved in voluntary activities aimed at the welfare of women and children.

Ajaya Kumar Sahoo is an Assistant Professor and Director of the Centre for the Study of Indian Diaspora, University of Hyderabad. His areas of research interests comprise international migration, South Asian diaspora, transnationalism, religion and ageing. Some of his publications include *Indian Transnationalism Online: New Perspectives on Diaspora,* co-edited with Johannes Kruijf (Ashgate, 2014); *Indian Diaspora and Transnationalism,* co-edited with Michiel Baas and Thomas Faist (Rawat, 2012); *Tracing an Indian Diaspora: Context,*

Memories, Representations, co-edited with Parvati Raghuram, Brij Maharaj, Dave Sangha (Sage, 2008); *Sociology of Diaspora: A Reader*, co-edited with Brij Maharaj (Rawat, 2007).

Trilok Chandan Goud is a PhD Research Scholar at the Centre for Study of Indian Diaspora, University of Hyderabad, India. His areas of research include understanding the nature and dynamics of changing diasporic communities in general and of Indian diasporic communities in particular. He is currently working on 'Return Migration from Gulf Countries to Andhra Pradesh'.

Chitra Natrajan has recently been awarded her PhD degree from the Centre for West Asian Studies, Jawaharlal Nehru University, New Delhi. Her areas of research interest include international migration and Indian diaspora. She has presented papers in many national seminars and international conferences about the Indian labourers in the Gulf countries, mainly focusing on their working and living conditions, policies governing the migration process and protection, current trends and patterns of international migration and human rights situation in the Gulf countries.

Introduction

Indian Immigrants in the Persian Gulf

Ajaya Kumar Sahoo

This volume mainly addresses the issue of international migration of Indians to the Persian Gulf countries in the era of globalization and transnational migrations. All the contributors in the volume examine the diverse areas in which the Indian immigrant communities in the Gulf countries face including their issues and concerns after returning to the homeland. By way of doing this, the majority of chapters also touch upon the migrant policy issues of the home country as well as the host countries. The volume mainly addresses three themes: diaspora, development and distress. The chapters are divided into four sections: the first section gives the background on migration policy of the Gulf countries and the country of origin including the recent economic crisis and its impact on the migrant labourers; the second section discusses an emerging issue in the present context, that is, the issue of diaspora and networks; the third section addresses the issue of development and social change; and the fourth and final section discusses the consequences of international migration on migrants and their families back home.

International migration is not a new phenomenon for the globe-trotting Indians who today constitute more than 25 millions living in different countries around the world. After India became independent, the first wave of Indian migration took place to the United States,

United Kingdom, Canada and Australia and with smaller scale to Western Europe; this flow began in the early 1950s and continued until mid-1970s. The second wave of migration took place to the Middle East, especially to oil-exporting countries broadening the Persian Gulf, the six countries belonging to the Gulf Cooperation Council (GCC)—the United Arab Emirates (UAE), Saudi Arabia, Oman, Kuwait, Bahrain and Qatar. Although Indian migration to the Persian Gulf started as early as 1930s after oil was discovered in the region (Khadria 2006; Pradhan 2010), it was in the early 1970s that the large-scale migration took place as a result of the price hike of oil and the consequent earnings of large revenues accelerated the process of industrialization and social change in the GCC states characterized by massive investment in social and economic infrastructure necessitating the service of large number of foreign workers.

The migration to the Gulf countries started with few thousands per year during the middle of 1970s and assumed large proportions during the 1980s and 1990s. Migration from India mainly took place from the states such as Kerala, Tamil Nadu, Andhra Pradesh, Karnataka, Punjab, Goa, Delhi and Gujarat. Migration from Kerala only accounts for about more than 50 per cent of the total stock of Indian migrants in the Gulf, Tamil Nadu ranks second, followed by Andhra Pradesh, Karnataka, Uttar Pradesh and Punjab (Prakash 1998; Zachariah et al. 2002).

Migration of Indians to the Gulf countries is not only influenced by economic factors, but also by many other factors such as caste, religion and geographical location. The lower castes and tribes had a greater propensity to migrate, and many of them migrated for short-term; they are low skilled and low paid workers with the highest levels of vulnerability and the lowest level of social protection. Although the literature on Indians in the Persian Gulf is overwhelmed with the economic contribution of Indians to the homeland in the form of remittances, the reality is that the majority of the immigrants, especially under the unskilled and semi-skilled categories, do not earn enough of money either to maintain a decent living in the host country or to sustain their family back home, let alone contributing towards economic development of the homeland. They face discrimination in getting salaries and sometimes they are ill-treated by their owners. They have to live in the labourers' camps, which are in some cases located near to the workplaces and in other cases they are located in isolated places far away from the workplaces. The difficulty in accommodation, food and salary is not an end to the miseries of migrants. Migrants with a tourist visa in the Gulf countries face severe hardships than other migrants as they are treated illegal once their visa period expires, which resulted in severe punishments, deportation or being sent to jail. The social and economic impact on the returnees and their families back home is further complicated once they return from the Gulf without major savings. They also do not get significant support from the government in order to rehabilitate in their local settings. This volume addresses some of these issues.

Diaspora, Development and Distress

This section outlines the chapters included in the volume. All the chapters in the volume share the common themes: diaspora, development, and distress. The chapters show that the Gulf countries do not have a uniform policy towards the migrant workers. While some countries in the GCC are concerned more towards immigrant workers and their safety during their stays by implementing different policies, others are more strict in terms of imposing rigorous working culture. However, despite all these stricture immigrant policies, Indians in the GCC countries have developed a diasporic life that can stretch beyond the homeland and host societies by connecting their links through further migration to other countries, thereby producing a transnational community in the making. As Khachig Tololyan (2007: 23) rightly pointed out, today the term 'diaspora' has extended its scope by sharing 'meanings with a larger semantic domain that includes words like immigrant, expatriate, refugee, guest-worker, exile community, overseas community, ethnic community'.

The first chapter by Binod Khadria in Section I outlines the different policies of the GCC countries. He argues that the Gulf economic crisis and the Iraqi invasion of Kuwait in the early 1990s led to the significant changes in the demographic composition of the Gulf, especially in Kuwait and Saudi Arabia. This has resulted—on the one hand—in large-scale return migration to the home country, while—on the other hand—it led all 'major labour importing countries to consciously introduce policies of indigenization of their labour force'. The chapter evaluates the different policies of the Gulf countries and its impact on the labour migration in the present context. Discussing the Gulf economic crisis and its impact on South Asian labour migration, S. Irudaya Rajan and D. Narayana in their chapter analyse how the migrant workers cope up with the crisis in their destination countries and how this has impacted back home especially on the remittances and return migration. The chapter is based on the large-scale survey conducted by the Centre for Development Studies (CDS), Trivandrum. There has been a steady increase in the recent trend of women's migration to the Gulf countries. Basant Potnuru and Vishishta Sam in their chapter examine the challenges that the women face in the process of migration and trace the causes for this challenge. They also highlight the important policy initiatives taken by the national and state governments in the context of women migrant workers.

The first chapter in the Section II by Marie Percot discusses the development of a Malayali diaspora in the Gulf countries. According to her, for many migrant nurses and for their husbands, the Gulf countries are now considered as a step for a further migration to the Western countries, which is described in the diaspora literature as 'twice migration' (Bhachu 1985). Migration has induced, for practical as well as symbolical reasons, a redefinition of traditional gender roles. She argues that today the migrant nurses aspire not only to a more lucrative career abroad, but also to a new life style, with more individualistic ambitions, in which in particular traditional gender-based restrictions are challenged, leading to an improved female agency. Ginu Zacharia Oommen's chapter deals with the changing sociocultural strategies of Kerala migrants in Kuwait, including the change in religious practice and the rise of radical religious groups. According to him, the involvement of religion, especially the church, has increased among the Syrian Christian immigrants from India in the post-liberation Kuwait. The chapter explores the reason behind the heightened religious revivalism among Syrian Christian immigrants in Kuwait. Sandhya Mehta's chapter focuses on the Indian diaspora in Oman from a different perspective, that is, the creative and artistic creations of the diaspora. She argues that while the literary achievements of the Indian expatriates in the West have been exhaustively documented, there remains a wide vacuum as far as the Middle East is concerned. This chapter tries to fill that gap by introducing historical narratives of the Indian diaspora in Oman as well as focusing on the contemporary Indian writers, painters, photographers, filmmakers and others to explore the multitudinous ways in which Oman has become a part of the consciousness of the Indian diasporic imagination.

The first chapter in the Section III by Anisur Rahman examines the changing patterns of Indian migration to the Gulf countries and its effect on migrant families back home especially on children's education and overall economic development. The chapter concludes that the Gulf migrations and remittances have a positive impact for the migrant families in particular and the nation in general. More than half of the Gulf migrants from the Kerala belong to the Muslim community, especially from the northern Kerala. Ajmal Khan's chapter shows how migration to the Gulf has made unprecedented social mobility among the Muslims of Kerala, especially in the areas of poverty reduction, educational and economic mobility of the migrant families. The last chapter in this section by Naresh Kumar outlines the recent trends and patterns of Indian migration to the Gulf countries and examines the role of migrant remittances. He argues that the remittances sent by migrants to their families not only help them to escape from abject poverty but also fuel economic growth of the country.

The fourth and last section of the volume contained three chapters. Habibul Khondker and Mehraj Jahan in their chapter argue that the experience of the migrant domestic workers suggest that they do not only remain passive subjects, due to their class situation, but also exercise a great deal of agency, albeit in a subtle fashion through whatever cultural resources they can muster. The chapter explores how domestic workers often use gender and/or religious solidarity with their employers depending on the circumstances. It concludes that the 'relationship between the domestic workers from South Asia and their employers, mostly female in the context of the UAE, asymmetric as it was, allowed them to mobilise resources such as religion and feminist solidarity to their advantage'. Based on a case study of returnees in Karimnagar district of Andhra Pradesh, Ajaya Kumar Sahoo and Trilok Chandan Goud in their chapter examine the reasons for return migration and coping patterns of returnees. The chapter concludes that extreme poverty, lack of employment opportunities and backwardness of the district led to the large-scale Gulf migration. However, because of the failure of jobs in the Gulf countries, the returnees are commonly called as 'Gulf victims' in their own villages. The chapter highlights some of the policy suggestions to address the problems of Gulf returnees in Andhra Pradesh. Chitra Natrajan's chapter explores the different forms of trafficking of Indian migrants in the Persian Gulf, the factors responsible for it and the socioeconomic background of the vulnerable migrants. It discusses the measures taken by the governments of host and sending countries to prevent trafficking of persons.

References

Bhachu, Parmnder. *Twice Migrants: East African Sikh Settlers in Britain.* London: Tavistock Publications, 1985.

Khadria, B. *India: Skilled Migration to Developed Countries, Labour Migration to the Gulf.* Singapore: Asia Research Institute, National University of Singapore, 2006.

Pradhan, S. 'India and the Gulf Cooperation Council (GCC): An Economic and Political Perspective'. *Strategic Analysis*, 34, 1 (2010): 93–103.

Prakash, B.A. (ed.). *Indian Migration to the Middle East: Trends, Patterns and Socio-Economic Impacts.* Rohtak: Spellbound Publications, 1998.

Tololyan, Khachig. 'The Nation-State and Its Others: In Lieu of a Preface'. pp. 21–27 in Ajaya Kumar Sahoo and Brij Maharaj (eds), *Sociology of Diaspora: A Reader.* New Delhi: Rawat Publications, 2007.

Zachariah, K.C., Prakash, B.A., and Rajan, S.I. 'Gulf Migration Study: Employment, Wages and Working Conditions of Kerala Emigrants in the United Arab Emirates'. Working Paper No. 326, Centre for Development Studies, Trivandrum, 2002.

Part I

Migration Impact and Policy

CHAPTER 1

Middle East Country Policies

Binod Khadria

Migrant 'Hubs' in the Middle East

Besides Europe and the United States (US), the six Gulf Cooperation Council (GCC) countries, namely, Bahrain, Kuwait, Oman, Qatar, Saudi Arabia and the United Arab Emirates (UAE) together make the third most important cluster of 'hubs', as I have elsewhere called the global destinations for migrants within Asia, the Middle East (see Khadria 2010b). This excessively high-immigration geographical region is one where non-nationals were estimated to constitute about 38.6 per cent of the population in 2009 (Table 1.1). Whereas the developed countries of the West are known to be the major importers of high skilled migrants, Middle Eastern countries are known to be the major importers of low or semi-skilled migrant worker prior to the 1970s, the countries in the GCC region maintained a liberal non-selective immigration policy. However, the 'oil boom' of October 1973 significantly affected the dynamics of their policies. The major oil-exporting countries or the GCC countries were earning vast revenues by exporting oil and decided to invest the revenue in major economic and social fields such as infrastructure and power stations, industrial and

First published as IMDS Working Paper No. 41 (December 2011), International Migration and Diaspora Studies Project, ZHCES, JNU, New Delhi. Reprinted by permission of the author.

agricultural sectors, health and education (Winckler 1997). The implementation of these projects, which were highly labour-intensive, resulted in a high demand for labour, both skilled and unskilled workers, in various categories. The demand could not be met locally due to two main factors—small domestic population, worsened in effect by very low rates of labour force participation, both contributing to limited number of workers being available for employment. Consequently, the governments had to look beyond their boundaries and import labour from other countries, mainly those having large populations and high unemployment rates. Although a substantial number of foreigners were already present in the GCC countries, the enhanced demand for labour led to a substantial rise in the inflow of foreign workers. The trend remained the same in the 1970s as well as in the 1980s until the Gulf crisis.

Table 1.1 *Total Population and Estimated Migrant Stock in the Six GCC Countries, 2010*

	Total Population	*Migrant Stock*	*Migrants as % of Total Population*
Bahrain	8,07,000	3,15,403	39.1
Kuwait	30,51,000	20,97,527	68.8
Oman	29,05,000	8,26,074	28.4
Qatar	15,08,000	13,05,428	86.5
Saudi Arabia	2,62,46,000	72,88,900	27.8
United Arab Emirates	47,07,000	32,93,264	70.0
Total	3,92,24,000	1,51,26,596	38.6

Source: United Nations Department of Economic and Social Affairs (UNDESA) (2009a, cited in Shah 2010).

In the early 1980s, the majority of workers in the GCC countries originated from Arab countries but thereafter South and Southeast Asian countries have emerged as the major source countries, or the 'hinterland' (*a la* Khadria 2010b). Out of the 8,49,000 low-skilled workers who went abroad for work in 2008, the highest in a single year in the quinquennial of 2005–2010, 41 per cent went to the UAE and another 27 per cent went to Saudi Arabia. Altogether 96 per cent of Indian low-skilled overseas workers who left India in 2008 moved to the GCC countries. In the closing decades of the twentieth century till 2009, the number of foreign labour steadily increased in the GCC countries. The numbers of foreign workers grew from 1.1 million in

1975 to 2.85 million in 1980, 4.12 million in 1985, 7.04 million in 1995 and 8.5 million in 2000, respectively (ILO 2009a). The share of foreign workers in total labour force was noticeably higher than in the populations, and been rising. In 2000, it was 56 per cent in Saudi Arabia, 59 per cent in Bahrain, 64 per cent in Oman, 81.9 per cent in Kuwait, 86 per cent in Qatar and 89.8 per cent in the UAE (Girgis 2002; Dito 2006). According to the latest United Nations estimates of population, foreign nationals in the Middle East region have been expected to be 15.1 million in 2010 (Table 1.2), up from 12.7 million in 2005, registering 18.8 per cent growth in five years. Between 2000 and 2005, stocks had grown 24.2 per cent. In individual GCC countries, the shares of non-nationals were estimated to have remained constant or increased (Table 1.2).

Table 1.2 *Stocks and Population Shares of Non-nationals in the GCC Countries: 2005, 2010*

Year	*Total*		*% of Total Population*	
	2005	*2010*	*2005*	*2010*
Bahrain	2,78,166	3,15,403	38.2	39.1
Kuwait	18,69,665	20,97,527	69.2	68.8
Oman	6,66,263	8,26,074	25.5	28.4
Qatar	7,12,861	13,05,428	80.5	86.5
Saudi Arabia	63,36,666	72,88,900	26.8	27.8
United Arab Emirates	28,63,027	32,93,364	70.0	70.0
Total	1,27,26,648	1,51,26,696	—	—

Note: Estimated Number of international migrants at mid-year.

Source: UNDESA, Population Division: Trends in International Migrant Stock: The 2008 Revision (May 2009).

The completion of major projects in the late 1980s had led to a fall in demand. The Iraqi invasion of Kuwait in August 1990 resulted in striking demographic changes in the Gulf, especially in Kuwait and Saudi Arabia. The impact of the war was immediately felt when a flight of large number of migrant workers left for their home countries. The ILO estimated that about 2 million expatriate workers left the region as a result of the Gulf crisis (ILO 1991). This was the beginning for major labour importing countries to consciously introduce policies of indigenization of their labour force. However, as the war ended, the reconstruction programmes in Kuwait led to a huge fresh demand for workers. Also a large number of migrant workers, who had fled during the war, returned.

Foreign workers in all the GCC countries have contributed significantly towards the development process. However, as is the case in most labour importing countries, after the completion of the projects, the governments tightened their immigration policies to reduce the number of foreign workers. In spite of such measures, demand for migrant workers in the Middle East remained high as more private projects came up in the construction sector.

A study by the Migration Policy Institute (MPI) and the British Broadcasting Corporation (BBC) also found that immigrants constituted the largest share of the labour force in the Gulf states. Foreign nationals accounted for 90 per cent of the labour force in the UAE, 86 per cent in Qatar, 81 per cent in Kuwait, 71 per cent in Oman, 59 per cent in Bahrain and 50 per cent in Saudi Arabia (UNDESA 2006: 16). More recently, in Kuwait, Qatar and the UAE, the total stocks of non-nationals relative to total populations have particularly been high. As indicated in Table 1.2, estimates for 2010 put their respective shares at 68.8 per cent, 86.5 per cent, and 70 per cent. In contrast, nationals from other Arab countries did not grow proportionately in GCC countries. Whereas they had represented 72 per cent of stocks in 1975, the proportion declined to 15–29 per cent in 2002. In Kuwait and Saudi Arabia, they dropped from 80 to 34 per cent and from 90 to 37–43 per cent respectively (Kapiszewski 2003). There are various reasons why Asians are preferred over Arabs: (a) the Asian labour force is viewed as more skilled than the Arab; (b) Asians accept lower wages and salaries; (c) they are prepared to live and work in harsh conditions and (d) they are characterized as obedient and easy to manage.

The 'Hinterland' for Migrant Labour in the Middle East Countries

To review and assess the immigration policies in the Middle East countries, it is important to relate them to the major migrant-sending countries, forming the 'hinterland', as I have called the source countries in Asia (Khadria 2010). Asia, namely, India, Pakistan, Bangladesh, Philippines, Sri Lanka and Indonesia, accounts for 60–70 per cent of all contract migrant workers in the Middle East (Kapizewski 2006). Asian workers from these countries now outnumber Arabs, although Egyptians are still present in large numbers in the GCC sub-region (Table 1.3). Girgis had ranked the presence of foreign nationals by

Table 1.3 *Number and Percentage of Foreign Migrant Workers in the Labour Force (LF), in GCC countries, by Nationality, 2005*

	Total	*% of LF*
Bahrain	3,06,000	58.58
Arab	38,000	12.42
Asian	2,45,000	80.07
European	6,000	1.96
American	6,000	1.96
Others	11,000	3.59
Kuwait	13,02,000	81.7
Arab	4,03,000	30.95
Asian	8,51,000	65.36
European	4,000	0.31
American	2,000	0.15
Others	42,000	3.23
Oman	6,05,000	66.13
Arab	34,000	5.61
Asian	5,59,000	92.4
European	—	—
American	—	—
Others	12,000	1.99
Qatar	3,15,034	56.69
Arab	1,26,013	40.07
Asian	1,44,915	45.64
European	5,954	1.99
American	—	—
Others	38,152	12.3
Saudi Arabia	48,94,000	64.57
Arab	15,27,000	31.2
Asian	29,02,000	59.3
European	1,59,000	3.25
American	1,03,000	2.1
Others	2,03,000	4.15
United Arab Emirates	27,38,000	82.26
Arab	2,38,000	8.71
Asian	23,86,000	87.14
European	41,000	1.5
American	15,000	0.54
Others	58,000	2.11

Source: ILO (2009a).

country of origin in the following descending order at the beginning of the twenty-first century: India, Egypt, Pakistan, Bangladesh and Yemen (2002: 10). Recent figures collected from different countries' consular services in the UAE suggest continuation of a similar ranking (ILO 2009a). Data on the distribution of temporary contractual workers in the private sector in Oman also depict a comparable pattern. For example, ILO (2009a) has cited the 2007 distribution of foreign workers by country of origin in the private sector in the following descending order: India, Pakistan, Bangladesh, Philippines, Egypt and Sri Lanka (Oman—Ministry of National Economy [MNE] 2008).

Structure of the Foreign Workers' Labour Market in the Middle East

Data on the sectoral distribution of foreign workers in countries of the GCC pose a major problem; they are generally scarce and often outdated (ILO 2009a). However, most migrants are estimated to be concentrated in construction, hotels and restaurants, wholesale and retail trade, and domestic work. In Oman, for example, the majority of foreign migrant workers in 2007 were concentrated in construction, repairs, domestic service, agriculture and forestry and manufacturing (Ministry of National Economy 2008: 5).

Women comprise about 25 per cent of all migrant workers in the GCC countries. According to the ILO, domestic work sector is a 'key factor in opening up legal channels of temporary migration for large numbers of women with few employment options at home' (ILO 2009b: 36). In recent years, this has consolidated further, raising the flow of women migrant labour to the GCC countries. They are mostly employed in the domestic service sector and health care (UNDESA 2006). Thus, migrant women work predominately in domestic services with only a minor presence in other branches of economic activity. However, there is significant presence of men in this sector as well. In Bahrain, at the end of 2007, there were a total of 64,000 domestic workers, of whom 35.3 per cent were men (Labour Market Regulation Authority [LMRA] 2008). In Qatar, the 2007 Labour Force Survey revealed that a total of 72,765 foreign workers were employed in domestic services, with 39.8 per cent being men (Qatar Statistics Authority 2008).

Employment terms and conditions for foreign workers are at great discrepancy with those for the nationals in the Middle East countries. In Bahrain, for example, average monthly wages for non-Bahraini workers, in 2007, were 58BD in agriculture, 48BD in fishing, 157BD in manufacturing, 98BD in construction, 147BD in wholesale and retail trade, and 108BD in hotels and restaurants. Given that the number of foreign workers employed in these branches was 2,29,462, accounting for 79 per cent of total foreign workers, their average monthly wages of amounted to 168BD, which was significantly lower than 'low wages' defined by GOSI (Bahrain—General Organization for Social Insurance [GOSI] 2008). Domestic workers, almost entirely of foreign origin, earned even lower average monthly wage of 128BD (LMRA 2008). In contrast, wages of Bahraini nationals were above the 200BD level in all branches, and the average wage at a much higher level of 507BD. In Qatar, average annual wages, to which only a very small minority of highly skilled foreign workers have access, were US$26,980 in construction, US$9,470 in distribution, US$7,785 in tourism, US$15,834 in transportation, US$25,431 in financial services and US$20,462 in education (ILO 2009a).

Working conditions for foreign migrant workers in the Middle East have drawn attention with regard to questions of rights at work. Although foreign workers, with the exception of domestic workers, are included in the scope of labour laws, the recruitment and contracting system is such that foreign workers are mostly unable or unwilling to report breaches to law enforcement officials. Even when they have reported, enforcement of laws has more often been found incomplete. For example, the latest labour regulations provide for suspension of work at construction sites during specified hours of the day because of high temperatures. Similarly, payment for overtime work is mandatory. However, in practice, noncompliance to these provisions is rampant. Laws also prohibit the retention of passports of foreign workers, but employers still carry on the practice. Smaller firms are hardly adhering to labour laws (Al Najjar, cited in ILO 2009a).

Like in most countries, household domestic workers are outside the purview of labour laws in Middle East countries as well, posing problems of monitoring their conditions of employment. The practice of paying low wages and getting long hours of work from foreign workers in the domestic household sector has made the demand high. Such conditions often lead to exploitation, especially of women domestic workers, who are particularly vulnerable to such situations. Cases of abuse and violence have been reported (Chammartin 2004).

Thus, there is visibly significant segmentation of the labour markets in the GCC countries, leading to foreign workers being concentrated in low-paid, low-skilled employment in the private sector and the local nationals in high-paid jobs in the public sector. In the private sector, national workers dominate the high-productivity, highly paid jobs only. This explains the coexistence of high unemployment rates for nationals and large volumes of foreign workers in low-paid jobs. Data are not available for all countries, but example of the UAE highlights the incidence of high unemployment among nationals. According to the 2008 Labour Force Survey, the rate of unemployment among nationals in the UAE was 13.8 per cent, whereas for foreign workers it was only 2.6 per cent (United Arab Emirates, Ministry of Economy, Central Department of Statistics, LFS 2008).

Policy Challenges Facing the Middle East Countries

Restricting Immigration

To ameliorate the high unemployment rates of national workers, governments in the Middle East initially tried to absorb new jobseekers in the public sector. This had the effect of increased disguised unemployment, inefficiency in the public sector and raising the share of wages in public expenditures (Awad 2007). This led to a shift in policy towards 'nationalization' programmes, with a number of GCC countries taking steps to replace foreign workers with nationals in the private sector. For example, the Kuwaiti government adopted a bill in 2000 designed to encourage Kuwaitis to seek employment in the private sector by extending most of the benefits of public sector employment to the private sector. The bill also sets a quota for Kuwaitis, which provides sanctions against companies that fail to respect it (ILO 2009a). However, most of these nationalization programmes did not result in the expected outcomes of reducing the unemployment rate among nationals and curtailing dependence on foreign migrant labour. Rather, an easy and abundant supply of workers coupled with the restrictive immigration policies result in the exploitation of the migrants.

Responding to a UN survey on opinions about levels of immigration and emigration, four out of the six oil-rich GCC countries—Kuwait, Oman, Saudi Arabia and the UAE—considered that the immigration level in their countries were too high and they wanted to reduce it. Such levels of migrant stocks are not what the governments of some GCC countries desire. A review of the opinions, attitudes and policies towards immigration in the Gulf region indicate that in all six countries the trend towards restricting migrant inflows has increased. Also, steps towards the actual implementation of the policies are more actively being taken and enforced. In order to lower the level of immigration, these countries are implementing highly restrictive immigration policies. However, the remaining two—Bahrain and Qatar—considered the levels to be satisfactory and had policies to maintain the inflow. There are several measures that are adopted by the governments of the GCC countries to discourage immigration[1]:

- Indirect taxes such as health taxes for expatriates not only raises revenue for the host country but also increases the cost of living for the expatriates.
- Owing to the lack of minimum wage legislation, the migrant workers get low wages.
- Apart from this, the ineffectiveness of the labour dispute settlement machinery results in no increments in wages, and non-payment of non-wage benefits as per the labour laws.
- Since mid 1990s, the Gulf countries have declared repeated periods of amnesty so as to encourage the departure of those residing in the host countries on an illegal visa, which is largely a result of being employed by a company that is not the legal sponsor of the worker.
- Governments are strictly monitoring the issuance of new work permits, and the transfer of existing work permits from one employer to another.
- GCC countries have policies to restrict the number of approved work visas.

Visa Trading

Another issue that the GCC governments have to deal with is visa trading by fictitious companies. The GCC has implemented a sponsorship (*kafala*) system whereby migrants receive an entry visa and work permit provided that a GCC citizen or institution employs them. Such a system gives the host countries the power to determine the source countries of migrants as well as the duration of their stay in the host countries. Under this system, each employee must have a sponsor or *kafeel*. For those working in the public sector, the government department employing the worker is the *kafeel*. Also, in the private sector, each worker must have a local sponsor who is expected to have a business for which it needs workers. A system of visa trading, however, emerged during the last two to three decades because the demand for visas to the Gulf exceeded supply. Some nationals thus opened up fictitious companies for which they procured work permits that they were able to sell to migrants willing to pay. Frequently, the work permit was not accompanied by a job. The migrant thus found employment with someone other than the sponsor, or remained unemployed.

In the UAE, it is estimated that the number of workers sponsored by these fictitious companies in 2004 was 6,00,000 or 27 per cent of the total workforce (*UAE-Gulf News*, 13 April 2004). As part of its efforts to curb the hiring of illegal workers, 11,600 bans were issued against the violating sponsors and companies during 2004 in the UAE (*Gulf News Online* [UAE], 22 February 2005). The Saudi Minister of Labour had said that 70 per cent of the visas issued by the government were sold on the black market and the government was determined to crack down on this (*Arab News* [Saudi Arabia], 29 April 2004).

Similar statements were repeatedly made by authorities in other GCC countries. The Bahrain Minister of Labour and Social Affairs lamented that the practice had plagued the Bahraini job market for the last 20 years. In August 2004, the government was undertaking a process of investigating 43 businesses and found them engaged in this practice (*The Arab News*, 4 August 2004).

The Kuwait Human Development Report of 1997 acknowledged the presence of visa trading as one of the factors that promoted the influx of foreign workers to Kuwait. It advocated for the implementation of serious steps to curb this practice. The report stated that one of the reasons for an uncontrolled import of workers was the existence, in countries of origin and in Kuwait, of elements that profited from trading in residence permits. Such workers were brought in simply to earn the fee rather than to satisfy the requirements of genuine economic activity (Ministry of Planning 1997). There have been repeated calls for the strict issuance of work permits in order to 'ward off unwanted elements from entering the country' (*Kuwait Times*, 20 April 2004). The scale of the problem clearly illustrates that visa trading is a highly lucrative industry.

A fundamental difficulty in the implementation of any policy aimed at curbing visa trading is therefore the ease with which an ordinary local sponsor can have a continuous source of income coupled with a market in sending countries where many are eager to buy such visas at any cost. The extent of adverse outcomes associated with visa trading is of course not known.[2] In June 2005, the International Labour Organization (ILO) representative to Kuwait made a proposal to the Kuwaiti government to change its sponsorship system. He recommended that the State of Kuwait should be the sponsor of all expatriate workers rather than individual sponsors and stated that the sponsorship system does not meet international standards and leaves the workers vulnerable to exploitation (*AMN*, 16–30 June 2005). In Qatar too, some citizens demanded that the state should be the sponsor of foreign workers and not individual citizens or business owners.

Select Country Policy Profile in the Middle East

Kuwait

Kuwait follows a policy to lower the permanent settlement of immigrants and its policy for granting citizenship is highly restrictive:

- It restricts the number of dependents of migrant workers by putting a ceiling on the salary of workers who are allowed to bring their family, so that cost of living and sustaining dependents in Kuwait becomes expensive (see Shah 2006: 2).
- Since the government does not want the immigrants to settle for long, there are no integration programmes and the unwillingness to integrate the migrants has become clearer after the crisis of 1990–1991.
- The workers are mostly on contracts, which last for two years. However, in reality there are workers who have been working for about 10 years.
- A migrant worker in Kuwait is required to buy health insurance for himself as well as each member of his family who is accompanying him. In the private sector, the employer often does not pay for such insurance. Around 92 per cent of all expatriates work in the private sector.
- Increasing cost of living for foreigners: rise in fees for issuance and renewal of residence permits, driver's license and registration and so on.
- Another mechanism that may indirectly affect the cost of living for a foreign worker is the policy to increase the fee that an employer must pay for hiring such a worker. In Kuwait, the cabinet had

deliberated on hiking the fee per worker to KD 50 (US$ 170) per year in 2005 (*Kuwait Times*, 28 February 2005).[3] This fee was highly likely to be passed on to the employee in the private sector.

Saudi Arabia

Saudi Arabia is one of the most active countries that have implemented policies to restrict migration.

- It had announced a measure limiting the number of new visas available to foreign workers to be reduced from the 8.8 million to only 2 million over the next eight years.
- It was also proposed that new visas would be available only for menial jobs that Saudi people were not willing to do or technical ones for which the citizens were not trained (*Washington Post*, 31 August 2004).
- There are also problems such as migrants coming on Haj pilgrimage overstaying and working illegally in Saudi Arabia. In order to counter this type of illegal migration, the government has imposed a bond deposit of $800 that the pilgrims are required to pay and which they have to forfeit if they do not leave within a month.

The basic elements of the migration policy regulations of Saudi Arabia are as follows:

- Foreign or non-Saudi workers cannot enter the country unless they have a sponsorship of an eligible employer or a permitted Saudi household in the case of domestic workers.
- When a foreign worker enters the country, he or she has to get a residency card or *iqama* and a work permit.
- Once the worker gets the *iqama* card, he or she has to give his or her passport to the *kafeel* (the sponsor); the passport will be returned only when he or she leaves the country, as the *iqama* card stands in place of the passport.
- A non-Saudi cannot change his or her sponsor or job unless the sponsor issues a release.
- The sponsor has the right to refuse to give a release, to deport the worker and to ask the authority to ban the worker from coming back to the country for two years.
- Foreign workers in professional, technical and managerial occupations with postsecondary education have the right to bring their families with them to Saudi Arabia, while relatives of

workers with lower education have the right to make only a short visit that might be extended to three months.

- In addition, a foreign worker is prohibited from checking directly with the passport department for any official arrangements concerning his residency or visa. He or she has to do this through the sponsor who hands over the worker's passport to an authorized person to make the arrangements.

Bahrain

Policies implemented by the Bahrain government to restrict immigration comprise:

- Indirect taxes that raise revenue for the host country and make life more expensive for the migrant workers aiming to reduce attractiveness of the Gulf market as a destination site.
- The Bahraini Cabinet also approved the implementation of a health fee for migrant workers around 2001. It was decided that expatriates or their Bahraini employers must buy health insurance, which should cover primary as well as secondary health services including regular check-ups and surgery (*The Gulf News*, 9 March 2004).

United Arab Emirates

- Since the implementation of a new health insurance scheme introduced in the UAE in 2006, the employer has been required to pay for the mandatory health insurance for the workers. The employees would have to pay the premium for their national health insurance, thus bearing additional costs in a situation where the wages are already fairly stagnant (*AMN*, 15–31 January 2006).
- The UAE, which has had a policy of health insurance for the last several years, recently introduced a new fee for all surgical procedures, much to the unhappiness of migrant workers. A fee ranging from 500 to 4000 Dirhams (DH) (US$ 136 to $1089) was imposed, depending on the type and complexity of the surgery (*Kuwait Times*, 9 May 2005).
- The UAE has introduced exorbitant fees for the verification of the university degree certificates of the immigrants after the change in this process in 2005. Under the new degree verification programme, expatriates must send their attested degree certificates through IntegraScreen, a document verification company,

via Emirates Post. This process would cost Dh510 (US$ 139), whereas previously they had to pay only Dh100 (US$27) for attestation of the same documents at their home country and in the UAE (*AMN*, 15–31 January 2006).

Jordan

Jordan follows a very liberal immigration policy. On the emigration front, the government supports the emigration of its nationals for employment. It is more a source than a destination country in the Middle East, supplying migrant workers to the GCC countries. The government has appointed counsellors in its diplomatic missions in the GCC countries (and Libya) to advise the Jordanian government about the dynamics of the labour markets of these countries and facilitate the employment of Jordanian migrants. Jordanians who had fled Kuwait during the Gulf War find it difficult to re-enter owing to political tension between the two countries. Qatar has also restricted the entry of Jordanians by making it difficult for them to renew or obtain visas, as for other migrant workers from non-Middle East countries in Asia.

Abu Dhabi Dialogue and the Colombo Process: A Collective Policy Initiative between Countries of Destination in the Middle East and of Origin in Asia

The GCC countries follow a migration regime that promotes 'contract migration'. In this way, they minimize the cost of labour. Concrete policies aimed at enhancing indigenization and reducing the number of foreign workers have been implemented during the last decade or so. One of the major reasons for this is the rising level of unemployment among the nationals, which is posing difficult economic and political questions for the governments. The local youth in the population of this period having diplomas are ready to enter the labour markets, but they have no guarantee of being hired. For the first time, the labour markets were witnessing a competition between the nationals and the migrants and the government had to safeguard the interest of its own people. However, the Middle East countries have also realized that to achieve the desired results they have to work not only in harmony with each other in the region, but also in tandem with the countries of origin of migrant labour in Asia. This is what let the Middle East countries to join the Colombo Process, which is a conglomeration of countries of origin, through what was called the Abu Dhabi Dialogue.

'Colombo Process', a Ministerial Consultations on Overseas Employment and Contractual Labour for Countries of Origin in Asia, was established in 2003, in its first meeting in Colombo, Sri Lanka, with the objective to provide a forum for Asian labour-sending countries. The stated aim of the Colombo Process has been to provide a forum for Asian labour-sending countries to:

- Share experiences, lessons learned and best practices on overseas employment;
- Consult on issues faced by overseas workers, labour sending and receiving states, and propose practical solutions for the well-being of vulnerable overseas workers;
- Optimize development benefits from organized overseas employment, and enhance dialogue with countries of destination and
- Review and monitor the implementation of the recommendations and identify further steps for action.

To review and monitor the implementation of previous recommendations and identify areas of future action, the member nations of the 'Colombo Process' have subsequently met thrice in countries of origin—in Manila (Philippines) in 2004, in Bali (Indonesia) in 2005 and in Dhaka (Bangladesh) in 2011. The Third Ministerial Consultation of the Colombo Process, which took place in Bali, Indonesia, in September 2005, was greatly enriched by the active participation of countries of destination (such as UAE, Bahrain, Italy and Malaysia) as observers. However, after the Bali meeting, the Colombo Process lost its momentum, and it took six years for its revival in Bangladesh, in 2011, which also partly explains the lull in the availability of data and information during the intervening period till the present (Khadria 2011).[4] As a landmark exception, however, the UAE had taken the groundbreaking step of hosting the inaugural Ministerial Consultation between Asian destination countries and Colombo Process countries in Abu Dhabi on 21 and 22 January 2008.[5] The Ministerial Consultation, referred to as the 'Abu Dhabi Dialogue, brought together for the first time the Colombo Process countries with the Gulf Cooperation Council (GCC) states, plus Yemen and two additional Asian countries of destination, namely Malaysia and Singapore'. The Abu Dhabi Dialogue therefore constitutes a milestone in regional cooperation on contractual labour mobility in the Middle East.

The Abu Dhabi Declaration launched a collaborative approach to short-term labour mobility in Asia in order to maximize benefits for all.

It focuses on developing four key, action-oriented strategic partnerships between countries of origin and destination for development around the premise of temporary contractual labour, based on a notion of partnership and shared accountability: The Abu Dhabi Dialogue was established in 2008 and currently has 20 member states. The eleven countries of origin are Afghanistan, Bangladesh, China, India, Indonesia, Nepal, Pakistan, Philippines, Sri Lanka, Thailand and Vietnam. The nine destination countries are Bahrain, Kuwait, Malaysia, Oman, Qatar, Saudi Arabia, Singapore, United Arab Emirates and Yemen.[6]

The main purpose of the first meeting of the Abu Dhabi Dialogue was to provide a forum for the discussion of new ideas and concrete activities towards the development of a comprehensive and practical framework for the management of temporary contractual labour mobility in Asia. Particular focus was placed on promoting the welfare and well-being of workers, on the development of both origin and destination countries through labour mobility, and on fostering greater intergovernmental cooperation and collaboration, with the active support of international and regional partners. The key foci of the dialogue are as follows:

- Developing and sharing knowledge on labour market trends, skills profiles, workers and remittances policies and flows, and the relationship to progress.
- Building capacity for more effective harmonizing of labour supply and demand.
- Preventing illegal recruitment and promoting welfare and protection measures for contractual workers.
- Developing a structure for a comprehensive approach to managing the entire cycle of temporary contractual work that fosters the common interest of countries of origin and destination.

These are supposed to have an interface with the main focus of the Colombo Process:

- Protection of and provision of services to migrant workers: In particular, protecting migrant workers from abusive practices in recruitment and employment, and providing appropriate services to migrant workers in terms of pre-departure information and orientation and welfare provisions.
- Optimizing benefits of organized labour migration: This includes the development of new overseas employment markets, increasing remittance flows through formal channels and enhancing the development impact of remittances.

- Capacity building, data collection and interstate cooperation: This includes institutional capacity building and information exchange to meet labour migration challenges. Increasing cooperation with destination countries in the protection of migrant workers and access to labour markets; and enhancing cooperation among countries of origin.

The current priority of the dialogue is to identify the role and responsibilities of both the government and the private sector at every stage of the contractual work cycle. This includes every phase beginning with recruitment, preparation, movement, working in the host country, return and finally reintegration in the country of origin. It also focuses on the implementation of projects with tangible outcomes so that all partners are benefited. One other priority is strengthening the regional framework on temporary contractual labour mobility. The collective effort for the Abu Dhabi Dialogue and the Colombo Process Member States to make progress in forging a broad platform has resulted in a greatly enhanced framework for cooperation between origin and destination countries of migration in the Middle East.

Acknowledgements

I am grateful to my graduate students Shantanu Sarkar, Umesh Bharte and Rashmi Sharma for research assistance in collecting information for this paper and discussing an earlier draft. I am also thankful to Melissa Siegel and Mark Lopez for their comments and suggestions on an earlier draft. Any remaining shortcomings are however my sole responsibility.

Notes

1. See, for measures adopted by individual countries, Shah (2006, 2008).
2. Occasionally, some tragic outcomes of visa trading catch the attention of the media. An Indian worker, who bought a visa for UAE, could not find a job once he landed in Sharjah and ended up becoming a beggar. He was a diabetic and suffered minor abrasions on his legs, which eventually turned to a level of severity when both his feet had to be amputated (*AMN*, 16–31 October 2005).
3. See Shah (2006). According to latest estimates, the overall average annual administrative and recruitment costs per worker in UAE are estimated at Dh2,674. For skilled workers, this cost is Dh3, 404 and for unskilled workers Dh2,296. Wages and both cash and non-cash benefits are estimated at Dh41,000 per worker annually. http://gulfnews.com/news/gulf/uae/employment/uae-s-per-worker-cost-to-companies-isdh55-000-a-year-study-shows-1.695337 (accessed on 26 June 2011).

4. For speculation on whether the Colombo Process would lead to relatively freer migration within Asia in the next 20 years, see Khadria (2011, 11–16).
5. http://www.colomboprocess.org/index.php?option=com_content&view=article&id=46&Itemid=29 (accessed on 25 June 2011)
6. In addition, France, Germany, Mauritius, the Republic of Korea, Japan, Poland and the United States have observer status while the European Commission (EC) is a partner of the Dialogue.

References

AMN various issues. http://www.smc.org.ph/amnews/amnews.htm, as cited in Shah, 2006.

Arab News (Saudi Arabia). http://arabnews.com/saudiarabia/, as cited in Shah, 2006.

Awad, I. 2007. 'Migration and Human Security in the Arab Region'. Paper prepared for the Arab Human Development Report 2009: Challenges to Human Security in the Arab Countries, New York: UNDP, 2009.

Bahrain – General Organization for Social Insurance (GOSI), 2008. http://www.gosi.org.bh/

Chammartin, G. 'Women Migrant Workers' Protection in Arab League States'. In *Gender and Migration in the Arab World: The Case of Domestic Workers.* Beirut: ILO, 2004.

Dito, M. 'Governing labour migration policies in the GCC countries: Risks and opportunities'. Paper presented at the *Expert Group Meeting on International Migration and Development in the Arab Region*, organized by the United Nations Economic and Social Commission for Western Asia (UNESCWA), Beirut, 15–17 May 2006 (in Arabic); cited in ILO (2009a).

Girgis, M. 'Would Nationals and Asians Replace Arab Workers in the GCC?' Paper submitted to the Fourth Mediterranean Development Forum, Amman, Jordan, 2002.

ILO. 'Gender Equality at the Heart of Decent Work, Report VI'. International Labour Conference, 98th Session, Geneva, 2009b.

ILO. 'International Labour Migration and Employment in the Arab Region: Origins, Consequences and the Way Forward'. Thematic Paper, Arab Employment Forum, Beirut, Lebanon, October, ILO, Geneva, 2009a.

ILO. 'Structural Change and Labour Migration within the Asian Region'. *Regional Development Dialogue,* 12(3) (1991): 3–19, ILO, Geneva.

Kapiszewski, Andrzej. 2003. The Changing Status of Arab Migrant Workers in the GCC. *Journal of Social Affairs*, 20 (78): 33-60.

Kapiszewski, Andrzej. *Arab versus Asian Migrant Workers in the GCC Countries.* UN Expert Group Meeting on International Migration and Development in the Arab Region, Beirut, 15–17 May 2006.

Khadria, B. 'Migration Patterns in the Asia-Pacific Region'. Paper presented at the ASSA Workshop on Rethinking Australian Research on Migration and Diversity, 9–10 August, University of Sydney, sponsored by the Academy of Social Sciences in Australia, 2010.

Khadria, B. 'What would be the impact on the future global migration system—and, specifically, on environmental migration—if the Colombo Process succeeded in its aims (i.e. relatively free mobility takes place within Asia, including to the Gulf region)?' Background Paper No. SR 20 of Foresight, Migration and Global Environmental Change, Final Project Report, The UK Government Office for Science, London, 2011.

Kuwait Times Online. http://www.kuwaittimes.net/, as cited in Shah, 2006.

Labour Market Regulation Authority, Bahrain, 2008. http://lmra.bh/portal/en/home

Ministry of Planning, Kuwait, 1997. http://www.e.gov.kw/sites/kgoenglish/portal/pages/kgd.aspx

Oman-Ministry of National Economy. *Monthly Statistical Bulletin*, 19 (5), May 2008.

Qatar Statistical Authority. *Qatar in Figures*. Doha: Qatar Statistical Authority, 2008.

Shah, N.M. 'Building State Capacities for Managing Contract Worker Mobility: The Asia-GCC Context'. Background Paper World Migration Report 2010, IOM, Geneva, 2010.

Shah, N.M. 'Recent Labor Immigration Policies in the Oil-Rich Gulf: How Effective Are They Likely To Be?' ILO Asian Regional Programme on Governance of Labour Migration, Working Paper No. 3, ILO Regional Office for Asia and the Pacific, Asian Regional Programme on Governance of Labour Migration, Bangkok, 2008.

Shah, N.M. 'Restrictive Labour Immigration Policies in the Oil-Rich Gulf: Effectiveness and Implications for Sending Asian Countries'. UN/POP/EGM/2006/03 5 May, Population Division Department of Economic and Social Affairs United Nations Secretariat, 2006.

UNDESA. Summary of Ad Hoc Expert Meeting on 'Strengthening the Business Sector and Entrepreneurship in Developing Countries'. New York, 5 October 2006.

United Arab Emirates, Ministry of Economy, Central Department of Statistics, LFS 2008. http://www.economy.gov.ae

Washington Post. (31 August 2004). http://www.encyclopedia.com/The+Washington+Post/publications.aspx?date=20040831&pageNumber=2, as cited in Shah, 2006.

Winckler, O. 'The Immigration Policy of the Gulf Cooperation Council (GCC) States'. *Middle Eastern Studies*, 33(3) (1997): 480–493.

CHAPTER 2

The Financial Crisis in the Gulf and Its Impact on South Asian Migration and Remittances

S. Irudaya Rajan and D. Narayana

The financial crisis had its origins in the United States (US) in 2008, spread to Europe and then to Japan. The effect of the crisis has been slow to manifest in the six Gulf Cooperation Council (GCC) countries.[1] Their basic strengths—a public-funded banking sector and huge trade surplus due to the export of oil, the price of which saw an unprecedented increase in a span of six months in 2008—shielded the GCC economies from the adverse impact during the initial days of the crisis. This, coupled with significant inward foreign direct investments to all GCC countries, except Kuwait, also had a beneficial impact (ESCWA 2008).

The GCC economies, however, began to feel the impact of the global crisis from the last quarter of 2008. The most significant indicator was the slowdown in the gross domestic product (GDP) growth rate in 2008 and the negative growth rate in 2009 in some of

---

First published in *India Migration Report 2012: Global Financial Crisis, Migration and Remittance*, pp. 74–93, edited by S. Irudaya Rajan. New Delhi: Routledge. Reprinted by permission of the author.

these economies. In the financial sector, the stock markets in all the GCC countries recorded a decline owing to the withdrawal of the foreign institutional investors. A number of privately funded domestic and international projects in the Gulf region had reportedly been cancelled or abandoned, leading to a large number of layoffs or retrenchment of the workforce. Countries that are more exposed to global capital, investment and consumption demand face a greater risk of being affected by crisis than others. For instance, Dubai in the United Arab Emirates (UAE), which depends heavily on international capital, tourism and real estate, seems to be more adversely affected than other countries. On the other hand, Saudi Arabia, which has only 25 per cent foreign workers compared to much higher proportions in the other GCC economies, might be much less affected than others (Zachariah and Rajan 2009a). The slowdown in the growth rates of GCC economies has particular significance for the GCC countries. This would, it was expected, affect the flow of migration and cause unforeseen large-scale return emigration and falling remittances (Kapiszewski 2006).

In this context, the following research issues become important:

(a) How has the crisis affected the demand for South Asian migrant workers in the Gulf countries?

(b) What strategies did the emigrants adopt to cope with the situation at their place of work (countries of destination), and what is the likely impact of the crisis on the home country in the terms of decline in remittances, if any?

(c) Did countries in South Asia see large-scale return emigration? Did they find a decline in the outflow of emigrant labour to Gulf countries and inward remittances from them?

The chapter is a modest attempt at analysing these issues in detail.

Approach and Methodology

Following an assessment of the trends in expatriate workers and the employment structure in the GCC countries based on published data, mapping the trends and patterns of international migration, preferred countries of destination and trends in remittances over a long period of time is attempted. In addition to macro assessment of the situation, the study is based on two surveys: (a) return emigrants in the countries of origin who lost their jobs in the countries of destination due to financial crisis and (b) return migrants who come back as per the terms of contract migration.

Return Emigrant Survey

This survey was conducted among the emigrants who lost their jobs and were forced to return home because of the financial crisis in the Gulf. It was also aimed at examining their coping mechanism after their return to their home country. The survey canvassed among 50 return emigrants each in the four countries of South Asia—Pakistan, Bangladesh, Nepal and Sri Lanka. In India, the survey was canvassed among 250 return emigrants in five states of India, selecting 50 each in Andhra Pradesh, Tamil Nadu, Kerala, Maharashtra and Punjab. Thus, the total number of return emigrants surveyed was 450 among the five countries of origin in South Asia. However, we confess that it was difficult to locate the emigrants who lost their jobs in the countries of destination and returned to the countries of origin. The return emigrant survey collected information on household details, the profile of return emigrants, household economic assets, employment, remittances and their utilization, household expenditure pattern, reasons for return, adaptation and coping mechanisms.

Return Migrant Resurvey, 2009

Return migration from the Gulf is the normal process of contract migration. Migrants from South Asia go on contract work to the destination countries; and once the contract ends, they—in the normal course—return to the countries of their origin. As of now, we have no estimate of return emigration from Gulf to South Asia. However, the Centre for Development Studies (CDS) has completed four large-scale migration surveys (1998, 2003, 2007 and 2008) over the last decade. One of the research objectives of this project is to assess the flow of forced return emigration, or return emigrants before the expiry of contract from the Gulf region to South Asia. To assess both regular migrants and the crisis-led return emigrants from the Gulf, we revisited emigrant households from the 15,000 households of the 2008 Kerala Migration Survey (KMS). We estimated the extent of crisis-led return emigrants to Kerala after the revisit. Further, in this chapter, we are applying the same methodology and projecting the figures to estimate the number of return emigrants from the Gulf to South Asia. In addition, the return migration resurvey 2009 also estimated the number of emigrants who lost their jobs in the Gulf, but had chosen to remain there without returning to their countries of origin. This is new information (lost job, but have not returned), which will also be generated for South Asia.

Financial Crisis and Growth in the Gulf[2]

The global crisis originating in the United States, spreading to Europe and to Japan, has affected the Middle East through a large fall in price of oil, reversal of capital inflows, depression of property and equity markets, and losses in sovereign wealth funds. The effect of the crisis varies across the countries depending upon country characteristics, such as high share of oil in total exports, large quantum of re-exports and sizeable share of services in GDP, especially transportation, trade, hotel and restaurants.

In the region as whole, growth declined from 5.1 per cent in 2008 to 2.4 per cent in 2009. Among the oil-producing countries, the sharpest slowdown was in the UAE, where the exit of external funds contributed to a large contraction in liquidity, a sizeable fall in property and equity prices, and substantial pressure in the banking system. At the other end of the spectrum is Qatar, which grew by about 9 per cent in 2009 (Table 2.1).

Interestingly, the comparison of growth forecast for 2009 and the realized growth for the countries shown in Table 2.1 presents some important patterns. For the developed countries, the contraction forecast and the realized hardly reveal much of a difference but the recovery is also rapid. The GCC countries show a mixed pattern: both the UAE and Kuwait witnessed contractions greater than the forecasts, the rest of the countries except Qatar reported growth rates higher than the forecasts; the growth recovery in 2010 and 2011 is on the expected lines (Table 2.1).

Gulf Economies: Population and GDP Growth

The population of the GCC countries has increased by 8.39 million between 2000 and 2008, which is almost the size of GCC excluding Saudi Arabia in 2000. The large increase in populations of almost all the Gulf countries is spawned by the high average growth of GDP between 2000 and 2009. Only Kuwait showed a large increase in population with a relatively low increase in GDP (Table 2.2). Along with population growth, the proportion of expatriates in the

Table 2.1 *Selected Economies: Real GDP Growth Rates (Annual Per cent Change)*

	2001	2002	2003	2004	2005	2006	2007	2008	2009	2010	2011
			Country of Destination								
Bahrain	4.62	5.19	7.25	5.64	7.85	6.65	8.07 (8.38)	6.12 (6.31)	2.64 (3.11)	3.47 (3.96)	3.94 (4.50)
Kuwait	0.22	3.01	17.33	10.24	10.62	5.14	2.51 (4.46)	6.33 (5.53)	–1.14 (–4.82)	2.39 (2.33)	4.34 (4.44)
Oman	7.51	2.57	2.01	5.33	6.02	6.79	6.38 (6.81)	6.18 (12.84)	3.02 (3.59)	3.80 (4.72)	6.00 (4.68)
Qatar	6.32	3.20	6.32	17.72	9.24	15.03	15.35 (26.76)	16.40 (25.42)	17.99 (8.65)	16.37 (15.96)	8.90 (18.58)
Saudi Arabia	0.55	0.13	7.66	5.27	5.55	3.03	3.52 (2.02)	4.63 (4.23)	–0.91 (0.60)	2.90 (3. 42)	4.40 (4.51)
United Arab Emirates	1.70	2.65	11.89	9.69	8.19	9.39	6.34 (6.06)	7.41 (5.15)	-0.60 (-2.47)	1.55 (2.43)	3.29 (3.18)
			Country of Origin								
Bangladesh	4.83	4.85	5.78	6.11	6.30	6.53	6.32 (6.31)	5.59 (5.96)	5.00 (5.64)	5.38 (5.78)	6.01 (6.26)
India	3.89	4.56	6.85	7.90	9.21	9.82	9.30 (9.89)	7.29 (6.40)	4.52 (5.68)	5.61 (9.67)	6.89 (8.37)
Nepal	5.63	0.12	3.95	4.68	3.12	3.72	3.19 (3.41)	4.70 (6.10)	3.60 (4.86)	3.25 (2.98)	4.81 (4.01)

Cont'd...

...Cont'd

Pakistan	1.98	3.22	4.85	7.37	7.67	6.18	6.02 (5.64)	5.95 (1.64)	2.50 (3.37)	3.50 (4.79)	4.50 (2.75)
Sri Lanka	−1.55	3.96	5.94	5.45	6.24	7.67	6.80 (6.80)	5.95 (5.95)	2.20 (3.54)	3.59 (7.0)	4.98 (7.0)
			Major Developed Countries								
Japan	0.184	0.262	1.414	2.744	1.934	2.039	2.392 (2.36)	−0.641 (-1.20)	−6.197 (−5.22)	0.515 (2.82)	2.168 (1.50)
United States	0.751	1.599	2.51	3.637	2.939	2.779	2.028 (1.95)	1.1111 (0)	−2.751 (−2.63)	−0.049 (2.64)	3.53 (2.31)
United Kingdom	2.462	2.097	2.818	2.758	2.058	2.838	3.022 (2.69)	0.707 (−0.07)	−4.086 (−4.89)	−0.396 (1.70)	2.121 (2.02)

Sources: International Monetary Fund (IMF), World Economic Outlook (WEO) Database, April 2009; IMF, WEO Database, October 2010.

Note: Figures within parentheses are from WEO 2010; Data for 2009–2011 and 2010–2011 are forecasts in WEO 2009 and WEO 2010, respectively.

population has shown an increase. In Qatar and UAE, expatriates constitute more than 80 per cent of the total population, and in Kuwait they account for close to 70 per cent of the total population. While in Saudi Arabia and Oman expatriates constitute slightly over a quarter of the population, Bahrain has over 40 per cent non-nationals in the total population. The proportion of expatriates in the labour force moves with the proportion in the population. More than 60 per cent of the expatriates are from South Asia and in some countries such as Oman and Bahrain, they account for more than 90 per cent of the expatriates (Table 2.3). Overall the flow of South Asian migrants to the GCC countries is a function of GDP growth in the latter.

Table 2.2 *Growth of Population and GDP in GCC Countries*

Country	*Population (million)*				*GDP Growth 2000–2008 (%)*
	2000	*2009*	*Increase*	*Increase (%)*	
Kuwait	2.217	3.443	1.226	55.30	6.68
Qatar	0.606	1.098	0.492	81.19	11.17
Saudi Arabia	20.474	24.897	4.423	21.60	3.91
UAE	2.995	4.764	1.769	59.07	7.74
Bahrain	0.670	0.779	0.109	16.27	6.29
Oman	2.402	2.769	0.367	15.28	5.36
Total	29.364	37.750	8.386	28.56	—

Source: World Economic Outlook Database, April 2009.

Table 2.3 *Profile of Expatriates in the Gulf, 2009*

Country	*Population (in Thousands)*	*Expatriates to Total Population (%)*	*% of South Asian Expatriates to Total Expatriates*	*% of Expatriates in the Labour Force*
Kuwait	3,443	68.8	52.8	83.9
Qatar	1,098	86.5	68.4	92.5
Saudi Arabia	24,897	27.8	54.9	55.8
UAE	4,764	81.0	68.7	89.8
Bahrain	779	43.0	95.1	58.3
Oman	2,769	28.4	89.0	64.3
GCC	37,750	40.3	61.8	—

Sources: Compiled from various sources such as 'Country Reports' prepared by the CDS team, Reported figures by the respective Embassies in the Gulf and the following four publications: (a) UN (2009), (b) Kapiszewski (2006), (c) Taattola (2006) and (d) Shah (2009).

Employment Structure in the GCC Countries

In the GCC countries, more than 50 per cent of the workforce is employed in manufacturing, trade and construction. Kuwait and Saudi Arabia are the exceptions, where the share of public administration and defence is rather high (Table 2.4). The share of construction in total employment increased rapidly during 2001–2008 in some of the GCC countries. For instance, in the UAE the share of construction sector employment increased by 5 per cent points during the period. In Saudi Arabia, the increase in employment in the construction sector during the period was of the order of 3,00,000.

Table 2.4 *Share of Employment (%) across Economic Activities in GCC Countries, 2007*

Activity	*Bahrain*	*Oman*	*Kuwait*	*Qatar*	*Saudi Arabia*	*UAE*
Agriculture, hunting and forestry	0.47	9.09	2.60	1.92	4.69	5.0
Fishing	0.01	0.44	0.08	0.43		
Mining and quarrying	0.49	1.96	1.90	5.27	1.32	1.3
Manufacturing	17.54	10.77	4.43	8.69	7.28	13.0
Electricity, gas and water Supply	0.13	0.33	0.01	0.66	0.96	1.2
Construction	29.86	34.68	14.23	37.14	10.22	20.6
Wholesale, retail trade and car repairs	24.62	16.18	14.03	12.28	16.10	20.0
Hotels and restaurants	6.55	5.97	2.89	1.96	3.20	4.2
Transport, storage and communication	4.20	1.30	3.85	4.33	4.42	6.2
Financial intermediaries	3.46	0.29	1.21	1.09	1.08	1.4
Real estate and renting services	7.54	1.77	5.59	3.43	3.22	3.3
Public administration and defence	0.01	0.02	14.75	6.35	18.03	10.8
Education	1.24	0.76	5.23	3.16	11.96	
Health and social work	0.24	1.91	2.40	2.55	4.33	
Community and personal services	2.11	1.08	4.18	1.54	2.26	4.5
Domestic services	0.06	9.96	21.86	8.79	10.79	8.4
Extraterritorial Organizations and bodies	0.21	2.59	0.11	0.21	0.13	—
Not classified by economic activity	0.30	0.90	0.66	0.18	0.01	0.01
Total	100.00	100.00	100.00	100.00	100.00	100.00

Source: ILO Labour Statistics, ILO; Statistical Year Book 2008, Ministry of National Economy Oman; For Saudi Arabia and UAE the figures are taken from the country reports.

Note: For Bahrain and UAE figures show the paid employment by economic activity. For Oman figures show expatriate workers in private sector. Kuwait figures show for year 2005.

[a] Fishing is included in agriculture, hunting and forestry.

[b] Education and health are included in public administration and defence.

Table 2.5 *Projects Affected by the Crisis in the Gulf*

Country	*Projects and Finance Involved*			
	Projects under Construction	*Projects Cancelled/ On Hold*	*Total Project Worth (US$ Billion)*[a]	*% Cancellation*
Kuwait	90	18	114	17
Qatar	124	7	42	—
Saudi Arabia	442	106	387	19
UAE	1,372	566	900	29
Bahrain	148	54	36	27
Oman	95	8	38	8

Source: Proleads.

[a] All projects including cancelled/on hold.

Table 2.6 *Projects Affected by Subsectors, UAE*

Subsector	*Projects under Construction*	*Total Number of Projects*	*% Cancellation*
Commercial projects	340	487	147 (30)
Hospitality business	288	406	118 (29)
Residential properties	495	712	217 (30)
Retail projects	249	333	84 (25)
Total	1,372	1,938	566

Source: gulfbase.com.

Table 2.7 *Government Expenditure in the GCC Countries, 2006–2011 (% of GDP)*

Country	*2006*	*2007*	*2008*	*2009*	*2010*	*2011*
Kuwait	31.83	29.94	40.15	47.36	43.22	44.28
Qatar	26.42	25.37	24.52	26.66	23.22	22.47
Saudi Arabia	31.96	34.36	30.81	44.54	42.80	40.75
United Arab Emirates	18.39	18.98	21.22	32.11	28.34	23.07
Bahrain	28.48	28.70	28.00	31.42	30.83	29.53
Oman	34.44	35.33	29.42	38.72	37.38	37.02

Source: WEO Database, October 2010.

As construction is one of the major sectors attracting expatriate labour, it is important to analyse the effect of the crisis of that sector. Housing finance on private utilities has taken severe beating along with finance institutions in the current crisis. A survey of projects (worth at least US$ 10 million) in mid-2009 reported 10–30 per cent cancellations or orders to put on hold in the GCC countries (Table 2.5). Dubai, which has about 60 per cent of all projects in the GCC, has taken the largest hit, which in turn has affected the GCC has a whole. Interestingly, the crisis has affected all sub sectors—from commercial projects to residential properties—as the illustration from the UAE would show (Table 2.6).

While new projects have come down in the UAE, there is persistent high-level activity in ongoing projects that would be 'the envy of many' elsewhere in the world. There is evidence of increased construction activity in Abu Dhabi, Sharjah and Ajman. Thus, while new starts have come down and those about to be initiated have been put on hold, a lot of work continued to be carried out for current projects.

Gulf Crisis and South Asian Labour: The Links

The link between economic growth and labour flow is through the growth in manufacturing, trade and construction. Construction, in particular, attracts large numbers of expatriate labour from South Asia. Any of the factors adversely affecting construction would affect the labour. The quick rebound of oil prices by mid-2009 and the not too depressing current account and budget balances have made the government of the GCC countries bolder and induced them to continue major infrastructure investment. The increase in government expenditures (as per cent of GDP) was close to 10 points in most of the countries (Table 2.7), except in Bahrain and Qatar. Fiscal policy has played a crucial role in cushioning the impact of global crisis in the GCC countries.

The interventions in the banking sectors have also been decisive. The further boost has been healthy, albeit lower, GDP growth in the whole of South Asia in 2009, 2010 and 2011, and the forecast of higher growth rate in 2012. South Asia and China have emerged as the major trading partner of GCC economies and the trade outlook does not look very depressing.

However, the continuing adverse factors have been the depressed real estate and equity prices in the GCC countries, particularly in Dubai. The recovery would remain fragile as long as private investment does not stimulate growth. FDI, which had played a major role in the high growth of the pre-crisis days, fell drastically in 2009 in almost all GCC countries, except Oman, Qatar and Saudi Arabia. The fall in the UAE was from US$ 13.7 billion in 2008 to US$ 4 billion in 2009 (United Nations Conference on Trade and Development, UNCTAD, 2010). It is unlikely that the situation will improve till the Dubai world[3] crisis is resolved.

Impact of the Crisis on South Asian Migrant Workers

This section is devoted to an assessment of the impact of the crisis—on the South Asian migrant workers in terms of return emigration—on flows of labour emigration from Asia to the Gulf; and on inward remittances to South Asia. The assessment is based on the summary results of the emigrant household survey and survey of return emigrants carries out to understand the coping mechanisms of individuals and families in time of crisis.

Return Migration to South Asia from the Gulf, 2009

All agencies working on migration and remittances in the South Asian countries and the Gulf region predicated an exodus of return emigrants from the Gulf to their countries of origin following the crisis. The CDS, which has undertaken four large-scale migration surveys in Kerala during the last 10 years to estimate the number of emigrants, return emigrants and remittances, revisited the households of the 2008 survey in 2009 (Zachariah et al. 2006)[4] to arrive at reliable estimates of return emigrants. All those in the original sample who had returned were asked to cite the reasons for returning to Kerala. The questionnaire provided 10 possible reasons for return, among which the following three could be attributed to recession: job loss and return due to financial crisis, expiry of contract (renewal of contract did not take place as expected due to recession) and compulsory expatriation. The estimates of return migrants due to the crisis had provided in Table 2.8.

Table 2.8 *Number of Return Emigrants to Kerala Due to Recession in 2009*

	Sample	*Kerala*
Total Emigrants in 2008 based on 2008 Kerala Migration Survey	3,953	21,93,412
Return emigrants among emigrants of 2008 in Return Migration Survey in 2009	304	1,68,681
Return Emigrants to Kerala due to financial crisis and recession	110	61,036

Source: Zachariah and Rajan (2009c).

If we deduce that out of the stock of 2.19 million emigrants from Kerala, about 61,036 migrants returned due to crisis, then what could be the number of return emigrants from the Gulf to South Asia? According to the database available from various sources (both formal and informal), we arrived at a figure of 9.5 million South Asian emigrants in the Gulf; and the projected return emigrants from the Gulf region to South Asian at about 2,63,660.[5] The countrywise estimates of return emigrants are provided in Table 2.9. One can also estimate the number of return emigrants from the countries of destination in the Gulf to countries in South Asia. For instance, India had a stock of 1.7 million migrants settled in the UAE; and in the projected number of return emigrants from the UAE, there were 47,000 Indians.

Table 2.9 *Estimates of Return Emigrants to South Asia from the Gulf Due to Financial Crisis, 2009*

Country	*Stock of emigrants*	*Return emigrants due to crisis*
Kerala	21,93,412	61,036
India	50,50,000	1,40,526
Pakistan	23,00,000	64,002
Bangladesh	9,00,000	25,044
Nepal	2,50,000	6,957
Sri Lanka	9,75,000	27,131
South Asia	94,75,000	2,63,660

Source: As estimated by the authors.

Why the number so small has been compared with the large prediction? We postulate two important features of Gulf migration from South Asia as responsible for this: (i) the cost of migration to the Gulf and (ii) the peculiarities of the channel of migration. South Asians incur huge cost to migrate to the Gulf. According to the Kerala Migration Survey 2008, the cost of migration to the Gulf varied between ₹ 53,951 to Kuwait and ₹ 74,606 to Saudi Arabia—between US$1,200 and 1,660 at an exchange rate of ₹ 45 per US$ (see Table 2.10). This applies to all the South Asian countries (also see United Nations Development Programme, UNDP, 2009; Zachariah and Raja 2009b; Rajan and Prakash 2009). The high cost of migration to the Gulf caused many emigrants to borrow from various financial sources. Under such conditions, even if the expatriates lost their job in the Gulf, they would prefer not to return home fearing inability to repay the debt already contracted there. They would rather accept any job at a lower wage and send home remittances to repay their loans during a crisis in the destination country.

Table 2.10 *Average Cost of Emigration for Different Migration Corridors from Kerala to the Gulf, 2008*

Countries	*Average Cost (in ₹)*
Kerala—Bahrain	57,172
Kerala—Kuwait	53,951
Kerala—Oman	56,840
Kerala—Qatar	66,316
Kerala—Saudi Arabia	74,606
Kerala—UAE	61,308
Kerala—UK	56,589
Kerala—US	42,080

Source: Zachariah and Rajan (2009b).

Another characteristic of South Asian migration to the Gulf is the part played by the social network, which consist of friends and relatives who perform a major role in the channel of migration flows by arranging visas and other requirements for the emigration process. For instance, an all India survey conducted by the CDS for the ILO and the Ministry of Overseas Indian Affairs (MOIA) revealed that close to 80 per cent of Indian emigrants utilized their friends and relatives as an important channel for migration (Table 2.11). This also ensured that in the event of the job lost, they could rely on someone to provide them temporary support.

Table 2.11 *Channels of Migration by Emigrants, 2007*

Channel	*Male*	*Female*	*Total*	*Male*	*Female*	*Total*
Friends and relatives	330	185	515	74.20	88.52	78.7
Government agency	3	0	3	0.70	0.00	0.5
Foreign employer	41	7	48	9.20	3.35	7.3
Private recruitment agencies	71	17	88	16.01	8.10	13.5
Total	445	209	654	100.00	100.00	100.0

Source: Rajan et al. (2011).

Lost Jobs in the Gulf and Have Not Returned to the Country of Origin

So there is a category of migrants, termed 'lost jobs in the gulf and have not returned to the country of origin' (Zachariah and Rajan 2009c: 21), who remain unemployed in the destination country and continue to look for jobs in sectors less/not affected by the crisis, at lower wages and poorer working conditions (see Zachariah et al. 2004). The Return Emigrant Survey 2009 conducted in Kerala offered a unique opportunity to estimate the number of those who lost their jobs in the Gulf countries due to the crisis. According to the estimate made by the authors, of the 2.2 million emigrants from Kerala, about 39,396 persons lost their jobs between 2008 and 2009 but have not returned to their country of origin (Zachariah and Rajan 2009c). Applying the same methodology to estimate the number of South Asian migrants who lost their jobs in the Gulf yields the number 1,70,181 (Table 2.12).

Table 2.12 *Estimates of Emigrants Who Lost Their Job in the Gulf but Have Not Returned, 2009*

Country	*Stock of Emigrants*	*Number of Those Who Lost Their Jobs but Have Not Returned*
Kerala	21,93,412	39,396
India	50,50,000	90,703
Pakistan	23,00,000	41,310
Bangladesh	9,00,000	16,165
Nepal	2,50,000	4,490
Sri Lanka	9,75,000	17,512
South Asia	94,75,000	1,70,181

Source: As estimated by the authors.

Outflow of Workers from South Asia to Gulf, 2009

As there was no official data to show the extent of outflow from South Asia to the Gulf, we estimated the possible trends using reasonably well-managed databases from these countries. All the countries in South Asia, except Sri Lanka, have reported decline in the flow of workers to the Gulf. The projected decline for India is huge—about 2,80,000—followed by Pakistan with just 12,000 (see Table 2.13).

Table 2.13 *Outflow of Migrant Workers from South Asia to Gulf, 2005–2009*

	India	*Pakistan*	*Bangladesh*	*Nepal*	*Sri Lanka*
2005	4,54,628	1,27,810	2,07,089	88,230	1,92,004
2006	6,18,286	1,72,837	3,07,620	1,28,306	1,70,049
2007	7,70,510	2,78,631	4,83,757	1,82,870	1,88,365
2008	8,18,315	4,19,842	6,43,424	1,69,510	2,15,793
2009	5,38,090	4,07,077	NA	1,52,272	2,26,299

Source: This table is based on the country papers prepared by the respective country team at the countries of origin for this project.

With regard to the destination, the decline was large for the UAE, which has been more severely affected by the crisis than other countries in the Gulf. But this was more than compensated by the increase in the number of people who left for Saudi Arabia. This pattern holds for India, Pakistan, Sri Lanka and Nepal. Thus, the crisis has changed the migration and demographic dynamics of South Asian workers in the Gulf region.

Inward Remittances to South Asia, 2009

The money that migrants send home is important not only to their families, but also to their country's balance of payments (BOP). In many developing countries, remittances represent a significant proportion of the GDP as well as foreign exchange receipts. In a 2009 World Bank Migration and Development Brief (Ratha and Mohapatra 2009), India was ranked number one in terms of the volume of remittances with US$52 billion in 2008 (94.2 per cent of GDP) among the South Asian countries. Bangladesh was ranked eighth and Pakistan ranked 11th in terms of remittances. On the other hand, Nepal is listed as one of the top 10 countries with the highest share of remittances for the rest of 2008 and 2009–2010 remains as uncertain as the outlook for the global growth, oil and non-oil commodity prices and currency exchange rates. After several years of strong growth, remittance flows to developing countries began to slow down significantly in the third quarter of 2008 in response to a deepening global financial crisis.

In late 2008, on request from the government of Kerala, the CDS prepared a report called the 'Global Financial Crisis and Kerala Economy: Impact and Mitigation Measures' (CDS 2008). The report predicted that the remittances to Kerala were expected to increase from ₹ 30.122 crore in 2007 to ₹ 42.917 crore in 2008. Both the World Bank and the CDS reports predicted that the inflows of remittances to

South Asia and Kerala were likely to continue, when the general expectation was that it would drastically fall.

Our estimates based on the simple average of remittances for the available months from the country reports prepared by the teams suggest that all the countries of South Asia are resilient to the crisis in terms of remittances (Table 2.14). Our estimates put the growth in remittances to India at 3 per cent, from US$52 billion in 2008 to US$53 billion in 2009. The World Bank report 'Migration and Remittances Trends 2009' (Ratha et al. 2009) confirmed our estimates and said that the outcomes were better than expected, but that there were significant risks ahead.

Table 2.14 *Inward Remittances to South Asian Countries from Migrant Workers, 2000–2009*

	India	*Pakistan*	*Bangladesh*	*Nepal*	*Sri Lanka*
			US$ Million		
2000	12,890	1,075	1,968	111	1,166
2001	14,273	1,461	2,105	147	1,185
2002	15,736	3,554	2,858	678	1,309
2003	20,999	3,964	3,192	771	1,438
2004	18,750	3,945	3,584	823	1,590
2005	22,125	4,280	4,314	1,212	1,991
2006	28,334	5,121	5,428	1,453	2,185
2007	37,217	5,998	6,562	1,734	2,527
2008	51,581	7,039	8,995	2,727	2,947
2009a	47,000	8,619	10,431	3,010	2,892
2009b	53,227	8,856	10,525	2,812	3,308
			Percentage Change		
2000–2001	10.73	35.91	6.96	32.43	1.63
2001–2002	10.25	143.26	35.77	361.22	10.46
2002–2003	33.45	11.54	11.69	13.72	9.85
2003–2004	-10.71	-0.48	12.28	6.74	10.57
2004–2005	18.00	8.49	20.37	47.27	25.22
2005–2006	28.06	19.65	25.82	19.88	9.74
2006–2007	31.35	17.13	20.89	19.34	15.65
2007–2008	38.60	17.36	37.08	57.27	16.62
2008–2009[a]	-8.88	22.45	15.96	10.38	-1.87
2008–2009[b]	3.19	25.81	17.01	3.12	12.25

Source: World Bank and the country reports prepared by the research team for this project from five countries of South Asia.

[a] World Bank Estimates.

[b] As estimated by the authors.

Why did remittances not decline in South Asia? From our study, the following six observations can be made: (a) the debts contracted to meet the high cost incurred during their migration kept the emigrants from returning to the countries of origin in spite of the lay offs; (b) the predictions of a large exodus of return emigrants from Gulf did not come true; (c) though the outflow declined in the first half of 2009, it has still not significantly affected the stock of South Asian migrants in the Gulf; (d) the appreciation of the US dollar vis-à-vis South Asian currencies, for instance, the current exchange rate of the Indian rupee to the US dollar is the same as in 2001–2002; (e) the continuous rise in oil prices generating more income in the Gulf and (f) the 'reverse migration' of the crisis-led return emigrants back to the Gulf.

Conclusions

The unravelling of the impact of the crisis on output and employment in the United States had generated an anticipation of large-scale retrenchment of expatriate labourers in the Gulf region. The anticipated misery and the need for rehabilitation had got some governments in South Asia thinking about plans for the returning migrants. We find that the dimensions of the impact were not as large as was feared earlier. For a stock of approximately 9.5 million South Asian emigrants in the Gulf, the number who returned due to the crisis was about 2,64,000 (just around 2.78%); and the number of those who lost jobs but continued to stay in the Gulf was about 1,70,000 (1.8%). Overall, less than 5 per cent of the South Asian emigrants had lost jobs owing to the crisis. But such an impact had not adversely affected the yearly flow of out-migrants from South Asia. Compared with the outflow of about 2.2 million workers in 2008, the number in 2009 was close to 2 million, which was higher than the corresponding figure in 2007.

With regard to remittances (in US$), the annual percentage increase since 2004–2005 has been more than 20 per cent for the South Asian countries, except for Sri Lanka. The magnitude of the increase has taken a hit all over South Asia, except Pakistan from where the outflow of migrants had been increasing at around 50 per cent every year since 2005. But remittances have not fallen following the crisis; it either has remained stagnant or has shown a mild rise depending upon the estimates. As most of the South Asian currencies have depreciated against US$ (to which the GCC currencies are pegged) from late 2007, remittances in terms of domestic currencies would have shown an increase. Survey of migrant households in South Asia confirmed these estimates as 94 per cent of the households reported regular remittances during the crisis period as in previous years and recorded no significant change in the use of remittances.

Overall, less than 5 per cent of the stock of South Asian migrants in the Gulf had lost jobs and had either returned or were struggling to continue in the Gulf. The flow of workers from South Asia to the Gulf had also not been affected to any significant extent, but there were changes in the origin (in favour of Pakistan) and the destination (in favour of Saudi Arabia) of the flow. The volume of remittances into South Asia too did not show any remarkable decline.

In sum, the crisis of 2008–2009 is a blip on the radar of labour migration to the GCC countries as far as South Asia is concerned. A few thousands lost jobs and had to come back but the number migrating to the Gulf has hardly fallen. With the quick recovery experienced in 2010 and 2011, the migration flow is going to increase and the resultant outcome—remittances—will follow.

Acknowledgements

This project was funded by the Asian Development Bank, the Ministry of Overseas Indian Affairs, Government of India; and the Department of Non-Resident Keralite Affairs, Government of Kerala.

Notes

1. GCC Countries are United Arab Emirates, Saudi Arabia, Qatar, Bahrain, Kuwait and Oman.
2. This section is based on the six country reports prepared by the research teams at the CDS. Most of the members of the research team have already visited the Gulf to assess the reality by talking to several stakeholders, and additional research is done by the authors of this report.
3. Dubai World, a holding company owned by the Government of Dubai that manages about the 90 entities, asked to delay payment on US$26 billion of debt for 6 months, shaking the confidence of investors holding government's debt.
4. Return Emigrant Survey 2009 was conducted at the CDS and sponsored by the Department of Non-Resident Keralite Affairs, Government of Kerala (for more details of the survey report, see Zachariah and Rajan [2009a]). The field work was carried out during 16 June–September 2009.
5. These could be underestimates as the composition of migrants from Kerala would have a lower proportion of unskilled workers.

References

Centre for Development Studied (CDS). 'Global Financial Crisis and Kerala Economy: Impact and Mitigation Measures'. Report submitted to the Government of Kerala, 2008.

Economic and Social Commission for Western Asia (ESCWA). 'Foreign Direct Investment Report'. E/ESCWA/EDGD/2008/Technical paper. 13 September, UN, New York, 2008.

Kapiszewski, Andrzej. 'Arab versus Asian Migrant Workers in the GCC Countries'. UN Expert Group Meeting on International Migration and Development in the Arab region, 15–17 May, Beirut, 2006.

Rajan, S. Irudaya and B.A. Prakash. 'Migration and Development Linkages Re-examined in the Context of the Global Economic Crisis'. Invited Paper for the Civil Society Days of the 3rd Global Forum on Migration and Development, 2–3 November, Athens, 2009.

Rajan, S. Irudaya, V.J. Verghese, and M.S. Jayakumar. *Dreaming Mobility and Buying Vulnerability: Overseas Recruitment Practices and Its Discontents in India.* New Delhi: Routledge, 2011.

Ratha, Dilip and Saket Mohapatra. 'Revised Outlook for Remittance Flows 2009–2011: Remittances Expected to Fall by 5 to 8 Per cent in 2009'. Migration and Development Brief 9, Migration and Remittances Team, Development Prospects Group, World Bank, 2009. http://sistersources.worldbank.org/INTPROSPECTS/Resources/MD_Brief9_Mar2009.pdf (accessed 27 October 2011).

Ratha, Dilip, Saket Mohapatra, and Ani Silwal. 'Migration and Remittances Trends 2009: A Better-Than-Expected Outcome So Far, but Significant Risks Ahead'. Migration and Development Brief 11, Migration and Remittances Team, Development Prospects Group, World Bank, 2009. http://sistersources.worldbank.org/INTPROSPECTS/Resources/334934-1110315015165/MigrationandDevelopmentBrief11.pdf (accessed 27 October 2011).

Shah, Nasra M. 'Trends and Polices for Contract Worker Mobility of Asians to the Gulf Cooperation Council Countries'. Paper presented at the 2009 International Union for the Scientific Study of Population (IUSSP) International Population Conference, Marrakech, 27 September—2 October, 2009.

Taattolo, Giovanna. 'Arab Labor Migration to the GCC States'. Working paper, Jean Monnet Observatory on trans-Mediterranean relations, Project on Arab Labour Migration, 2006.

United Nations (UN). *International Migration 2009*. New York: United Nations Department of Economic and Social Affairs, Population Division, 2009.

United Nations Conference on Trade and Development (UNCTAD). *World Investment Report: Transnational Corporations, Agriculture Production and Development.* New York: United Nations, 2010.

United Nations Development Programme (UNDP). *Human Development Report 2009: Overcoming Barriers: Human Mobility and Development.* New York: United Nations, 2009.

Zachariah, K.C. and S. Irudaya Rajan. 'Impact of the Global Recession on Migration and Remittances in Kerala: New Evidences from the Return Migration Survey 2009'. Research Report, Centre for Development Studies, Thiruvananthapuram, 2009c. http://www.cds.edu/wp_content/uploads/2012/09/wp432.pdf (accessed 31 October 2011)

Zachariah, K.C. and S. Irudaya Rajan. 'Migration Monitoring Study, 2008: Emigration and Remittances in the Context of Surge in Oil Prices'. Research Report, Centre for Development Studies, Thiruvananthapuram, 2009b.

Zachariah, K.C. and S. Irudaya Rajan. *Migration and Development: The Kerala Experience.* New Delhi: Daanish Publishers, 2009a.

Zachariah, K.C., B.A. Prakash, and S. Irudaya Rajan. 'Indian Workers in UAE: Employment, Wages and Working Conditions'. *Economic and Political Weekly*, 39, 22 (2004); 2227–2234.

Zachariah, K.C., P.R. Gopinathan Nair, and S. Irudaya Rajan. *Return Emigrants in Kerala: Welfare, Rehabilitation and Development.* New Delhi: Manohar Publishers and Distributors, 2006.

CHAPTER 3

International Migration of Women from India to the Gulf

The Case of Domestic Workers

Basant Potnuru and Vishishta Sam

There were an estimated 215 million migrant workers living in the world in 2010 (International Organization for Migration; IOM 2011). Forty-nine per cent of these migrants worldwide were women and an estimated 94 million women migrant stock was economically active (UNDESA 2008). Given the gradual increase of women migrant workers, international migration has entered into a phase where it can no longer be viewed from a gender-neutral lens. This gradual increase in the number of women migrants has often referred to as the phenomenon of 'feminization' of international labour migration (Piper 2008). International migration of women occurs due to a variety of reasons, such as family reunification, labour migration, asylum and natural disasters. However, the inherent differences between the experiences of migrating men and women present differential opportunities and challenges at every stage of the migration process. Thus, the problems women migrant workers endure vis-à-vis their role and access to resources, facilities and services within the migration cycle are central to understanding and forming policies mitigating these challenges.

The feminization of migration also resonates through the migration trends from South Asian countries. Reflecting global trends, women from South Asia have consistently accounted for almost 40–45 per cent of its total international migrants over the last one decade (UNDESA 2008). In some parts of Asia, however, the number of women migrating has surpassed that of males. For example, approximately two-third of migrant workers from Sri Lanka in 2002 were women. Larger proportions of female migration have also been observed in countries such as Indonesia and the Philippines (Esim and Smith 2004). The Gulf continues are the dominant destination followed by the neighbouring East Asian countries for these migrants.

Although the number of women migrating from India is not very large compared with its neighbouring countries, there has been a steady increase in the trend recently. The number of women migrated seeking Emigration Check Required (ECR) clearance increased from 10,416 in 2008 to 14,636 in 2009 and peaked at 20,000 in 2010.[1] This constitutes about 3–4 per cent of the total labour migration from India under the ECR category. However, informal estimates put the actual flows of women to the Gulf three times that of the numbers reported above. The majority of these women migrate to Gulf countries under contractual terms as housemaids.[2] This reflects the dominant sexual division of labour with relatively lower-end position that are being filled by the migrant women (Thimothy and Sasikumar 2012). Apart from the domestic work, migrant women are also engaged in other low-end services as beauticians, babysitters, caregivers and cleaners.

Since most migrant women work at the bottom rung of the occupational hierarchy as housemaids, they are extremely vulnerable to exploitation. Housemaids are particularly vulnerable because they work in closed doors of the houses where their conditions of work and exploitation are outside of the ambit of societies and authorities concerned. These occupations are neither legally protected nor clearly defined. Although the protection of many existing ILO conventions technically apply to domestic workers, they have not been often extended or applied to protect domestic workers due to traditional perceptions of domestic workers as 'helpers' rather than 'workers' and the location of employment is in private households rather than in commercial enterprises (Sharma and Iyer 2010). This along with the prevalent *Kafala system*[3] in the Gulf countries leaves many women migrant workers dependent on employers for legal status and basic needs such as housing, food and payment of due wages, which employers may and often arbitrarily withhold in order to ensure compliance to their demands.

> I worked in a family of 26 members. They used to beat and deprive me of adequate food and sleep. I was expected to rear cattle and look after the family including its extended family members. Though, I was shouted at and harassed by the employer's sister, I never complained because the employer was working in a local police station. Finally, I had to escape with the help of my sister's son who brought me here to the shelter home at Muscat in the early morning hours. (Smriti, Tamil Nadu, [name changed], interviewed on 5 July 2011, at the shelter home, Muscat)

Of late, there have been increased concerns on the issues of safety and security of Indian women migrating as housemaids to Gulf countries. Given the patterns of work and nature of migration, these women mostly come from disadvantaged sections of society, which in turn exposes them to severe vulnerabilities at each stage of the migration cycle. Therefore, envisaging migration as an empowering process for women will entail comprehensive strategies. These strategies will have to analyse the social milieu under which women seek to migrate, the challenges that they face in the event of migration and the impacts that the entire process has on their sense of being.

This chapter underlines the issues and concerns of women migrant workers from India to the Gulf. In pursuance of the same, it also suggests policy for smooth facilitation of informed processes making migration an empowering experience for both men and women. This chapter is divided into five sections: the second section discusses recent data trends of women migration; the third section analyses the current practices and policy on emigration, the fourth section discusses the limitations and policy challenges and the fifth section concludes with key policy recommendations.

Trends of Women Migrant Workers

The data on international migration, specifically gender disaggregated, are difficult to come by. Under the Emigration Act, 1983, emigration check is mandatory for individuals who do not qualify above class X and migrating for employment purposes to any of the listed 17 ECR countries: Afghanistan, Bahrain, Indonesia, Iraq, Jordan, Kingdom of Saudi Arabia (KSA), Kuwait, Lebanon, Libya, Malaysia, Oman, Qatar, Sudan, Syria, Thailand, UAE and Yemen. Rest of the 175 countries have been notified as Emigration Check Not Required (ECNR) countries.[4] Under the existing regulatory framework, data pertaining to only ECR migrants are captured by the office of the Protector General of Emigrants (PGE).[5] This effectively means that the number of women with qualification of above class X (non-ECR category) migrating abroad and women who migrate showing any other purpose other than work are not captured under this process. The data on women migrant workers under the ECR category are presented below.

Table 3.1 shows that there is a sharp rise in the number of women migrated in 2009 from the 2008 mark. The rise is approximately 40 per cent in 2009 from the number migrated in 2008. The figures indicate that Protector of Emigrants (PoEs) such as Hyderabad, Mumbai, Cochin and Trivandrum account for high volumes of ECR clearances. Among these, Hyderabad accounted for the highest number of clearances, that is, about 43 per cent of the total in 2008 and 68 per cent in 2009. Clearances from Kerala (combining Trivandrum and Cochin) accounted for approximately 15.6 per cent (third highest after Hyderabad and Mumbai) in 2008 and 17.3 per cent (second only to Hyderabad) in 2009.

Table 3.1 *ECR Clearance Granted to Women Migrants Workers by PoE, 2008–2009*

PoE Location	*2008*	*2009*
Chandigarh	15	21
Chennai	517	954
Cochin	872	1,648
Delhi	134	97
Hyderabad	4,475	9,960
Kolkata	30	28
Mumbai	3,614	1,030
Trivandrum	759	898
Total	10,416	14,636

Source: Data collected and compiled from PGE office, MOIA, New Delhi.

Table 3.2 shows that between 2008 and 2010, the top three destination countries for Indian women migrant workers under the ECR category were Kuwait, Oman and UAE. These three destinations together account for about 97 per cent of all women migrant workers under the ECR category. In 2010, Kuwait alone accounted for 61 per cent of the total flow of women migrant workers to the Gulf.

Table 3.2 *ECR Clearances Granted to Women Migrant Workers by Major Destinations 2008–2010*

Country	*2008*	*2009*	*2010*
Bahrain	219	140	122
Kuwait	3,319	9,602	11,901
Lebanon	17	10	14
Malaysia	3	14	29
Oman	6,707	6,625	5,884
Qatar	52	19	45
KSA	121	131	340
UAE	1,358	1,333	1,334
Yemen	13	6	12
Total[6]	11,909	17,880	19,681

Source: Data collected and compiled from PGE office, MOIA, New Delhi.

Table 3.3 *ECR Clearances Granted to Women Migrant Workers by Occupation and Major Destinations, 2010*

Category of Unskilled Occupation	*UAE*	*Qatar*	*Oman*	*Kuwait*	*KSA*	*Bahrain*	*Total per Occupation*
Labour	6	0	2	6	11	1	26
Cleaner	21	1	45	41	17	5	130
Helper	5	0	0	1	0	0	6
Housemaid	74	3	5,734	11,736	93	94	17,734
Domestic cook	4	0	0	3	0	0	7
Servant	860	4	4	4	0	0	872
Domestic servant	0	0	3	0	0	0	3
Messenger	7	0	0	0	0	0	7
Office worker	4	0	0	0	0	0	4
House boy/girl	0	0	1	9	0	0	10
Domestic driver	0	0	1	9	0		10
Other unskilled	109	19	53	61	50	7	299
Total	1,090	27	5,843	11,870	171	107	19,108

Source: Data collected and compiled from PGE office, MOIA, New Delhi.

Table 3.3 provides a further breakdown of the data on women migrant workers by occupation and destination. It clearly demonstrates that among the ECR migrant women workers, housemaid is the most dominant occupation and comprises approximately 93 per cent of all women migrant workers. Kuwait and Oman recruited the highest number of Indian women migrant workers as housemaids with 11,736 and 5,734 respectively in 2010. Bahrain, KSA and UAE recruited 94, 93 and 74 women as housemaids respectively. It may be noted that UAE also recruited an additional 860 women as servants.[7]

Table 3.4 *Average Monthly Wage of Housemaids by Destination and Sex, 2010 (in ₹)*

Country	*Male*	*Female*
Bahrain	13,855	12,387
KSA	16,945	12,208
Kuwait	10,557	8,082
Oman	9,340	8,623
Qatar	NA	10,750
UAE	NA	13,422

Source: Data collected and compiled from PGE office, MOIA, New Delhi.

Table 3.4 provides an indication of the average wage of Indian migrant workers employed as domestic workers. The average wage paid to Indian women migrant workers in the UAE is approximately ₹ 3,422 per month, followed by Bahrain at ₹ 12,387, KSA at ₹ 12,208 and Oman at ₹ 8,623 per month. It is also interesting to note that Kuwait, the top destination country with about 61 per cent of all Indian domestic workers in the Gulf, paid an average wage of about ₹ 8,082 per month. In other words, it would mean that majority of Indian migrant domestic workers in the Gulf earn only little more than ₹ 8,000 per month.

Current Practices and Measures

The Government of India and the major origin state governments have undertaken several initiatives for the protection and welfare of its migrant workers. Some initiatives or measures that are of relevance to women migrant workers are presented under the four broad categories: (i) regulatory measures, (ii) information dissemination, (iii) protection and social welfare and (iv) skills training.

Regulatory Measures

Under the regulatory framework, individuals who require emigration clearance are required to furnish the following documents: (a) valid passport with a minimum period of six months validity; (b) valid work visa; (c) employment contract from the foreign employer duly attested by the Indian Embassy or permission letter from the concerned Indian Embassy/Post; (d) Receipt of prescribed fee and, (e) Insurance policy under Pravasi Bharatiya Bima Yojana (PBBY). Furthermore, the Government of India has imposed a restriction on emigration of women below 30 years of age for work in ECR countries. This regulation was imposed at the recommendation of the National Commission for Women with the aim of protecting women from being abused in the cycle of migration as well as reducing the risk to trafficking.

Other regulatory measures include initiatives such as attestation of the employment contract at the Indian Embassy in the country of employment, which is a mandatory requirement for the employment of housemaids and other unskilled workers. Since June 2011, employers are also required to deposit a security amount of US$2,500 in the form of a bank guarantee with the Indian Embassy. Upon completion of the contract, this security amount is reimbursed to the employer. However, this is subject to the condition that the migrant worker reports back to the Indian Embassy and the Indian Embassy verifies that all the terms and conditions of her employment have been respected and adhered to. A failure to adhere to the terms of employment by the employer, not only nullifies the employer's claim to the deposit money, but in extreme cases can also lead to *suo moto* action by the Indian Embassy in the destination country.

Information Dissemination

Migrant Resource Centres (MRCs) set up by the Ministry of Overseas Indian Affairs (MOIA), Government of India, have been strategic in providing migration-related information to the potential migrants. Currently, three such centres are in operation in Hyderabad, Cochin and Panchkula. The primary objective of these MRCs is to provide valid information on legal emigration processes and assist migrants to organize their migration in a systematic manner. MRCs are also expected to assist aspiring migrants in the job search, counselling and training opportunities. Services provided at these centres include walk-in and telephonic counselling and assistance in verification of documents and information.

The MOIA has also initiated preparation of country-specific manuals for the GCC countries. These manuals contain general as well as specific information and data about the relevant destination countries. They provide useful information to the prospective Indian migrants. These initiatives have also been supplemented by awareness campaigns through the medium of print and visual media. The major migrant origin state governments are also taking keen interest in disseminating information to potential migrant workers. For example, the Government of Kerala has organized pre-departure orientation trainings, job portal and training opportunities through the Norka Roots.[8] The Government of Andhra Pradesh has also recently undertaken similar measures through its state recruiting agency called Overseas Manpower Company Andhra Pradesh Ltd. (OMCAP).[9]

Protection and Social Welfare

Consular support, verification and follow-up measures are important steps to ensure the safety of migrant workers in the destination. This is facilitated through Indian Embassies (Labour Attaches) that are entrusted with the responsibility of intervening on behalf of workers in the destination country. Protection and welfare of migrant workers is also propagated through establishment of institutions such as the Indian Workers Resource Centres (IWRC) abroad (currently, in Dubai only) and Overseas Workers Resource Centre (OWRC) in New Delhi. These institutions register, respond and monitor complaints received from emigrant workers.

Shelter homes have been instituted in the select Indian Embassies in the Gulf to accommodate and address the issues of run-away women migrant workers. These services have been adapted within the framework of Indian Embassies and IWRCs. Other services common to all migrant workers are the Pravasi Bharatiya Bima Yojana (PBBY),[10] Indian Community Welfare Fund (ICWF),[11] Pension and Life-insurance Fund (PLIF)[12] for Overseas Indian Workers scheme, and so on.

Pre-departure Orientation and Skills Training

Pre-departure orientation and skills enhancement are other essential components of the organized migration. Training is important to acquaint women migrant workers about the working conditions, principles, use of technology, and so on, in a foreign country. Skill training is essential not only to enhance the productivity of workers but also to command better wages and position in the job market. Under the current framework the central and major migrant origin state governments are providing pre-departure orientation and skills training through agencies such as OMCAP and Norka Roots in Andhra

Pradesh and Kerala respectively. OMCAP is being mandated by the state government to provide trained and qualified human resources for overseas employment; Norka Roots provides training and orientation to prospective emigrants.

Limitations and Policy Challenges

The foremost challenge in the current regulatory practices is that the legal processes and the formal institutions of emigration are undermined by the extensive networks of unscrupulous middlemen. These middlemen act as a road-block between the migrants and the formal institutions and channels, thereby making it difficult for the women to access reliable information. These hurdles in the current regulatory practices and lack of adequate schemes/services on information dissemination, pre-departure orientation, skills training, and so on contribute to the risks and vulnerabilities of intending women migrants. The registered recruiting agents,[13] on the other hand, are unwilling to formally recruit women for employment abroad in order to avoid the responsibility of ensuring accountability and safety of women.

> 'I'm 35 years old, unmarried and going to Kuwait'. (Laxmi [name changed], interviewed at PoE office, Hyderabad)
>
> However, she looked much younger than the stated 35 years of age. When she was asked to frank and genuine, she had replied that her actual age was 21 years. She stated that she had lied while applying for the passport for getting ECR clearance.

The policy of restriction on women below 30 years of age from emigration to the ECR countries has come under sharp criticisms from scholars and practitioners alike. Kodoth and Varghese (2011) have argued that this 'protectionism' by the state has contributed to the production of underground operation of emigration activities for women. Moreover, it is also argued that 'protection by exception' may not offer any substantial improvements since the exercise of verification can be reduced to document verification exercise (Rajan et al. 2009). While the intent of the policy has been to safeguard the interests of women workers, the actual implications of the policy have been counterintuitive. Furthermore, this age restriction on emigration goes against the spirit of gender equal laws promoted by international instruments such as Committee on the Elimination of Discrimination against Women (CEDAW), to which India is a signatory. The government may also want to take into consideration General Recommendation Number 26, which requires the sending countries to lift bans on migration.[14] This principle is also reiterated under Article 8 of the International Convention on the Protection of the Rights of All Migrant Workers and Members of their Families[15] and its subsequent General Comment Number 1, Para 61 on Migrant Domestic Workers.[16]

Familiarization with work environment and culture is essential for any worker. In this context, it is crucial to provide intending migrants and their families with adequate and accurate information. Some of the information dissemination, pre-departure orientation and training programmes initiated in the past by the major origin state governments and the central government have been discontinued now. For example, housekeeping training for intending migrant housemaids initiated in Andhra Pradesh by the OMCAP was halted shortly after inception. A lack of awareness on aspects such as rights and duties, language, culture and other work-related skills has proven to be a severe delimiting factor for women migrant workers.

> When I first visited to Kuwait, my recruiting agent promised me a salary of ₹ 9,000, however, I have been paid only ₹ 6,000. I also have been given additional work like car washing, etc. and offered insufficient food to eat. Despite, these problems, I continued my work just to fulfil the contract obligations and returned back home. I Could not report my problems to the Embassy because I was unaware of the Indian Embassy and its services. (Ruchi Andhra Pradesh, [name changed])

Upon arrival in the country of employment women workers require continued support and monitoring by the respective Indian Mission in the destination country. Systemic support at arrival is essential as it would provide the opportunity of first contact point for both the migrant and the Indian Government Machinery in the destination country. It would also give the opportunity to document the migrant workers local contact details and initiate meetings and gatherings with them eventually for promoting social welfare of migrant workers abroad. Most women migrant workers have limited access to the support and welfare services at the embassy and IWRC. This can be attributed in part to the lack of awareness among women workers about the various schemes and policies of the government. Furthermore, given the isolated nature of work, at times the physical distance from the embassies, women workers are unable to get support in the country of destination. Therefore, policies and mechanisms in the destination countries should ensure easy access of these services and facilities to the women migrant workers.

Conclusions and Recommendations

Thus, the discussion in the preceding sections highlights the need for a coherent strategy for an orderly and humane experience of international migration. The entire emigration process or cycle can be divided into four stages, that is, pre-recruitment, recruitment and emigration, work and living and finally return and re-settlement. The nature of the problems and stakeholders associated within each of these stages of migration cycle are different and, therefore, need different strategies or measures for addressing them. However, these measures need to be coherent to substantiate and compliment the good practices in each stage of the migration cycle with the other so as to make the migration process smooth.

For example, under the current emigration framework, legal channels and process are largely undermined by the extensive networks of unscrupulous middlemen who reach out better to the migrant communities. Therefore, it is important to reverse the current environment of emigration that is highly dependent on middlemen/brokers to the one that draws the migrants and migrant families close to the formal institutions and channels of emigration. This can be done either by pushing the informal middlemen/brokers away or by mainstreaming them in the formal mechanisms and practice to ensure their accountability. The state machinery and mechanisms needs to be expanded and strengthened to reach out to the migrant communities effectively. The activities of the MRCs needs to be enhanced and upgraded accordingly for providing valid and useful information, assistance, guidance and direction. In addition, the MRCs should frequently take up awareness-generation campaigns and set up extended help desks for a fixed time periods at the village/districts in order to disseminate information and assist potential migrant workers.[17] Similarly, workshops at state and national levels may also be organized to educate and spread awareness among all stakeholders of migration such as concerned centre and state government officials, media, police, civil society organization and local self-governments. For all this to happen effectively, MRCs need to function as autonomous and independent service providers. The centres also need to be widely publicized to promote their wider usage by the migrants. Lastly, the centre and state governments must mobilize resources to provide skills training initiatives to the women migrant workers.

Similarly, during the stage of recruitment and emigration, it is important to ascertain fair and transparent recruitment system with clearer terms of contract (wages, duration, working hours and living conditions), hassle-free and easy access to emigration services, proper documentation and pre-departure orientation. It is important to examine and review the ban on emigration of unskilled women migrant workers below 30 year of age so as to ensure equal opportunities for both men and women. The regulation compels the young women migrant workers to take the illegal recourse. Apart from these, it is important to build, maintain and share a database of women migrant workers on their socioeconomic profile, employer details and focal points of contact in the destination country.

After arrival at the destination, the institutions such as Labour Attaches at the Indian Embassies, IWRCs, OWRC and MRCs should coordinate with each other for facilitating follow-ups on the well-being of migrant workers. The Labour Attaches may organize gatherings and meetings of women migrant workers with the help of IWRC and Overseas Indian Centres in order to ensure that the living and working of women abroad is an empowering, enjoyable and risk-free process. Setting up of help desks at the departure and arrival airports would also be helpful for assisting women migrant workers as well as for surveillance of their movements.

These measures are important because, despite all the regulatory requirements of work contract, attestation of the work contract, security deposit, and so on, there have been no mechanisms or maintained database in place to reach out to the migrant domestic workers during the period of employment. If, such a database is made available; IWRC, OWRC or MRCs can follow up periodically on the well-being of women migrant workers and report to the concerned authorities accordingly. These measures are also important to keep the employer under periodic scrutiny and check.

On return, most women migrant workers need counselling and assistance on resettlement issues. Some returnee women also need assistance in rehabilitation and distress management, especially those who suffer from adverse consequences of migration such as financial loss, exploitation, loss of family member(s), abandonment by family, and so on. Thus, maximizing the benefits of remittances while abroad and reintegration upon return are essential towards ensuring labour migration benefits. The governments have a key responsibility in providing assistance to returnee workers through providing opportunities for skill upgradation and remittance linked investment products.

Acknowledgements

Authors would like to thank women migrant workers in Hyderabad, Malikipuram, Vijayawada, Trivandrum and Kochi for their time and interaction during the situational analysis study carried out by the joint team of ICM, UN Women and MOIA. Authors also thank Mr K.V. Swamy and Mr Durga Prasad, PoEs of Hyderabad and Trivandrum, Dr Irudaya Rajan, Officials of the Indian Embassies in the UAE, Kuwait and Oman for their time, support and sharing of views. The views and opinions expressed and any errors in the chapter are solely of authors, and not that of the ICM.

Notes

1. See the second section for trends of women migrant workers from India to the Gulf and detailed explanation of the term ECR.
2. See second section on trends of women migrant workers from India.
3. Under the *Kafala* system, the employer sponsors the visa for the migrant worker, which authorizes the migrant to temporarily reside in the country. On withdrawal of the job/employment by the employer, the migrant automatically losses the right to stay in the country and thus becomes irregular (Thimothy and Sasikumar 2012: 32).
4. The list of 175 ECNR countries may be seen in the MOIA Annual Report 2011–12, Annexure C, pp. 52–53.
5. The PGE is the statutory authority under the Emigration Act 1983, who is responsible for all operational matters relating to emigration, the provision of emigration services to emigrants and the enforcement of the Emigration Act, 1983. He also oversees the ten field offices of the Protector of Emigrants (PoEs) across the country for governing the emigration process. The ten field offices are located at Chandigarh, Chennai, Cochin, Delhi, Hyderabad, Jaipur, Kolkata, Mumbai, Rae Bareli and Thiruvananthapuram.
6. The discrepancy in the total number of ECR women migrants in 2012 as seen in Tables 3.1 and 3.2 are owing to the interpretation of authors on sex of the migrants on the basis of occupations for data cases/entries where sex was of the migrant was not reported.

7. The application form for ECR clearance comprises many questions pertaining to the socioeconomic profile of the intending migrant. Under the occupation subgroups, applicants can choose to fill from a variety of occupations. Therein housemaids and servants appear as distinct occupations.
8. Non-Resident Keralites' Affairs Department was set up by the Government of Kerala in 1996 to ensure the welfare of the Non-Resident Keralites (NRK), redress their grievances and safeguard rights. Norka-Roots is the field agency of the Department of NORKA, set up in 2002. It acts as an interface between the NRK and the Government of Kerala and a forum for addressing the NRKs' problems, safeguarding their rights and rehabilitating the returnees.
9. OMCAP is a recruiting Agency launched by the Government of Andhra Pradesh. OMCAP maintains Data Bank of Doctors, Engineers, other skilled and unskilled workers and provides overseas employers the best suited short-listed candidates by screening from the data bank. If the required candidates are not available from the data bank, OMCAP mobilizes applications through advertisement in print and electronic media. Interviews of the candidates are arranged by OMCAP at its premises or any other centre convenient to the foreign employer.
10. PBBY is a compulsory insurance scheme for emigrant workers that provides for a life cover of ₹ 10 lakhs (in case of death) and medical cover up to ₹ 75,000 (in case of accident) for the actual period of employment contract. In case of death or permanent disability during employment, the worker, his/her family including spouse and up to two children are entitled to a hospitalization cover of ₹ 50,000 per annum till at least any one child of the deceased attains 21 years of age.
11. Indian Community Welfare Fund (ICWF) is another important onsite service for migrant workers. It is aimed at providing the following welfare services to workers in distress: (i) Boarding and lodging for distressed overseas Indian workers in household/domestic sectors and unskilled labourers; (ii) Extending emergency medical care to the overseas Indians in need; (iii) Providing air passage to stranded overseas Indians in need; (iv) Providing initial legal assistance to the overseas Indians in deserving cases and (v) Expenditure on incidentals and for airlifting the mortal remains to India or local cremation/burial of the deceased overseas Indians.
12. The Pension and Life Insurance Fund (PLIF) for Overseas Indian Workers, renamed as Mahatma Gandhi Pravasi Suraksha Yojana (MGPSY), has been instituted for the return and reintegration needs of migrant workers. It is an integrated scheme meant to encourage and enable overseas workers to voluntarily save for their return and

resettlement, save for their old age and obtain a life insurance cover of ₹ 1,00,000 against their natural death.

13. The Emigration Act, 1983 (Section 10), requires that those who wish to recruit Indian citizens for employment abroad shall register themselves with the Protector General of Emigrants (PGE). In pursuance of the same, a guideline for recruiting agents has been prepared by the Ministry of Overseas Indian Affairs and can be accessed on the ministry's website.
14. General Recommendation 26: 24 (a) Countries of origin must respect and protect the human rights of their female nationals who migrate for purposes of work. Measures that may be required include, but are not limited to, the following: Lifting of discriminatory bans or restrictions on migration. States parties should repeal sex-specific bans and discriminatory restrictions on women's migration on the basis of age, marital status, pregnancy or maternity status. They should lift restrictions that require women to get permission from their spouse or male guardian to obtain a passport or to travel abroad (CEDAW 2008).
15. International Convention on the Protection of the Rights of All Migrant Workers and Members of their Families, Article 8 (1): Migrant workers and members of their families shall be free to leave any State, including their State of origin. This right shall not be subject to any restrictions except those that are provided by law, are necessary to protect national security, public order (order public), public health or morals or the rights and freedoms of others and are consistent with the other rights recognized in the present part of the Convention.
16. General Comment Number 1, Para 61: States parties should repeal sex-specific bans and discriminatory restrictions on women's migration on the basis of age, marital status, pregnancy or maternity status (Articles 1 and 7), including restrictions that require women to get permission from their spouse or male guardian to obtain a passport or to travel (Article 8) or bans on women migrant domestic workers marrying nationals or permanent residents (Article 14), or securing independent housing.
17. Women migrant workers being illiterate and alien to foreign country and language often face difficulties at the arrival airport in the destination country. It is imperative to provide support and assistance to the migrant workers for immigration clearances, establishing contact with employers and so on. Systemic support at the airports of departure in the origin and arrival in the destinations is necessary for safe travel and arrival of women migrant workers at the destination.

References

CEDAW General Recommendation 26. 2008. http://www2.ohchr.org/english/bodies/cedaw/docs/GR_26_on_women_migrant_workers_en.pdf (accessed on 5 December 2012).

Esim, Simel and Smith, Monica. *Gender and Migration in Arab States: The Case of Domestic Workers,* 2004. http://www.ilo.org/public/english/region/arpro/beirut/downloads/publ/publ_26_eng.pdf (accessed on 3 December 2012).

International Organization for Migration. *World Migration Report 2011.* http://publications.iom.int/bookstore/free/WMR2011_English.pdf (accessed on 7 December 2012).

Kodoth, Praveena and Varghese, V.J. 'Emigration of Women Domestic Workers from Kerala: Gender, State Policy and the Politics of Movement'. CDS Working Paper No. 445. Centre for Development Studies, Trivandrum, 2011.

Piper, Nicola. *New Perspectives on Gender and Migration.* London: Routledge, 2008.

Rajan, S. Irudaya and B.A. Prakash. 'Migration and Development Linkages Re-Examined in the Context of the Global Economic Crisis'. Invited Paper for the Civil Society Days of the 3rd Global Forum on Migration and Development, Athens, 2–3 November 2009.

Sharma, Seetha and Iyer, Asha. *Domestic Workers and Trafficking,* 2010. http://www.labourfile.org/CurrentArticleDetails.aspx?id=536 (accessed on 6 December 2012).

Thimothy, Rakhee and Sasikumar, S.K. *Migration of Women Workers from South Asia to the Gulf.* UN Women and V.V. Giri National Labour Institute, 2012.

UNDESA. *International Migrant Stock: The 2008 Revision,* 2008. http://esa.un.org/migration/p2k0data.asp (accessed on 3 December 2012).

Part II

Diaspora and Connections

CHAPTER 4

Malayali Nurses in the Gulf Countries

Migration as a Factor of Women Empowerment

Marie Percot

Indian nurses' migration—and more precisely Malayali nurses' migration—has started nearly four decades ago. Nowadays, most nursing students choose this profession in order to leave, at least for a few years. Migratory strategies not only have been developed by families but also among the concerned women over three generations of migrants: from a sort of a 'passive' experience it used to be for the first migrant nurses in the 1970s, it is now a very active life task. The development of a Malayali diaspora in the Gulf countries has also open ways to a renewed sociability compared with the home country. Moreover, for many migrant nurses and for their husbands, the Gulf countries are now considered as a step for a further migration to the Western countries. Migration has induced a redefinition of traditional gender roles.

In this chapter, I argue that today migrant nurses aspire not only to a more lucrative career abroad but also to a new life style with more individualistic ambitions, in which in particular traditional gender-based restrictions are challenged, leading to an improved female agency. As skilled workers, being often the bread earner of the family, nurses indeed get an increased negotiation and decision power within the family. I will also argue that life in the Gulf presents some advantages for nurses compared with life in a Western country.

Since the middle of the 1970s, Gulf countries recruit nurses whose large majority comes from Asia. Although no accurate statistics exist, one considers that more than 70,000 of them come from India, mostly from Kerala. Recruitment in the Gulf was an unexpected opportunity for the first generation of migrant nurses whose profession in their own country was altogether badly considered and poorly paid. But for the following generations, these are indeed the migratory opportunities that decided the choice of profession. Moreover, in the 1990s, many Western countries also started to recruit foreign nurses, giving them new migratory opportunities. One even observes recently that more and more young men are entering the nursing schools with the same plans of migration as their female counterparts.

Until now, most researches on female migration have focused on unskilled migrants, particularly in the care sector (Parrenas 2001; Ehrenreich and Hochschild 2002; Falquet 2006). Yet, as Kofman and Raghuram (2006), for instance, remarked, there is a growing number of skilled women migrants whose strategies and stakes do not correspond those of less qualified migrants. Nurses are part of this category. I shall try to demonstrate here that, in their case, migration is not only considered as a way of climbing social ladder, but also the result of an aspiration to get another life style than the one they could have expected in their place of origin, regarding women status especially. I will also argue that, even if the legislation poorly protects the migrant, migration to the Gulf countries happens to often offer more well-being to the nurses and their family than a migration to Western countries.

This chapter is based on a research started in 2001, with nearly two years of ethnographic fieldwork in Kerala, in Delhi and Mumbai, in the UAE and Oman as well as in Ireland, one of the latest recruiting countries. I have been able to interview more than 300 women (nursing students, migrants or ex-migrants) and have been invited to stay in 15 nurses' families (in Kerala, Muscat, Dubai and Dublin) with whom I am still in touch through phone or Facebook. Interviews were also conducted with nurses' husbands, members of the extended family and with nursing school principals or hospital directors.

Nurses' Background and Family Strategies

Most Malayali nurses come from low middle-class or middle-class families: father is most often a farmer employing a few agricultural labourers and/or he works as a petty clerk. Most nurses belong to the first generation in their family who has been able to attend higher studies and the first women of their family to work in a salaried job (Percot 2006). Until the middle of the 1980s, stipends were given for nursing studies. In a context where salaried job for women was developing in Kerala and was more and more accepted socially, nursing was a good option for not so wealthy families to ensure a job opportunity to their daughters, although nursing was not a prestigious and well-paid profession. Later, the increasing migratory opportunities lead to a growing number of candidates to this profession and to the blossoming of private nursing schools. However, families managed to pay, considering that their investment will surely be covered by their migrant daughter's remittances.

The first generation of migrants constituted of married women in their 40s. In the course of time, younger and younger women started to leave, to the point that, nowadays, nurses migrate as soon as they have got the two years of experience required by recruiting countries. Indeed, for the parents, migration of a daughter who is still single presents some advantages. First, they beneficiate from her remittances until her marriage; then, their daughter will be able to save for her own dowry.[1] In addition, a migrant nurse gives her future husband a way to migrate himself, whether it is by legal family reunification in the Western countries or—in the Gulf countries—by first getting a 'visiting visa', which will afterwards easily be transformed into working visa. This opportunity actually often plays a role in reducing the dowry amount asked by the groom family. Moreover, only 20 years ago, nurses were considered as a poor match because of the stigma attached to this profession, but they are now looked after on the matrimonial market as it can be checked, for instance, on the matrimonial websites.[2] As a consequence, nurses' families can now pretend to have more prestigious sons-in-law: a few decades ago, the latter were generally blue collars (mechanics, electricians, etc.); today, most of them are degree holders.

Even if the choice of the nursing profession is not only an individual decision of the young women, they however find their own interest in this choice and often push their family to let them take this path. They first want to have a professional career and not to remain—like their mothers—'housewives'. Then, the time of their studies (most often far from their family home) and their first years as professionals in an Indian metropolis are unanimously considered as a liberation from a social control that all these young women describe as too strongly burdening them in their native town or village. As one of them explains:

> In Kerala, without my brother, my father, or at least my mother, there was no place I could go to. Here, I can go to the market on my own. I also go to meet some friends who work in other hospitals. I come back at 8 or 9PM. Nothing happens to me and I am not doing anything wrong. But if I was doing so in Kerala, it would be a scandal. Neighbours would gossip about my morality. (Raji, 23, working in Delhi and preparing to leave for Abu Dhabi)

All these young women are also well aware that, once married, migration will—*de facto*—free them from the tight control of the extended family and, particularly, from the authority of a mother-in-law. Almost all of them praise the model of nuclear family, a model that is still not the norm in their social milieu. At last, like male migrants, they share the ambitions attached to migration: discovering other countries, climbing the social ladder and also gaining more professional and individual experience. For most of these women, to become a nurse is a passport for the world.

Having started nearly four decades ago, the migration channels are now well established for nurses. Recruiters and 'travel agencies' are still largely used, but the feminine networks also play an essential role: colleagues or friends who are already abroad never stop to inform new migrant candidates of the job opportunities, thus reducing a lot the possible scams attached to such an adventure: indeed, very few nurses are alone when leaving for the Gulf countries at least; most of them leave in small groups, with women they have already met earlier (Percot & Naïr 2010).

Nowadays, most young nurses' final goal is a migration to a Western country (whether it is United States, United Kingdom, Australia or New Zealand). They not only consider it as more prestigious than migrating to a Gulf country, but also look for certain advantages: an easier family reunification, a free and better education for their young children, the possibility to invest in a house abroad and they also aim at getting another citizenship with which displacement will be easier than with an Indian passport. Such things are not possible in a Gulf country. Yet, to reach a Western country is more difficult since it requires altogether more capital and some diplomas in addition (IELTS in all cases—NCLEX-RN for the United States). One thus more often observes a step-by-step migration, starting with a first sojourn in a Gulf country. However, this step in the Gulf may last for long: by default if one has not been able to pass the required exams or to gather the capital; and by choice, if the couple has succeeded enough in the Gulf and choose not to venture further.

Life in the Gulf

The first nurses who reached the Gulf in the 1970s describe their life at that time as rather difficult. They used to live in the hospitals' hostels and barely got out of these premises. They had to deal with patients who were not accustomed to modern medicine and to work with a medical staff they had some difficulties to communicate with (most doctors at that time were coming from Arabic countries). They had few contacts with their family at home, phone being very expensive and mail being very slow. Yet, slowly, with the development of a Malayali diaspora, especially in the UAE, their life started to change. If nurses still live in hostels as long as they are single, they now dare to go out and, as soon as they get married, they settle in town: most Gulf cities have now Malayali neighbourhoods with not only housing, but also shops, movie theatres, churches and temples, schools, sportive grounds and so on. Cultural and religious organizations are also very active (Oommen 2011). To be in contact with the motherland is not a problem anymore, due to the massive use of phone and Internet; moreover, the development of international airports in Kerala has made it easy to go back home regularly for holidays or family functions, at least for people who, like the nurses, have enough income to afford it. The opportunity of having a rich social life, without suffering really from home sickness, is acknowledged by the vast majority of nurses working in the Gulf and they consider that it is particularly true for women. Actually, if the Malayali community in the Gulf does not deny the traditional values of its own society, it has nevertheless taken some freedom with some of its codes, whether it is out of pragmatism or due to a more modernist thinking:

> When you live abroad, it opens your mind. You also understand that some traditions are pointless or then they cannot be followed everywhere. At home [in Kerala], one does not trust enough our women. Yet, most of them are serious women. Here, anyway, we have no choice but to trust them: my wife works on night duty and I have a daytime work. She cannot wait for me for everything she has to do. On my side, I also have to manage when I am alone at home. (Philip, a nurse's husband, who has settled in Muscat 7 years ago)

In the Gulf, Malayali women indeed have more presence in the public space than in Kerala: going to watch a movie with colleagues, to go shopping in the malls, to have a lunch at a fast-food restaurant, to meet in a church for a prayer afternoon or a philanthropic action, as many moves for which they would most probably have been chaperoned in Kerala. Nurses spontaneously remark that, due to migration, they earn in autonomy and authority:

> When you live with your husband alone and that in-laws and neighbours are not around, your husband is not so much influenced by other people's discourse. He is less afraid of being considered as a coward or as a weak man in his relation with his wife and there is a lot more of equality [...] It also helps to know each other better and to develop a good couple relation. (Lethika, 37, who has been working in Fujairah for these last 12 years)

Nurses also underline the added power of negotiation they get in family matters regarding spending, children education or choice for the future like new migratory destination, plan to build a house at home or use of the savings. They attribute this new power to their capacity of earning well as well to the distance with their homeland. In a more anecdotic aspect, they also praised new freedoms as the one to dress as they like or to put up make-up without critics from relatives or neighbours.

However, the women' role is still marginal in the diasporic institutions, whether they are religious or cultural (George 2005). In public situations, women carefully keep a low profile:

> You should not hurt your husband's pride [...] You should not try to play it smart in front of other people. For instance, if I do not agree with what my husband is saying or doing, I wait to be back home to tell him. (Teresa, 33, living nowadays in Ireland after 8 years in Oman)

Migration in the Gulf also often induces for the nurses a life far from their children. Since child care is a difficult task with no crèche and few possibilities to hire a maid, young children at least are generally left to the care of in-laws. This painful aspect is a strong pushing factor to try to migrate in a Western country where it is easier to take the children, although most nurses are well aware of the specific difficulties they will face there.

Gulf *versus* the West

Academic literature on Indian migration to the Gulf, considering mostly unskilled migrants, tends to stress on exploitation and on harsh conditions of living that the migrants have to face (Khalaf and Alkobaisi 1999; Rahman 2001; Prakash 1998). This is particularly true for literature concerning female migrants who work as housemaids (see, for instance, Varghese and Rajan 2001). Yet, in the Gulf, skilled migrants and successful Indian entrepreneurs can be found, especially Malayalis (Gardner 2008; Venier 2011). For this category of people—which the nurses belong to—I argue that, in the course of time, the Gulf countries—except perhaps for Saudi Arabia—have become a well-appreciated destination and, in a certain way, a more 'comfortable' one than the Western countries, even if they do not offer the same rights to migrants.

A strict segregation exists in the Gulf countries between the different communities. Outside the professional field, relations between locals and migrants or between migrants of different origins hardly exist at all (Longva 1997). This is, however, a situation that nurses rather appreciate. The judgement of Malayalis—and of Indians in general—concerning the Gulf people is indeed rather severe. If, on the one hand, they feel looked down upon by the locals—as migrants and, moreover, as people coming from a developing country—most Malayalis despise in return these locals that they consider as uneducated and incompetent people:

> They are racist towards Indians. They consider us as slaves, just good enough to work. But, look, actually they are absolutely uneducated and unable to do anything by themselves. Foreigners have built everything here and foreigners continue to manage everything. If they were not lucky enough to get oil, they would still be walking behind their camels.

The old Indian tradition of culture is always reminded by my informants, compared with the newly created Gulf states. The migrant nurses share this general opinion about Gulf and, as women, add a more precise appreciation, taking into account the absence of local nurses:

> Look how they behave with their women. They do not let them work. How many Emirati nurses are there? What are they doing with their women? They just sit at home all day long, idle, their foreign maids

> taking care of everything. They have no education, they have no ambition. (Beemole, 33, who has worked for two years in Saudi Arabia and four years in Abu Dhabi, before migrating to Ireland)

Having no personal relation with the locals is thus not felt as a problem; indeed, Malayali nurses also have few personal relations with their colleagues who are coming from other countries; Filipinos who represent the second higher group of foreign nurses appear, for instance, as having too many cultural differences:

> We do not have the same habits. [...] We don't like the smell of their food [...] They enjoy partying, some of them even drink alcohol. As Malayali women, we do not consider such behaviour as good. (Anita, 26, living in Dubai since 2 years)

In the Gulf, living mostly within one's own community, but far from home, authorizes Malayalis to take some distance with the social norms of the motherland, without however having to question one's identity, something that nurses particularly appreciate. This is another story when migrants go to a Western country and more especially to those that have a link with the colonial past (UK, Ireland, Australia). In those places, nurses are well aware that one expects them to adopt the local codes of behaviour and to adopt the local values, particularly regarding gender relations. That is something they are particularly uncomfortable with, which is against their own traditions and values. According to K.M. Zentgraf (2002: 639), Salvadoran female migrants who studied in the United States considered as a benefit to live in a country whose 'sociocultural context was such that women were regarded as valuable and treated with respect'. I argue that in the case of Malayali nurses, their status of female migrant in a Western country leaves them alone to face clichés attached to them as 'coloured women', coming from an ex-colony, where the status of women is notoriously low and in addition whose job not so many Western women are willing to do anymore:

> My Irish [female] neighbours are nice with me. But they are a little bit too quick to teach me lessons or to give me all sorts of advices, regarding my family life especially. That it is because they consider that I come from an underdeveloped country. They consider that their own culture is superior to our own culture. (Teresa, 33, today in Ireland after 8 years in Oman)

It is therefore in terms of gender, class and race (Allan and Larsen 2003; Falquet et al. 2010) that they have to justify their behaviour, a task that they have some difficulties to face. Actually, if, from the beginning of their migratory plans, they were aiming at escaping a social control they felt as too strong, in no case were they engaged in a frontal struggle against the traditional values of Kerala and in no case do they reject all of them. They indeed continue to largely praise the virtues of this social system, particularly when confronted with Western norms that they judge altogether too permissive and lacking familial solidarity. If they take some freedom with tradition, if they have chosen and appreciate to be in a position to do so and present themselves as 'modern [Malayali] women', it does not mean that migrant nurses drastically question the social gender relations of their native land. S. George (2005: 122) remarks, for instance, that a group of migrant nurses in the United States had chosen as a philanthropic action to participate in the payment of dowry for 'poor young women in Kerala'. As a matter of fact, living in a Western country obliges to question one's own identity in a way which does not exist in the Gulf countries. In order to get rid of the patriarchal norms of their country, in a way that they feel rather humiliating, Malayali nurses may end up having a less comfortable life in the West than in the Gulf.

They also face another problem. In the Gulf, due to the development of a large Malayali diaspora, a nurse's husband is almost sure to find a job, whether he has useful qualifications or not, as long as his wife has been able to get a legal entry for him in the territory. If, very often, the wife remains the main family earner, husband may also achieve professional success (Venier 2011).[3] On the contrary, in the Western labour markets, these men are frequently in a situation of professional disqualification, when they are not simply 'house husbands', taking care of the young children (Gallo 2006; Percot 2011). It is even more frequent with the last generation of migrant nurses whose husbands are degree holders, such degrees (Masters in Social Sciences or Law for instance) being more prestigious than useful in the labour market. Therefore, the nurses as main—if not only—bread earners for sure earn some power in the family, but they also have to constantly negotiate with an unsatisfied husband, frustrated by his inability to succeed by himself. This is particularly difficult in a country like Ireland for instance where the lack of a Malayali community does not provide space until now for a real masculine sociability, with its arena of distinction and power.

Conclusion

It may not be true for female migrants without qualification or for migrant housewives, but in the case of migrant nurses, migration is clearly a factor of empowerment: the choice of the profession in order to migrate is indeed a choice towards such result. Contrary to their elder counterparts who migrated in the 1970s or 1980s, young nurses or nursing students do not consider migration as a parenthesis in their life, but as a chance to escape a too traditional and too predictable future. Considering the social milieu they come from, it is certainly the easiest way for them to achieve their personal aspirations. To become a nurse in order to leave is for sure a way to climb social ladder, but it is also the choice of modernist values (from an emic point of view) regarding the status of women.

To live far from one's homeland authorizes to take some distance with its social norms, something that migrants acknowledge as good, considering themselves as modern men and women. However, in the case of nurses at least, there is no claim for a revolution in gender relationships. To behave as 'modern Malayalis' is a rather easy task in the Gulf countries where many places can now be considered as actual Malayali metropolises with a very lively social life. Moreover, the segregation which is the norm in the Gulf actually allows avoiding questioning one's identity in a too painful way. It is more difficult in Western countries, at least where no Malayali community has settled, for migrant nurses have to justify their position in front of locals who often question the migrants' traditional values. The lack of good job opportunities for nurses' husbands reinforces the potential discomfort generated by such a migration.

Let us finish with the story of Teresa. After several years passed in the Gulf, she and her family reached Ireland. When I came to visit them in Dublin two years ago, Teresa's idea was to settle in this country. They bought a house, she got trained in oncology and got a new nursing degree, her two young children attend a Gaelic catholic school and are perfectly well integrated in the Irish society; at last, she has recently got Irish citizenship. Since more than ten years I know her, Teresa has successfully achieved all of her plans and got much more self-esteem and confidence. But her husband has not been able to find a suitable job in Dublin: he spent most of his time at home, taking care of the children and of the house or work in petty jobs, which are poorly rewarding. Lately, I got a call from Teresa to tell me that they were leaving for Qatar:

> Now that I have a European Passport, we can travel easily. It was the important thing to get here. In Qatar, Teresa said, with no taxes I will indeed earn better. For John [her husband], it will also be better for he will find a job on the spot [...] I also consider that it will better for the children since there will be many Malayalis there and they will have more chance not to forget their culture. At last, it will be easier to visit Kerala regularly.

When asked if they were not considering going back home instead of resettling in the Gulf now that they had rather good savings, Teresa answered that she does not think that, as a still rather young woman, it would be easy for her to re-adjust: 'Gulf is the best option for us'. Not too far, but not too close.

Notes

1. Among all the informants, no case has been found where a dowry was not paid.
2. See, for instance, *keralamatrimony.com* or *shaadi.com*
3. The nurses working in governmental hospitals may get loan easily and this can be the starting point of a business.

References

Allan, H. and Larsen J.A. *'We Need Respect': Experiences of Internationally Recruited Nurses in the UK.* European Institute of Health and Medical Sciences, University of Surrey, 2003. Available at http://www.hrhresourcecenter.org/node/449 (accessed on 11 December 2012).

Ehrenreich, B. and Hochschild, A. *Global Women: Nannies, Maids and Sex Workers in the New Economy.* New York: Henry Holt and Company, 2002.

Falquet, J. 'Hommes en armes et femmes 'de service': tendances néolibérales dans l'évolution de la division sexuelle et internationale du travail'. *Cahiers du Genre,* 40, 1 (2006): 15–37.

Falquet, J., Hirata, H., Kergoat, D., Labari, B., Le Feuvre, N., and Sow, F. *Le sexe de la mondialisation. Genre, classe, race et nouvelle division du travail.* Paris: Presses de Sciences Po, 2010.

Gallo, Ester. 'Italy Is Not a Good Place for Men: Narratives of Places and Masculinity Among Malayali Migrants'. *Global Network,* 6 (2006): 357–372.

Gardner, A. 'Strategic Transnationalism: The Indian Diasporic Elite in Contemporary Bahrain'. *City and Society,* 20, 1 (2008): 54–78.

George, S.M. *When Women Come First. Gender and Class in Transnational Migration.* Berkeley: University of California Press, 2005.

Khalaf, S. and Alkobaisi, S. 'Migrants' Strategies of Coping and Patterns of Accommodation in the Oil-Rich Gulf Societies: Evidence from the UAE'. *British Journal of Middle Eastern Studies*, 26, 2 (1999): 271–298.

Kofman, E. and Raghuram, P. 'Gender and Global Labour Migrations: Incorporating Skilled Workers'. *Antipode*, 38, 2 (2006): 282–303.

Longva, A.N. *Walls Built on Sand. Migration, Exclusion and Society in Kuwait*. Oxford: Westview Press, 1997.

Oommen, G.Z. 'The Assertion of Religion among Indian Immigrants in West Asia: A Case Study of the Syrian Christians of Kerala in Kuwait'. *International Politics*, 4, 7 (2011): 43–66.

Parrenas, R.S. *Servant of Globalization: Women, Migration and Domestic Work*. Stanford: Stanford University Press, 2001.

Percot, M. 'Indian Nurses in the Gulf: Two Generations of Female Migration'. *South Asian Research*, 26, 1 (2006): 41–62.

Percot, M. 'Masculinity in Transnational Migration: Indian Nurses' Husbands in Ireland'. *Emigrinter*, 9 (2011): 74–86. Available at http://www.mshs.univ-poitiers.fr/migrinter/e-migrinter/201208/e-migrinter2012_08_074.pdf (accessed 11 December 2012).

Percot, M. and Naïr, S. 'Comment s'ouvrir les frontières du monde: la migration des infirmières indiennes'. pp. 211–239 in V. Dupont and F. Landy (eds), *Circulation et territoire dans le monde indien contemporain*. Paris: ed. de la MSH, coll. *Purushartha*, no. 28, 2010.

Prakash, B.A. 'Gulf Migration and Its Economic Impact: The Kerala Experience'. *Economic and Political Weekly*, 33, 50 (1998): 3209–3213.

Rahman, A. *Indian Labour Migration to the Gulf: A Socio-Economic Analysis*. New Delhi: Rajat Publications, 2001.

Varghese V.J. and Rajan S.I. 'Governmentality, Social Stigma and Quasi-citizenship: Gender Negotiations of Migrant Women Domestic Workers from Kerala'. pp. 224–248 in S.I. Rajan and M. Percot (eds), *Dynamics of Indian Migration: Historical and Current Perspectives*. New Delhi: Routledge, 2001.

Venier, Philippe. 'Development of entrepreneurial initiatives in the UAE among Kerala emigrants'. pp. 164–194 in S.I. Rajan and M. Percot (eds), *Dynamics of Indian Migration: Historical and Current Perspectives*. New Delhi: Routledge, 2011.

Zentgraf, K.M. 'Immigration and Women's Empowerment: Salvadorans in Los Angeles'. *Gender and Society*, 16, 5 (2002): 625–646.

CHAPTER 5

Blurring the Boundaries of Belief

The Transnational Religious Dynamics of the Syrian Christians of Kerala in Kuwait

Ginu Zacharia Oommen

The subject of this chapter is the changing sociocultural strategies/dynamics of immigrants from the southern Indian state of Kerala, in Kuwait. According to the Government of India, nearly 5.5 million Indian immigrants currently live in the Gulf region (Rajan 2004: 27) and out of which nearly 6,00,000 are in Kuwait. The chapter focuses on the changes in religious practices and the rise of radical religious groups among Kerala immigrants after the First Gulf War in 1990–1991. It is an attempt to understand the impact of religious revivalism by studying how religion has become a site for various identity-based community-centred networks among the immigrants.

The church is increasingly active among Syrian Christian immigrants of Kerala in post-liberation Kuwait. The chapter investigates the growing affinity of Syrian Christian immigrants, who have traditionally followed the church, towards sects/practices such as Pentecostalism. These religious groups are transnational in nature and are actively linked to both home and destination countries. At the macro level, the chapter would investigate the interconnection between the geo-political dynamics in the Gulf and the expansion of religious spaces in Kuwait. Finally, this chapter would analyse the increasing popularity of Pentecostalism and will examine the influence of the American Evangelical movement among second-generation Syrian Christian immigrants.

This is an empirical study based on my Post-Doctoral (Hermes) field research conducted by the author in Kuwait from December 2009 through January 2010. The main methods of documentation were through detailed interviews of immigrants and observances at various cultural performances and festivities.

During the fieldwork, in-depth interviews of 70 immigrants, along with professionals, Indian journalists, community leaders, priests and academicians of the Kuwait University, were conducted through a detailed interview schedule. A convenient sampling was followed in the study whereby the informants were selected through the links established within the community. The key persons of each parish helped to identify the possible respondents.

The interviews were conducted in both Malyalam and English, the languages the respondents/subjects and the author were comfortable with. It is significant to note that much of the background information of the workers, professionals and analysts came mostly from the older generation who experienced both invasion and liberation phase of Kuwait. The author's close association with the vicars of various Christian denominations, Kerala Associations and Clubs further helped conduct the research more thoroughly. Moreover, the author had the opportunity to attend various social gatherings such as marriages, baptism, Christmas carols and other church celebrations that provided an opportunity to interact and get responses from people outside of the subject list. This undoubtedly helped to understand the internal dynamics of the community. For the purposes of this chapter, the names of the respondents have been changed to hide the real identity.

Conceptual Framework

Contemporary migration is marked by an acceleration of the pace of interaction between the host and home setting through multiple networks. Transnational migrants simultaneously live at best in two settings. Patterns of immigration have changed since technology enabled distances between the home and the host society to contact as never before. Margolis argues that, 'immigrants establish and maintain familial, economic, political and cultural ties across international borders, in effect making the home and host society a single arena of social action' (cited in Baia Ruiz 1999: 95).

Religious communities simulate transnational movements that challenge the way in which we imagine religion and politics traditionally. The current phase of international migration has set in motion a plethora of such transnational movements. They are transnational in the sense that they refer to movements that come into being within the social intricacies and specificities of certain communities, yet are increasingly identified and appropriated outside (Waldinger and Fitzgerald 2004). Migrants often retain their religious beliefs and traditions through various kinds of social and economic links with the home country (Levitt 2003: 853). Technological advancements have further strengthened the migrants' links with the home countries on a day-to-day basis. Yang and Ebaugh (2001: 278) identified a number of immigrant congregations that kept in daily contact with the sending country through the Internet. The migrants make efforts to sustain their relations with the sending country through transnational religious practices as well (Levitt 2004: 5).

Although social scientists have written extensively on the role of religion in the diaspora, very little research has been done on the impact of transnational religious groups in the sending countries. *Transnational Religion and Fading States* (1997) by Rudolph and Piscatori concludes that in today's postmodern age, religious communities have become vital agents in the creation of a transnational civil society. Immigrants lean towards religious institutions to escape the hostility and discrimination of their settings and also to achieve social recognition. Hirschman (2004: 1228) argues that for immigrants who are separated from their homeland and from many relatives, religious membership offers a refuge in the sense that it creates a sense of belonging and participation in the face of loss and the strains of adjustment. Yang and Ebaugh (2001: 278) noted that religious mobilization also helps immigrants cope with marginalization by providing fellowships, social services and leadership positions to compensate for the downward mobility that many of them experience.

Vertovec (1997: 273–275) argues that the new rituals and religious practices reinforce the homeland ties of the immigrants. At the same time, newly moneyed migrants rely heavily on the religious trajectory for the strategic conversion of their economic capital into prestige and status (Oscella and Oscella 2003) and also to sustain their relations with the sending society. As pointed out earlier, there have been no studies on the subject of the impact on Indian migrants with respect to religion. As there were no precedent studies, the author used the opportunity to conduct an empirical study highlighting various aspects of the dynamics of transnationality of religious practices and beliefs among the Syrian Christians of Kerala in Kuwait.

In the context of Kuwait, the factors such as social alienation, work pressure, geo-political dynamics and the lack of social space have prompted the Kerala immigrants to move closer to religious spheres in an alien setting. In the case of Syrian Christian immigrants, the transnational religious institutions are operating as one of the viable networks connecting sending and receiving countries. Moreover the unique social situation in Kuwait has reshaped their religious and ritual practices, thereby reinvigorated community/denominational-centred identity.

The Indian migration to Gulf countries is both transitory and circulatory in nature, which heightens the transnational activities of the immigrants and their links with the sending country. Moreover the lack of social interaction with the local people and social alienation felt by the immigrants in GCC countries has only strengthened their quest for spiritual and religious identity. Participation in religious rituals provides comfort to those enduring hardships in an alien land, especially in a socially alienated environment such as Kuwait. In the host setting, the transnational religious practices enhance the transformation and reshaping of identity, perception and ritual practices of immigrants. Openness and acceptance drives immigrants towards integration of ethnic groups within the social structure. Denial and rejection of cultural diversity produces a violated, hurt and suppressed ethnic consciousness. Intolerance towards the ethnic immigrants in the Kuwait has resulted in ghettoization of groups preventing successful integration. Nonacceptance and alienation of the immigrants have strengthened their quest for spiritual and religious identity. Hence, radical transnational religion groups and new places of worship have emerged as 'community centres' to fulfil the identity vacuum the alienated immigrants experience in these societies.

In this context, the volatile situation in an alien setting is being exploited by conservative groups such as Pentecostal and Neo-Pentecostal, with large number of migrants, especially the youngsters, are moving away from the traditional churches towards these groups. The activities of these radical Christian groups and their membership have increased to a great extent in post-Gulf War Kuwait. The precarious and alienation in the host setting has strengthened the quest for spirituality and doctrine of 'prosperity gospel', and Pentecostal groups are making deep inroads among the socially alienated immigrants. The prosperity gospel is a unique theology that blends 'faith and wealth' within the framework of Bible and globalized market. Interestingly, this new version of the gospel, which promotes accumulation of wealth and consumerist culture, has a greater appeal among the immigrants whose main objective is to make maximum wealth in a shorter period of time. The Pentecostal spirituality or prosperity gospel plays a major role in reshaping the religious identity of immigrants. Therefore, in the host setting one could witness an intense conflict between the 'traditional religion' and 'popular religion' along the prevalence of new and ostentatious religious practices and rituals. Moreover, the unmatched influence of 'popular religion' has eroded the traditional nature of religion, giving rise to a more exclusionary and dogmatic transnational religious identity (Born again).

Syrian Christian Migration to Kuwait

The Christians, including the Syrian Christians of Kerala, constitute 18.6 per cent of the population of Kerala accounting for 6 million people (Zachariah 2006). Of them, the Syrian Christians—one of the oldest Christian sects in the world—comprise nearly 3 million (Zachariah 2006). Syrian Christians of Kerala are defined as persons born to Syrian Christian parents and who follow the 'Syrian rite' (Mathew and Thomas 2005). The Syrian Christians comprise different denominations such as Syro-Malabar, Malankara Catholics, Jacobites, Orthodox Syrian Church, Marthomites, Chaldean, Canaanites and Protestant Syrians. Earlier, the community was concentrated in and around five or six districts of Kerala. But, with the high rate of education, occupational diversification and few local job opportunities in the community, Syrian Christians have migrated to other states in India and abroad.

The history of Syrian Christian migration dates back to early 1900 AD when there was a massive flow of them to South East Asia—mainly to Singapore and Malaysia. The hostile situation in East Asia (a traditional area of emigration since colonial times) and the discovery of oil in the Persian Gulf diverted the flow of Syrian Christian Migration to West Asian Countries (Zachariah 2006).

Kuwait was the first Arab Gulf country that opened doors to the indigenous Christian community of Kerala. In the late 1940s, a small group of members of the Marthoma Syrian Church was the first to set up worship services in the region. The oil boom of the 1960s allowed for an immigration of Syrian Christians as a community to GCC countries that consequently led to the establishment of the Syrian Churches across the Gulf countries except Saudi Arabia. Since the late 1960s, remittances from the Gulf States have been a major source of income for Syrian Churches in Kerala. It is to be noted that all the Syrian Churches have separate Gulf Diocese/Diocesan Bishops and serving in a diaspora diocese is considered a very prestigious assignment among the clergy.

Currently, there are nearly 60 Malayalam churches in the GCC countries that include both Syrian Christian and Catholic denominations, besides various Pentecostal and Charismatic groups. Until the 1990s, the church trying to woo immigrants was nothing more than a routine and low key affair. However, in the last one decade or so the role of religion has dramatically increased among Indian immigrants, especially within the Syrian Christian (SC) community.

In 1990, the total number of Indians expatriates in Kuwait was nearly 1,70,000 and according to Centre for Development Studies (CDS) data nearly 80,000 Keralites returned to Kerala during the Iraqi invasion of Kuwait in 1990 (Zachariah et al. 2003). Presently in Kuwait, there are nearly 5,90,000 Indians of which Keralites account for around 40–50 per cent. Of the total number of Indian immigrants in Kuwait, Andhra Pradesh ranks second with roughly 1,20,000 members followed by Tamil Nadu with 80,000; Karnataka 40,000; Goa 40,000; Bihar 40,000; Punjab 15,000; Rajasthan 20,000; Bengal 3000 and Orissa 1000.[1] In Kuwait, out of the total emigrants from Kerala roughly 40–50 per cent are Christians and another 40 per cent are Muslims and the rest are Hindus.

The first group of Syrian Christians came to Kuwait in the late 1940s as workers at the Kuwait Oil Company (KOC) and also at the American Hospital. Syrian Christian expatriates flocked together under the banner of Kuwait Town Malayalee Christian Congregation (KTMCC) that was founded in 1956 for inter-denominational worship in Kuwait City at the American Hospital Chapel. It was the first non-White congregation of GCC states and comprises various Syrian denominations. KTMCC consists of seven Kerala non-Catholic churches: Marthoma, Orthodox, Jacobite, CSI, St. Thomas Evangelical, Brethren and Indian Pentecostal. At present, there are nearly 13 priests from Kerala who serve in the various Syrian churches of Kuwait. The Indian churches are not permitted to construct churches in Kuwait and the member churches of the KTMCC worship at the

NECK (National Evangelical Church of Kuwait) premise except Catholics. The Kerala Catholic denominations such as the Syro-Malabar and the Malankara Syrians conduct their worship at the Catholic Church at the Vatican Embassy premise in Kuwait city.

The main centres of Christian immigrants from Kerala are Abbasiya, Ahmadi, Salmiya and Mangaf. Currently, all the Syrian Christian denominations have more than three congregations in Kuwait.

Members of the Syrian Christian community engage in various occupations—they are nurses, doctors, company secretaries, managers, technicians, electricians, drivers, paramedics, industrial labourers, construction workers and so on. The membership and profile of the families are well documented by the churches and according to the church registers and documents most Syrian Christian emigrants belong to the moderate income group, with both husband and wife engaged in work. Many Syrian Christians work in the tertiary and secondary educational levels. The women of the community are mostly employed and pursue nursing, paramedical professions and secretarial jobs. Therefore, a substantial amount of Syrian Christian emigrants in Kuwait reside with their families unlike other immigrants. Syrian Christian males are predominantly engaged in blue-collar jobs, with some of the younger generation involved in professional jobs too.

Geo-political Dynamics and the Rise of Christianity in Kuwait

The history of Christians in Kuwait began in the early 1900s when Reverend Dr Samuel Zwemer and Reverend Fred Barney, missionaries from the American Reformed Church of America, arrived in Kuwait in 1900. Subsequently, in 1911 Kuwaiti Emir Sheikh Mubarak Al-Sabah granted permission to the American Reformed Church under the leadership of Dr Scudder to build a hospital, which was finally established in 1913 (Sharaf 2009). The KOC was established in 1934 as a partnership between Gulf Oil and British Petroleum. Since the majority of staff members were Christians, the KOC built two churches in Ahmadi in the late 1940s and up until now, the two churches are maintained by the KOC. The American hospital chapel was later converted into a church in the mid-1960s. Currently, the NECK is located on the premises of American Medical Mission premises.

The small Arab congregation of Kuwait consists largely of Kuwaiti Christians and there are approximately 150–200 families of local

Kuwaiti Christians. The first Christian family came from southeast Turkey and Iraq in the beginning of 1920s and they have been in Kuwait for more than 90 years. These Kuwaiti Christians belong to the Presbyterian congregation and Rev. Emmanuel Gharib is the lone native pastor of Kuwait (Sharaf 2009).

Kuwait gained independence from Britain in 1961 and the ruling Al Sabah family has been in power since then. In the 1970s and 1980s, the Kuwaiti ruling elite tried to maintain a degree of neutrality between the USSR and the United States. However, towards the end of the 1980s, Kuwait switched over completely to the United States in terms of its geo-political strategy. The Iran—Iraq War was the decisive factor in consolidating closer ties with the United States. The Iraqi invasion of Kuwait in 1990 and the subsequent intervention of the United States consolidated the Kuwait-US relations to a great extent.

In the post-1990s, after the liberation of Kuwait church activities have picked up, most probably because of the discernible presence of Americans in the country. For instance, the United States Department of State's report on the religious freedom (2010) says that 'the US. Government discusses religious freedom with the Government as part of its overall policy to promote human rights. Intensive monitoring of religious freedom matters remained an embassy priority. During the reporting period, embassy officials met with senior representatives from the major recognized Christian denominations, encouraged them to present their concerns in a unified manner to the Government, and advocated on their behalf in high-level meetings with government officials' (International Religious Freedom Report 2009).

The American intervention in Kuwait altered the social dynamics of the Arab Christian minority and also expanded the non-Islamic space in Kuwait. For instance, in January 1999 the Arab Congregation in Kuwait ordained Rev. Emmanuel Gharib as the clergy of NECK. Though he graduated from the Presbyterian Theological seminary in 1989, he was ordained as a priest in 1999 and he was the first Kuwaiti Christian to be ordained with the support of American Episcopal Church (Sharaf 2009). Second, in December 1999, the Bible Society established its distribution office—The Book House Company Ltd. Interestingly Kuwait was the first country to allow the Bible society to set up the office in GCC states. Currently, NECK has an agreement with the Kuwaiti government to import books and gifts that relate to the Christian faith through the Book House Company Ltd. Finally, Kuwait was notably the first member of the Gulf Cooperation Council to maintain diplomatic ties with the Vatican State. But in 2001 Apostolic Nunciature was upgraded from charge d'affaires to full ambassadorial status to represent Vatican's interest in the region.

Currently, the American Revival Church or the Light House Church is a well-established congregation with more than five American pastors. The website of the Light House Church shows the multiple spiritual activities of the American missionaries for expatriates. It is interesting to note that the senior priest of Light House Church has resided in Kuwait since 1985 and now the church has an official Bible college and an American school.

During the Christmas season in 2009, I witnessed the display of religious symbols such as stars, the bursting of crackers and loud carol singing in the streets by the immigrants. Some of the old respondents informed me that explicit and public display of Christian symbols is a more recent phenomenon—after the liberation of Kuwait. The non-intervention of the government regarding the public celebration of the Christian faith could be due to the strategic dependence of the Kuwaiti regime on the Americans.

However, the excessive expansion of Christianity has been sharply criticized by Islamists. For example, in February 2012 few Kuwaiti Members of Parliament openly called for a halt to the construction of new churches in Kuwait. Kuwaiti MP Osama Al-Munawar announced on Twitter that he was planning to submit a draft law calling for the removal of all churches in the country (Shane 2012). This was followed by the call of the Grand Mufti of Saudi Arabia for the demolition of all churches in the GCC states including Kuwait. The displeasure among some sections of the Kuwaiti population at the assertion of churches and also the intrusion of Christians in the country is increasing (Longva 1997: 46).

The Invasion Syndrome

On the first day of my stay in Abbasiya, a predominantly Keralite settlement in Kuwait, I was astonished to see immigrants, especially males walking with bibles in the streets as they were heading towards prayer meetings organized in individual houses and halls. By evening I could hear loud chants and Christian songs, mostly from the basement of buildings (normally called 'Underground churches') as is a routine affair in Abbasiya today. The spirituality and the role of religion have increased dramatically in the post-liberation phase in Kuwait.

For many respondents, worship and the church had been nothing more than a routine and low key affair till 1990. Life was more relaxed and often immigrants used to go on the weekends for picnics in Iraq or to drink alcohol. The Kuwaiti immigrants were relatively the richest immigrants due to the high pay scale and other welfare schemes of Kuwait. However, the invasion altered the socioeconomic and religious perceptions of the immigrants especially the Syrian Christians to a great extent. As Mathew Joseph, the marketing Manager of Kuwait Airways, said, 'the invasion had a deep impact on the minds of the people. It has increased the need for investment and need for spirituality'. Since the invasion there has been a drastic change in the activities of the church, as well as in the attitude of the people towards spirituality and religion.

Majority of the respondents admitted that the invasion had been a big setback in their life and the life in Kerala during the interim period was highly traumatic and dreadful. Indian emigrants had to leave Kuwait despite having debts in India and being burdened with social commitments such as the marriage of sisters, education of siblings and unfulfilled promises of bringing immediate family members and friends to Kuwait for employment.

As one respondent told me 'I came to Kuwait in September 1989 and I was the first member from my family to reach Gulf and had to pay a huge amount of money to the travel agent. So I pawned my property to obtain the required amount. After arriving in Kuwait I asked my sister to join the Nursing programme in Tamil Nadu and I had to pay donations to secure an admission for her. I took a loan thinking that I could repay it eventually. But the invasion was a big shock and I was clueless. It shattered all my dreams and I landed in Kerala with huge debts and finally left for Bombay in search of a job to support my family'.

Interestingly, many immigrants narrated about their difficult lives and unpleasant relations with siblings and family members back home in Kerala. The unexpected arrival of the immigrants from Kuwait was a sudden shock to the family and they were not ready to shoulder the responsibility of debt-ridden siblings from abroad. The invasion changed both the economic strategy and the spiritual strategy of the Kerala immigrants. A good number of immigrants who continue to be in Kuwait currently began investing in building homes and buying land in Kerala and they have also become more concerned about the needs of their immediate family members. Their attitude to investments in their children's education has also undergone a sea change.

Interestingly most of the immigrants I spoke to, including the recent immigrants, articulated a common phrase to me in Malayalam 'Anything can happen here. There is no sense of security and mental peace here. Our job is so insecure here and we are rotating our lives as a machine for making money without enjoying life qualitatively. Prayers at the Pentecostal Church is a big relief to us. We were Christians before migration but we found God in Kuwait'. The 'invasion syndrome' haunts immigrants deeply even today.

The 'invasion syndrome' has influenced the Kerala immigrants mainly at two levels. First, it has resulted in the ghettoization or clustering of immigrants from the same social setting in respective neighbourhoods. To quote an example, at present Keralites are mostly settled in Abbasiya apart from Mangaf, Salmiya, Riggae, Abu Halifa and a few in Kuwait city. Most Keralites, especially Christians, prefer to live in Abbasiya, which in turn is called 'mini Kerala'. Second, it has influenced the immigrants to increasingly turn to religion and transnational religious organizations.

The geo-political instability, economic recession and psychological stress have increased the attraction of immigrants to spirituality and thereby increased the assertion of religion, especially by radical religious groups among the immigrants. Economic growth and financial undercurrents in Kuwait were slow till 2003 and even the rich Kuwaitis were not ready to invest in their own soil. The American invasion of Iraq changed the 'insecurity phobia' to some extent, after which the internal economic trajectories attained momentum. An Indian diplomat at the Indian Embassy, whom I met, placed this feeling of insecurity in the context of geo-political dynamics in the region. He said 'until 2003, the Kuwaitis too were going through a great sense of insecurity and economic scrutiny. Even they were not ready to make any further investments and this further aggravated the sense of timidity in the economic market which inevitably heightened the nervousness of the immigrants and also heightened the feeling of uncertainty'. Working conditions in offices and hospitals have become stricter with stringent penalties even for mild errors and the work load has increased dramatically. Nurses and medical professionals explained to me the unprecedented level of psychological pressure and disgrace they have to endure in the workplace. The pre-war Kuwait had given many concessions and assistance to both natives and expatriates, but the government had withdrawn almost all the concessions in the post-liberation phase (Longva 1997: 60).

One of the main features of the post-liberation phase among Kerala immigrants is the proliferation of various religious and caste groups and the explicit display of religiosity in the day to day life in the host setting. The increase in the number of immigrants also has a direct impact on the proliferation of religious worship centres and transnational religious groups, particularly the so-called 'Charismatic Christian' groups. All the communities have opened their religious centres in post-liberation Kuwait.

In the case of Kerala Muslims, nearly seven Islamic organizations are functioning actively: the Kuwait-Kerala Islamic Group (affiliated to Jamati Islami), Kuwait Kerala Islamic Centre (affiliated to Mujahideen), Lizallie Study Circle (affiliated to A P Sunni), Friday Forum, Kuwait Kerala Islamic Centre (a factional group affiliated to Mujahideen) and Kuwait Kerala Muslim Association. Both spiritual and caste groupings are widespread among the community of Hindu migrants to Kuwait. Some of these groups are the AMMA, Ayyappa Seva Sangham, Nair Service Society (NSS) and Sree Narayana Dharma Paripalana Yogam (SNDP). Interestingly, National Sample Survey (NSS) also organizes spiritual meetings, especially the 30 days recital of the Holy Scripture Ramayana during the month of Karkataka (mostly in July or August). It is to be noted that in Kerala organizations such as NSS are hardly involved in the spiritual affairs of the people.

Church as a Place for Social Recognition and Refuge

The worship centres are also places for recognition and the display of individual success. The church designations such as Secretary or Trustee are seen as symbols of social mobility and recognition. Annual elections for electing the office bearers are very common in Kuwait in the Syrian Church. One of the vicars pointed that competition for leadership in the church often ends up in conflicts and personal rivalries. Elections for the church hierarchy are a month long affair with house to house campaigns by the candidates, which is not a very common practice in Kerala. Religious institutions are the only avenue to display one's success in a socially alienated host setting. Most males involved in 'Parish Politics' are middle-income groups and the educated/high-income groups generally abstain from the internal affairs of the Parish. One of the respondents commented that 'Nurse Husbands' were actively involved in the church politics to attain recognition and status in the community. Many respondents did not bother to discuss the internal skirmishes in the community and tried to project their contribution in the 'welfare of Parish'.

There are incidents of people leaving the parent church and moving to a Pentecostal church for not being properly accommodated in the church. The young migrants often complain about the monopoly of the 'veterans' (older immigrants) in church affairs and the unwillingness of the older immigrants to accommodate the newcomers in the church. During an interview, one of the leaders of the church boasted about his proximity to the Bishops and his living room was decorated with his photographs with the Bishop and political leaders on the occasion of various church functions he had organized.

I have observed that the church has become the 'epicentre' for many respondents and the frequency of their participation in religious activities have increased very high. However, the participation of women in church activities is very limited, though many of them earn more than the men.

As Hirschman notes, almost all studies of contemporary immigrant churches and temples in the United States describe the multiple services they provide to newcomers, from information about jobs, housing and business opportunities to classes in English and seminars on various practical topics (2004: 1230). The church also functions as a public organization among the immigrant community. It is also a major site of social networking in finding jobs for the newcomers with the help of senior members of the church, to establish joint business ventures and also to cater various needs of the members. All the major religious organizations in Kuwait have an employment cell to help newcomers or the members of the community to find jobs. The vicar of Marthoma Church narrated that members of other religious groups from Kerala also benefited from the employment cell of the church. In addition, the church provides short-term loans to people who have lost jobs or do not find a job in a stipulated time.

The most interesting feature of community networking is the 'social security scheme' or the 'family relief schemes' managed by different religious groups. The treasurer of the Kerala Muslim Cultural Centre (KMCC) told me that the KMCC was the first expatriate organization to introduce a unique 'social security scheme' or 'welfare schemes' for the community and many families have benefited from this scheme. Currently, all the churches have various schemes for the welfare of the members. The website of Indian Orthodox Church says, 'the objective of the family Relief Scheme shall be to provide financial assistance to the family of a member in the event of his/her natural/accidental death or physical disability within or outside

Kuwait'. The respondents explained that deaths or disability due to accidents are always a critical moment for an immigrant family and these schemes are extremely advantageous during an unexpected tragedy. In Kuwait, the religious/community organizations accomplish both spiritual and socioeconomic needs of the members and thereby consolidate the loyalty and dependency of the people towards the religious institutions. The intervention of religious groups in the immigrant life has reinforced the authority of religion among immigrants to a great extent. The NSS and SNDP also have similar schemes.

Rise of Pentecostalism/Charismatic Churches: Official versus Popular Religion

Steven Vertovec (2000) in his path breaking study on the Hindu Diaspora noted the trend among the immigrants to embrace 'Popular' religious movements instead of the official religion. Official religion is institutionalized with rituals, values under the leadership of clergy/proper organization with strong roots and lineage. On the other hand, popular religion is less hierarchical, maintained by lay persons with magico-religious/charismatic phenomenon.

The popular religion stresses healing, fighting evil and miracles. In the post-liberation phase, the major development among Syrian Christian community is the growth of Charismatic/Prosperity Gospel/Pentecostal churches. The Pentecostal churches are predominantly a Global Religion and emphasize the prosperity gospel. Pentecostalism connects faith and wealth within the broad structure of the Bible and the globalized market. Pentecostalism too emphasizes the 'war against evil spirits', healing, demonology, and the forsaking of worldly pleasures. Martin (1990) in his famous work 'Tongues of Fire' contended that 'Pentecostalism challenges the hierarchical and provides a new kind of religious space, which is a blend of neo-liberal materialistic values and spirituality'. The erosion of members from mainstream churches to these splinter groups is extremely high in Kuwait.

As one of the respondents said 'the main goal of every immigrant is to make as much wealth as possible in a limited span of time'. The accumulation of wealth remains a major concern for immigrants and the struggle towards this process is met with anxiety, stress, competition and insecurity. The Pentecostals operate in this 'diasporic space' of uncertainty and instability in the host setting. The 'healing ministry' of the Pentecostal church is the most appealing spiritual activity among the immigrants. Besides, this group gives a lot of priority to the economic well-being of the members and 'success in life' continues to be the favourite prayer item. Geographically separated 'Gulf Parents' and 'Gulf Wives' left behind in Kerala face many social problems at home. At present, there are nearly 1 million Gulf wives in Kerala. Immigrants are unable to keep their children with the family as most of the Gulf states lack proper institutions for higher studies. This separation remains to be a major cause of concern for parents living in the Gulf.

There is intense competition between the mainstream Syrian Church (which includes all the denominations) and the 'Popular Church' (Pentecostal church). Pentecostals members range from people who strive for spiritual needs, those who require social assistance such as workers and those marginalized in the mainstream churches. The major activities of the Pentecostal church are mainly in labour camps, which were neglected by the mainstream church for many years. For instance, the Relief Net Service (RNS) is a nongovernmental organization (NGO) associated with a Pentecostal church named Grace Fellowship and they have 19 branches in Kuwait. The President of RNS, a former communist activist in Kerala, told me, 'sometimes the labourers are left without salary for two to three months and without a renewal of the visa. Our organization provides food, medical kits and also short term loans for those who don't have a salary. We organize medical camps with the support of doctors from Kerala and also arrange vehicles to take them to good hospitals'. The RNS also has prayer halls in almost all the camps and a vibrant congregation in Abbasiya.

However, the mainstream church is of the opinion that charismatic groups such as Pentecostals exploit the precarious socio-physiological context that prevails in Kuwait. A prominent member of the Orthodox Church commented that splinter Pentecostal churches indulge in 'Spiritual terrorism' inflicting fear among people. It is interesting to note that unlike in Kerala the Syrian denominations do not excommunicate members who have joined the Pentecostal church. The majority of the members keep dual membership, as they attend the worship of Pentecostal churches, though they are members of the Syrian Church. However, the pastors carve boundaries of 'born again' and members are time and again reminded of the uniqueness of this membership.

Abbasiya is the nucleus of the splinter/Pentecostal churches, and the worship centres of these churches are known as the 'Under Ground Church', a term that comes from the fact that these churches usually conduct their prayers in the basement of the buildings as they cannot worship at the NECK premises. The caretaker of one of the buildings told me that one Pentecostal church has hired the basement for a full year at a high cost. On Fridays, the streets of Abbasiya are packed with cars and buses in which the members have been brought from far away labour camps. The church also conducts house prayers almost every day, according to the timing schedule of the members. Mary Suzan a nurse from Abbasiya pointed out that she attends the prayers a minimum three days a week except when she has night shifts. In Kuwait, a good number of immigrants spend an enormous amount of time on prayers and church-related activities compared with what they used to do when they live in Kerala. In his study on the Haitian community, Paul Brodwin (2003: 95) hinted that 'the Pentecostal churches become virtually the only communal space in Guadeloupe where Haitians can collectively articulate the sentiments of anger and exasperation produced by the migration experience'.

Popularity of the spiritual broadcasting channels is another key element for the members of the Pentecostal groups. The religious TV channels in Malayalam are extremely popular among the immigrants. Malayalam Christian channels such as Shalom, Jeevan and Power Vision were launched in the late 1990s and they resemble American Channels such as ECTV or GOD Channel. All the channels have offices across the Gulf, including Kuwait with high-tech equipments and TV crew. In almost all the Christian homes that I visited, Christian channels were followed avidly. Many of these channels function mainly on funding from the GCC expatriates. I could hear people talking with pride about the participation of children in the various channels. One respondent said that 'I watch Power Vision Channel every day and it gives a lot of peace. I also record the sermons on my mobile and listen while I am working'.

Interestingly, the concept of 'tithe' is also very popular among the Christian immigrants. Tithe is an Old Testament conception of contributing one tenth of one's income to poor and needy and this is not widely prevalent among the Syrian Church in Kerala. Nevertheless, it is the Pentecost church that popularized this concept among the immigrants as a mark of thanksgiving for economic success. However, the Pentecost church insists that the contribution be given to the pastors/church and that the church distributes the money for various needs. Thus, charity is highlighted as the prime duty of a born again Christian. In addition, spending a huge amount of money on religious ceremonies is another key aspect of the diaspora community. However commoditization of religion and the high spending of money on religious ceremonies such as Baptism and marriage are increasing among the Christian immigrants. The religious space is appeared to be the only arena in a host setting to express themselves and to release the feelings for many immigrants.

The pilgrimage to Israel/Palestine is another significant aspect, which is widely prevalent among Syrian Christian immigrants. Each year, almost all the churches in Kuwait organize a pilgrimage via Jordan to the Holy Land especially during the summer vacations. Perhaps due to the influence of Gulf immigrants, the pilgrimage to Israel/Palestine has become very popular in Kerala too.

Community Formation and Identity

Has the religious identity surpassed the national/ethnic identity of Syrian Christians in an alien setting? Prema Kurien (2004: 367) argues that 'the religious organizations became a preferred means for immigrants to maintain and develop ethnic identities, much of their process of group formation and mobilization is accomplished by using religious organizations and symbols'. In the host setting, religion makes a significant contribution in identity construction, community formation and maintaining the community. In some cases, immigrants make use of religious space to sustain their transnational connectivity with the sending and receiving countries. The transnational religious congregations at times reshape and restructure the ethnic identity of immigrants. Identity formation based on religion is another feature of immigrants from Kerala in Kuwait. Collective forms of worship have increased among immigrants as they grow in numbers and wealth. The salient feature of Pentecostal churches is 'Corporate Prayers'. The church or worship place is not just a centre of devotion, but also a haven of community solidarity and space of identity. The social networking and close interaction among immigrants are by and large confined within the community, especially among the Christians within the wider framework of religious pluralism that has traditionally marked Kerala society. Currently, the church seems to be one of the nodal points of interaction between sending and receiving societies. The President of Kuwait Arts Lovers Association (KALA), the largest secular association of Kerala immigrants attached to Communist Party of India (CPI, Marxist), told me that 'people are more comfortable in associating and connecting with religious institutions rather than the secular organizations. But this is the general trend'.

It is very important to note that there is no united Kerala Association or a Pan Indian Association in Kuwait. The strongest and largest organizations are the religious groups, which are systematic, neatly structured, well organized and with many units across Kuwait. There are many factors that make community centric organizations more appealing among immigrants. First, immigrants are socially isolated from the host society and their interaction with Kuwaiti nationals is strictly confined to the workplace. The social isolation of Syrian Christian immigrants has produced greater cohesion within the community and the church fills this social vacuum. The Vicar of Marthoma Church notes that 'in the isolated environment Church or the religious institution creates a sense of 'sharing and caring' among the immigrants'. Second, the absence of social/public space in the host country has created a strong cohesion and deep sense community bondage among the immigrants. The religious institution is turned to be the public as well as spiritual space and life is more centred on a 'trio' of office, home and church. The religious institutions to a large extent recompense for the lack of social space in Kuwait. Collective forms of worship create a communal/community identity among the immigrants.

The church is systematically organized and is divided geographically into various prayer groups in accordance with the convenience of the members. The Marthoma City Church has 42 prayers groups and each prayer group comprises 60–80 families with a 'Prayer Secretary'. The prayer group organizes picnics, sports and get-togethers and church members celebrate all personal events or achievements such as birthdays, wedding anniversaries or the academic success of children in the respective prayer groups. Hence, the prayer group is a very key element in the life of a Syrian Christian immigrant and the prayer secretary is the main nodal person of this network. Many interviewers responded that their close friends are from the church or from the prayer group since they interact within the community frequently.

One of the respondents from Syrian Orthodox church narrated a very interesting anecdote. He said '15 members of our Prayer group have bought six acres of land next to the Parumala Church (very popular church in central Kerala) and we are building cottages and a community centre there. We bought it together because we are members of the same prayer group in Abbasiya and we want to continue our friendship and we would like to live together after our retirement. Moreover Parumala Church is the sacred church of Syrian Christians and we would like stay very close to the church so that we can attend the Church service every day'. In this context, it is to be noted that the church is playing an important role in the creation of an alternative denominational identity and also to sustain the transnational links for the immigrants. I have observed a unique denominational identity being evolved among the Christian immigrants in the diaspora setting and the immigrants are categorized on the basis of Christian denominations.

Pilgrimages to various religious places in Kerala are increasingly popular among immigrants in Kuwait. Popular Christian shrines in Kerala such as Parumala, Manjanikara, Malayatoor and Puthuppally have a high participation of immigrants from GCC countries. These pilgrimages and participation of immigrants at the feast in native churches could be termed as expressing their attachment to the home society. The participation in the rituals and the visits to shrines reinforces their roots, an opportunity to express their attachment to the sending society and also to create an alternative category of belonging by the immigrant community (Levitt 2003: 855).

However, I have noticed a unique 'born again' transnational identity formed within the Pentecostal groups delinking them from the outside world. The charismatic groups separate themselves from the rest of the world and project an 'exclusive' spiritual identity from the rest of the denominations. Brodwin (2003: 98) argues that 'their alienation and exclusion from the dominant society is precisely the problem they address through the moral and theological doctrines of Pentecostalism'. An average member of Charismatic/Pentecostal groups normally confines within their own church members and their life are revolving within the daily prayer meetings and house visits. The 'born again Pentecostal' identity transcends the national boundaries as they envisage a global community of believers. One of the Pentecostal Pastors told me that 'the mission of the church is to evangelize to win maximum souls within the immigrant community. He further added that the church normally discourages the members to involve in the worldly groups like clubs and political associations'. The Charismatic groups evolve strong transitional networks of their members and the pastors from Kerala often visit Kuwait to assist the diaspora community. These radical groups reinforce and reshape communal identity of an exclusionary and very often fanatic nature.

Conclusion

Though several previous studies have examined the economic consequences of migration and remittances, no attempt has been made so far to explore how migratory movements and remittances affected the religion and religious practices of Indian immigrants in the host setting. The change in religiosity and religious practices were in turn influenced by the migrant experiences based on their religious beliefs in their host countries. These differential experiences made them reinvent their own religions in a transnational environment but exclusivist in spirit. These complex trajectories of migrant's experience perhaps strengthen group identity and reorient the socioeconomic life in Kerala towards increased 'exclusivism' and 'conservatism'. In the case of Syrian Christian immigrants, the public expression of religiosity has expanded manifold and ideologically immigrants has become more Christianized. The invasion of Kuwait and the subsequent departure of the immigrants to Kerala and the hardships they encountered in Kerala altered both the 'spiritual and economic strategies' of the immigrant community.

In Kuwait, I observed that religion is salient factor in a migrant's day-to-day life, as it fills the emotional hole created in the contexts of extreme social isolation that the migrants experience in foreign countries. For the Syrian Christian community, the major development has been the rise of Charismatic/Pentecostal churches. Digging deeper in this context, one sees a gamut of issues that has led to the assertion of the church in the life of expatriate workers. The region's political instability and economic slump, the hostile social environment and the community's continued social alienation from the host society has invigorated the phenomenon. One of the main features of the post-liberation phase has been the proliferation of various religious and charismatic and the explicit display of religiosity in everyday life among immigrants. The proliferation of evangelical prayer groups with charismatic pastors, huge donations to missionary activities, popularization of 'tithe', increasing dependence on pastors/clergy and emerging trends for pilgrimage to the 'Holy Land' reflects the exuberant presence of religion in immigrant's life.

Thus, religious revivalism among Syrian Christian immigrants in the host countries is abetting the assertion of communal/denominational identity, proliferation of radical religious groups, rise of cults/God men and the emergence of new forms of worship. The lack of public space, social alienation and the quest to achieve social recognition are being filled through the religious space. Diaspora religious practices play a major role in sustaining the transnational links between home and host settings and it also creates an alternative sense of belonging to the sending country. In the contemporary context, religion provides the opportunity for immigrants for community formation and produce intense conflict between the 'mainstream' and 'popular/conservative' religious groups and also helps to carve a unique 'denominational/Born Again identity'. Moreover the host settings have paved the way for the emergence of 'popular religion' and it creates a unique 'global identity', which transcends the national boundaries.

Note

1. Interview conducted by the Author with Indian Ambassador to Kuwait on 15 January 2009.

References

Baia Ruiz, Lariza. 'Rethinking Transnationalism: Reconstructing National Identities among Peruvian Catholics in New Jersey'. *Journal of Interamerican Studies and World Affairs*, 41, 4 (1999): 93–109.

Brodwin, Paul. 'Pentecostalism in Translation: Religion and the Production of the Community in the Haitian Diaspora'. *American Ethnologist*, 30, 1 (2003): 85–101.

Hirschman, Charles. 'The Role of Religion in the Origins and Adaptation of Immigrants Groups in the United States'. *International Migration Review*, 38, 3 (2004): 1206–1233.

International Religious Freedom Report. US Department of State, 26 October 2009. http://www.state.gov/j/drl/rls/irf/2009/127351.htm

Kurien, Prema. 'Multiculturalism, Immigrant Religion and Diasporic Nationalism: The Development of an American Hinduism'. *Social Problems*, 51, 3 (2004): 362–385.

Levitt, Peggy. 'Redefining the Boundaries of Belonging: The Institutional Character of Transnational Religious Life'. *Sociology of Religion*, 65, 1 (2004): 1–18.

Levitt, Peggy. 'You Know Abraham Was Really the First Immigrant: Religion and Transnational Migration'. *International Migration Review*, 37, 3 (2003): 847–873.

Longva, Anh Nga. *Walls Built on Sand-Migration, Exclusion and Society in Kuwait.* Colorado: West View Press, 1997.

Martin, David. *Tongues of Fire.* Oxford: Blackwell, 1990.

Mathew, C.P. and Thomas, M.M. *The Indian Churches of Saint Thomas.* New Delhi: Cambridge University Press, 2005.

Oscella, F. and Oscella, C. 'Migration and Commoditisation of Ritual: Sacrifice, Spectacle and Contestations in Kerala'. *Contributions to Indian Sociology*, 37, 1–2 (2003): 109–139.

Rajan, Irudaya. S. 'Dynamics of International Migration from India: Its Economic and Social Implications'. *The ICFAI Journal of Employment Law*, 2, 2 (2004): 25–46.

Rudolph, Susan and Piscatori, James. *Transnational Religion and Fading States.* Colorado: Westview Press, 1997.

Shane, Daniel. 'Kuwait's Image Tarnished by Church Fiasco'. *Arabian Business.com*, 8 April (2012): http://www.arabianbusiness.com/kuwait-s-image-tarnished-by-church-fiasco-453105.html

Sharaf, Nihal. 'Christians Enjoy Religious Freedom: Church-State Relations Excellent'. *Arab Times*, 15 April (2009).

Vertovec, Steven. 'Three Meanings of Diaspora Exemplified among South Asian Religions'. *Diaspora*, 6, 3 (1997): 277–299.

Vertovec, Steven. *The Hindu Diaspora: Comparative Patterns.* London: Routledge, 2000.

Waldinger, Roger and Fitzgerald, David. 'Transnationalism in Question'. *American Journal of Sociology*, 109, 5 (2004): 1177–1195.

Yang, F. and Ebaugh, H.R. 'Transformation of New Immigrant Religions and Their Global Implications'. *American Sociological Review*, 66, 2 (2001): 269–288.

Zacharia, K.C. *The Syrian Christians of Kerala: Demographic and Socio-Economic Transition in the Twentieth Century.* New Delhi: Orient Longman, 2006.

Zacharia, K.C., Mathew, E.T., and Rajan, S. Irudaya. *Dynamics of Migration in Kerala: Dimensions, Differentials and Consequences.* New Delhi: Orient Longman, 2003.

Chapter 6

Connecting Across the Sea

Imaginative Creations of the Indian Diaspora in Oman

Sandhya Rao Mehta

The image of the Indian deity of Shrinathji, the baby Krishna who was brought from Basra to Masqat towards the end of the seventeenth century, is an interesting image evoked among the Indian community in Oman to highlight the close ties between themselves and their host country. This deity catches attention because it is said to have been garbed in the traditional Omani dagger *(khanjar)* once it was established in a temple in the town of Masqat, a sign of the close ties between Indian merchants and the land they inhabited (Allen 1981). Although not much is known about this image, it remains a unique piece of evidence in the narrative of Indian presence in the coastal areas of the Persian Gulf, about which very little is known, even today. While this narrative allows for a fascinating insight into the religious zeal of Indians travelling and populating various parts of the world, it more relevantly points to, in this context, the significant role played by Indian traders in Oman in the later decades of the seventeenth century as they successfully established their religious and cultural roots in a society that has often been assumed to be less than liberal.

A focus on the historical presence of Indians in the eastern part of the Middle East emerges as an important area of interest in diaspora studies, for, to a large extent, it remains a geographical and, therefore, a cultural space that has been left unexplored by various studies on the

Indian diaspora. This, in turn, has made a particular section of the Indian diaspora invisible, which has been marginalized to a large extent for constituting of 'temporary residents' (Rahman 2009: 100–103) or of belonging to an unorganized sector of society, and therefore, not significantly visible in the present day context of skilled migration categories. In fact, the Indian community living in Oman and in many other parts of the Gulf are not only established members of their host country but contribute culturally, economically and socially to their development while establishing creative spaces in which debates on identity, home and return are made possible. This chapter attempts to trace the history of the Indian diaspora in the Middle East with particular reference to Oman as being a significant one owing to geographical proximity as well as cultural similarities. In addition, it looks into the way in which this diaspora has established itself in the region and immersed itself in the cultural and social processes of the adopted land. The artistic, creative and literary manifestations of this immersion are then explored, establishing a framework within which the Indian diasporic community in Oman could be examined and reflected upon.

Defining the Diaspora

While the term 'diaspora' has long shrugged off its inevitable associations with the conditions of the Jews across the world, it has also included, within its sphere, voluntary, economic travellers as well as refugees and exiles from conflict zones in various parts of the world. William Safran's definition of the requirements of the diaspora including their having dispersed to different parts of the world with a common original space, being bound by a connecting memory of the homeland, however imaginary and being still actively involved with the land left behind in terms of retaining spiritual and physical contacts along with the all-important hope to returning to the homeland, still remain useful frames of reference with which to view the experience of migration (Safran 1991: 83–84). All these qualities continue to be associated with the Indian diaspora to a large extent, albeit with various qualifications owing to the transformation in the very physical realities of a changing globalized world.

The extent, to which the Indian communities in the Middle Eastern countries, particularly countries in the Gulf, are brought under the umbrella of diaspora, is still an argument in its nascent stages.

While the presence of a large Indian population is generally accepted and largely known, there are very few studies on the nature of their migration and the specific contexts, problematics and issues emerging from these patterns of diaspora. While the middle eastern 'gulfies' seem to be widely known only in terms of the remittances they send back to their homes (Karayil 2007) and the way in which particular states have been transformed due to this movement, the status of this diaspora eludes the context of the Middle East. Emerging research, to some extent, is beginning to posit the idea that temporary stay could be included within the framework of migrant studies. Studies conducted by the Gulf Research Centre at Jawaharlal Nehru University and the Centre for West Asian Studies at Jamia Millia Islamia have begun to focus on the human face of this diaspora, moving beyond the emphasis on monetary considerations. The debate about whether residents in the kingdoms of the Arabian Gulf are to be considered expatriates or not remains contentious in diaspora studies, but the emphasis can be seen to be shifting. This is best brought out by a research on the Indian community in Oman by Veronika Deffner and Carmella Pfaffenbach entitled 'Zones of Contact and Spaces of Negotiations: The Indian Diaspora in Muscat', where, having discussed more traditional notions of diaspora, they suggest:

> Nevertheless, one should mention that there are important differences between diasporas and communities (Dahlman 2004: 486). Communities, that are not considered diasporas, can still exhibit 'diasporic dimensions to their practices and cultures' (Clifford 1999: 303) with some communities being 'more diasporic than others' (Clifford 1999: 310). This indicates the broad empirical and conceptual range of this social phenomenon. The concept of diaspora is changing and now has more positive connotations, be they anything from latent to openly positive (Mayer 2005: 9). Diasporic ties have become an economic success. For this reason, diasporas are now also conceptualized as a resource or asset (Kokot 2007) and are becoming important to (trans)-migration research (Deffner and Pfaffenbach 2011: 3).

It is in this context that an analysis of the Indian diaspora in Oman emerges as a useful study. By moving beyond the configurations of earnings and remittances, the emergence of creative voices seem to add a dimension to the story of expatriation, which is not entirely dissimilar to accounts in the metanarrative of migration and travel.

Within the Omani context, the Indian presence and role in the host country is not only significant in the last few decades, but also goes back to, literally, times immemorial.

Historical Relations between India and Oman

The earliest references to Indians residing in the capital town and kingdom of Masqat are to the period around 1650 AD when traders from Sind had arrived at the port in order to facilitate trade in the Persian Gulf region. J.E. Peterson, a consultant and historian with the Government of Oman until the last decade, traces the existence of more than 4000 Sindhi merchants in 1688, adding that at the beginning of the twentieth century, there were around 200 traders along with their families. He illustrates that a vibrant community lived inside the old walls of Masqat town in which there were two temples, a cow shed and a crematorium in the Sidab area. Peterson, in his study, then traces the established families of Oman today, including the Khimjis, Dhanji Morarji, Ratansi Purushottam and others (Peterson 2004: 38–40).

Further historical studies of Allen (1981), Risso (1986) and Bosworth (2007) trace the sporadic presence of Indian traders in the Umani Kingdom as well as its extension into Zanzibar, a move explored by Nicolini (2004) and Goswami (2011). Through the eighteenth century, the trade shifted from Sind and Kutch to the Malabar Coast, aided particularly by the power and ambition of Tipu Sultan. Indian representatives were then sent to the Umani coast in 1789 by the Sultan to focus on the special status being given to trade in these quarters. By 1798, however, a new 'dalal' by the name of Vishnu Das was appointed and this man employed the services of a British physician for the then Sultan Said, thus introducing the Umanis to the British and pitting them against the French (Risso 1986: 92). These examples go a long way in establishing the power of the Indian mercantile community in the medieval history of Omani politics and the way in which they were instrumental in filling up the power vacuum at significant points of history. In fact, Calvin Allen centres his argument on Omani history on the fact that, contrary to public perceptions, the Umani Kingdom did not fall with the shifting of base from Masqat to Zanzibar, but in fact, the economic power actually shifted into the hands of the Indian merchants until the beginning of the First World War. They were no longer trading in the traditional items but in fact had begun to trade in dry dates with the United States and weapons with Europe. This, Allen argues, firmly established the significance of the Indian community as being, not only participants in the history of the coastal kingdom but, in fact, transformed them into major players in the Middle Eastern political stage as well. Much of this clout, however, was lost with the conflicts of the world wars and the accompanying political uncertainties in the Persian Gulf as well, as a result of which most families fled back to their homes in India, only to return after 1970.

Indian Diaspora: The Omani Connection

Mass movements of population into the Gulf, including labour as well as trading classes, came to dominate the economic scene following the creation of political states in the early 1970s. While some of the families mentioned above continued to stay over the period in the middle of the twentieth century in Oman, most had returned home after the fall of the Muscat rule in the early part of the century. It was only after the accession of the present monarch Sultan Qaboos bin Said to the throne and the creation of modern-day Oman in 1970 that Indian traders returned to their old businesses and livelihood in Muttrah. By 2011, the Indian embassy estimated that more than 5,00,000 Indians resided in Oman, of whom 82 per cent are blue-collared workers in construction businesses and domestic workers. Ten per cent of the Indians in Oman occupy upper middle ranks in the executive circles and the remaining 5 per cent or so include consultants, financial advisors and scientists. While it is possible to establish figures for the majority of the working class, most often as a result of human rights groups and NGO's pressure on the Indian embassy and recruitment agencies, the remaining groups have largely been unexplored. These constitute the educated middle class, very often professionals whose experiences are linked with the notion of temporary migrancy, very often turning into more permanent settlement.

This peculiar experience of living in the countries of the Gulf defined in terms of its linguistic and cultural difference and yet, in many ways, being similar to India in respect to dress, food and other everyday details, is being explored for its impact on the families, its representations in art and its effect on the community as a whole. Inhabiting an in-between space of being near home but not quite 'in' it, this group is uniquely rewarded by its proximity to the homeland, yet having a distance from it to be able to achieve a sense of perspective from immediate experiences. The stories surrounding these groups of expatriates remain an interesting source of history and imagination, underlying essential conditions of diaspora and its various associations.

Predominantly, the narratives of the Indian community in Oman are couched in vocabulary, which is comforting, homely and protected. Very often, residents speak in terms of being near home and of being in a very friendly atmosphere where the locals are inviting and comfortably (although their lives run parallel to each other). The typical response is that of Sandhya Menon, an Indian journalist working in one of the most popular newspapers in the country:

> You are in a country that has a completely different culture from your own, yet you feel at home because of its adoptive nature and its multi-cultural and cosmopolitan fabric. I don't think my first novel would have happened it if wasn't for the fact that I live here (Menon, personal communication, 2010).

Menon speaks of the physical beauty of the country as a source of inspiration for her, an aspect for which the country is particularly well known, and in fact, officially promoted as well. She refers to the fact that 'the aesthetics and stunning landscape overwhelm me. I didn't realize how much being surrounded by so much beauty would impact me ...'

It is a landscape, the ruggedness of which is emphasized in terms of the raw energy and purity of the human form in other artistic medium such as that of Pinaki, a photographer and freelance writer. For Pinaki, Oman reminds him of the essential humanity of all beings and as he centres the human experience in a land which he strips of all sense of location and time and manages to explore the notion of man-in-nature. Pinaki notes: 'I like to think of myself as a world traveler and see beauty where it has not been explored before. I think that my work should speak for itself without being burdened with personal connections and associations' (Pinaki, personal communication, 2010).

Landscape, history and grandeur also come together in the form of the sculptural installations of Radhika Khimji whose cardboard cuttings set against the Barka fort installed in June 2010 express her quest for identity and fixity. Born in Oman and educated at the Royal Academy of Art in London, Khimji relates the story of how she was constantly being perceived as being an outsider, making her introspect on the role of artists' biographies in their productions. The result of that quest takes the form of installations entitled 'shifters', a reference to shifting of identities, perceptions and meanings: 'They are not drawings, they are not paintings, they are not sculptures. They are always on the edge of what they are not, they keep slipping out of every category' (Khimji).

Landscapes and natural sceneries in Oman remain an important source of inspiration for the Indian diasporic artists, but the gradual shift to more social issues remains a significant part of the way in which the community, not only creates contexts of identity and self, but involves itself in more proactive ways in the synergies of daily life. Sudha Sha, an immigrant and film maker produced a film, 'The Call', chronicling the daily life of another immigrant, this time a housemaid, living and working for a local family, 'living in a house that is not her own and performing the role of a mother and carer, while enduring the pain of living alone herself' (Sha, personal communication, 2010). The shared sense of alienation and empathy on the part of the producer allows for the empowerment of a creative space, giving voice to a hitherto unexplored subject, thus making possible the continuation of dialogue and, possibly, action towards affecting a social shift in the condition of the workers.

Artistic creations, inspired by, both, the natural beauty of the land and the historical connections of the host country with India, make possible a variety of artistic expressions, all of which point to the exploration of issues such as identity and home, both of which are central to the predicament of the diaspora. If art in its various manifestations has allowed for a creative expression of such concerns, literature points to the way in which the experiences could be harnessed in more liberating ways, pointing, at once, to the pain and joy of living in a foreign land. The literary works of two novelists help to establish the contours of Indian literature in Oman, a venture that is still in nascent stages but helps to frame the expatriate experience.

Both Sunaina Ahluwalia and Asha Iyer use the metaphor of the desert, the majesty of the land and the central image of water to reflect on the experience of migration and the various associations it hold for them. Sunaina Ahluwalia's *A Safe Harbour* revolves around family relationships in the nurturing backdrop of Omani landscape. Set in modern Muscat, the novel revolves around the personal struggles of an Indian mother and daughter pair, Trishala and Afreen Luthra who find solace in the changing social contexts of the Indian expatriate community in Muscat city. Trishala's content, self-contained life as the socialite wife of an affluent Indian executive is jolted by the realization that she is suffering from cancer. Her daughter, Afreen, meanwhile navigates her career graph in the world of advertising back in New Delhi, India, while struggling to exorcise the demons of her past. In order to gain a perspective on her ongoing strife and mental instability, she comes to Muscat to join her parents for a brief holiday, having lived there in her childhood. The serenity and beauty of the surrounding physical landscape become a refuge and calming influence in the central characters' lives:

> Clean, spacious and green beyond belief, this city was truly a model for gracious living. Managing the delicate balance of the traditional with the modern beautifully, the highly developed aesthetic sense of the Omanis was in evidence as far as the eye could see ... (Ahluwalia 2010: 42)

To a large extent, *A Safe Harbour* is exactly that: a place of refuge, a corner of hope and peace in a world that is rapidly disintegrating for and around individuals. Ahluwalia repeatedly reminds the reader of the way in which the city lends itself to meaningful interaction among the various different communities, thus making possible an experience rarely available in most cosmopolitan centres. As her protagonist observes about what she likes most in Muscat: 'Most importantly, the way all expatriates, Asians and Europeans alike, were welcomed, then integrated into the society and country'. In addition and more interestingly, it is the way in which the Omani background contributes to the resolutions of strife and doubts of the characters that adds to the curative quality much eulogized in the novel:

> Walking to the balcony, she looked out. The garden soothed her senses and restored her mental equilibrium. Further ahead, she could see the sea. It was calm, the waves gently lapping at the shore, and a few seagulls circled overhead, filling the air with their cries. There was also a small fishing boat, bobbing up and down on the waves, and a lone fisherman had his net cast out. To her, it was clear. His sojourn was undoubtedly solitary, but successful. (Ahluwalia 2010: 231)

The writer, Sunaina Ahluwalia, admits that a primary motive for writing the novel was her increasing sense of indebtedness to Omani society and the need to 'give back' to the community. As she elaborates:

> I have been living here for the last 20 years and have worked full time in advertising, PR and communication. I have engaged and interacted with Omanis—even mentored a few and am very familiar with their stories. I worked closely with the National Association for Cancer Awareness survivors and heard their stories and in a way, working around the theme of cancer was my way of 'giving back' to the society I had lived in for so long. I felt the need to inspire cancer survivors with hope and positivism as I feel that is what they need the most. (S. Ahluwalia, personal communication, 20 December 2010)

Ahluwalia's involvement with the community expresses itself in various other platforms such as newspaper columns and increasing interest in photography which, she feels, 'expresses the beauty of Oman' in a variety of perspectives. When asked about the notion of diaspora, Ahluwalia comments,

> I don't experience a great disconnect when I go back home to India. You are a transient visitor here; you are always planning your future back home, unlike the experiences of those living in US and UK—where the degree of permanence gives you mental security and shapes how and what you will contribute to life there. (S. Ahluwalia, personal communication, 20 December 2010)

Comforting and restorative as Ahluwalia's Oman may be, it is not the only version of immigration possible in the contemporary context. Migration is never without its associations of loss and pain and Asha Iyer's novel *Sand Storms, Summer Rains*, while using the background of the desert, as the title suggests, dwells on the more poignant angle of diasporic experience. While *A Safe Harbour* outlines the positive aspects of migration and the restorative powers of Oman, *Sand Storms, Summer Rains* positions immigration in the more painful framework of class and gender struggle, privileging the experience of a class of workers who remain in the margins of migrant societies. The novel revolves around the lives of Mustafa and Achu and their travels from Mumbai to the Gulf in search of the legendary Gulf wealth. Even as Achu meets Mustafa very early in the novel, Mustafa comes across as cynical and serious, inexplicably unexcited about having been earning for his family in the desert. Years later, Achu remembers Mustafa's tone and identifies with his increasing cynicism and self-loathing:

> You know, every man gets caught in his own web of destiny. It is hard to escape destiny. I had never wanted to go abroad, but I did. I was forced to. I was newly married then. It was tortuous to leave my wife

> behind. I don't know if you would understand my pain. I carry the burden of their farewell tears all the time. (Iyer: 92)

Iyer's acknowledgment of the Gulf as an inspirational starting point is clear when she articulates the way in which her novel began:

> Although I have been very fond of writing and have had great affinity towards the written word from my college days, a novel wasn't on my mind at all ... I used to write small things, shorter versions of fiction like stories and other articles of self opinion, but a novel was the remotest thing on my mind. But being a keen observer of people and things around me, I realised that over a period of time, I had collected in my kitty, a lot of things to which I was raring to respond in my own personal way. This included my numerous observations and experiences after I came to the Gulf in 1998. These impressions of people and life were such that they demanded a more serious treatment than an ordinary feature, article or a short story. Thus came about the idea to string the impressions together and create a novel. (Iyer, personal blog)

Asha Iyer's detailing of her novelistic technique in *Sand Storms, Summer Rains* provides an insightful take into the manner in which universal themes of class struggle, gender conflict and intergenerational strife can be effectively localized to create stories in a specific cultural milieu. Admitting that she wanted her novel to be more than 'just a document' on the ordinary lives of migrant workers, Iyer creates the picture of diaspora that is, in this case, deliberately different from narratives that etch success stories of workers going to the Gulf in search of unbelievable wealth capable of turning around lives. The tale, she says, is never so simple:

> It was one or many such things that told me categorically that there was much more to a working class expat's life in the Gulf than making money. With age, I discovered that the gulf dream wasn't as shimmering as it looked. It was a realisation that broke my juvenile fallacies and the novel is an outcome of this slow and systematic understanding of the living-alone expat people in the Gulf—the man out there who toils in the sun when the rest of the city cools it off in the interiors, the woman who puts the picture of her son on her desk and wonders every morning if he must have eaten his breakfast, gone to school or given a headache to his grandmother, the young son who lives in the perpetual fear of not being next to his aged parents when they pass away, the family back home that although enamoured of

> the new riches, still thinks it was better if the man of the family had not been so far away. The kaleidoscope of their lives presents endless patterns. Even today, when I see these men and women, my heart goes out to them. You can read the despair on their faces, if only you take a moment to read them. (Iyer, personal blog)

It serves to demonstrate that Oman provides much inspiration and influences for the artists to integrate into their works, whether simply through visually observing the vistas around them or actually incorporating the country's atmosphere, beliefs, and traditions into their existing artistic philosophies. Furthermore, the conjunction of their initial artistic encounter and subsequent relationship that they develop with Oman along with the artistic ideologies, style and techniques that they have nourished over the years results in exciting artistic work, showing how Oman has potentially impacted the artist and how the artist has responded to Oman. Interaction with Omani artists and learning more about their individual artistic approaches also contributes towards an enhanced awareness of the artistic scene in Oman as well as encouraging the arrival of new techniques and philosophies in their midst. Thus, the Indian artist's presence in Oman is not just merely limited to the act of physically observing the surroundings and replicating them on the canvas, but also the works that the artists go on to create reflect a new sensibility that they have developed after their interaction with Oman, its people, its culture and traditions and becoming aware of local arts and artists.

Rabab Zaidi, a young professional artist from Jamia Millia Islamia in New Delhi, admits to owing much to her new home. A new resident of the Sultanate, Rabab has previously exhibited in Lalit Kala Academy in Delhi as well as the National Museum in Riyadh. Her moment of pride, however, was when she was chosen to represent India for a mural based on 'Indo-Omani' relations. This mural was jointly composed by Rabab and Anwar Sonya, a well known Omani artist. The resulting painting was a testament to the continuing relevance of art and its capacity to transcend geographical borders. She was also awarded an honorary prize for her work 'Duality' in the recently concluded 15th Annual Youth Art Exhibition. Rabab views her role as being primarily as that of educating the viewer by sensitizing them to the finer nuances of the canvass. She says, 'My role as an artist is to instil a sense of appreciation and contemplation. As art emanates aesthetic pleasure, an artist must always sensitize the viewer to react to a thought. It can be as subtle as Monalisa's smile or as poignant as pain the Picasso's *Guernicas*. As the approach is based on human response, it is relevant at all times'.

In her time in Oman, Rabab has seen the art scenario change rapidly, often for the better. She says that Oman has changed significantly in terms of receptivity as artists are open to new media. She lauds the constant effort to encourage young talent and the frequent attempts to re-introduce tradition and heritage through modern and global visual vocabulary. She cites the Omani Society of Fine Arts as being primarily responsible for almost single-handedly transforming the art scenario in Oman. Rabab sees her latest work as being inspired by Islamic aesthetics, particularly the notion of repetition becoming central to a composition. Her current projects revolve around the attempt to decipher duality in repetition, inevitably occurring because of constant changing of contexts.

As far as Oman is concerned, Rabab attributes the serenity of space as an important source of inspiration for her. As she puts it, 'As a visual person, I found 'regularity' and 'absence' of polychrome' very fascinating. For me, it provokes introspection and explains ethereality, traces of which are reflected in my work of late'. The range and versatility in Rabab's work shows the ease with which she moves across cultures and willingly gains inspiration from them.

Another painter, Padmaja, thinks of the colours of the neighbouring sea and mountains as being the inspiration of her art. Having lived in Oman for the last decade, Padmaja frames her paintings in a more domestic context, using the typology around her house to create more metaphysical meanings of the condition of life. Her recent painting, 'The Bird', for example, catches a tiny sparrow outside the window of the artist's kitchen, hanging on to the electric pole. Caught between the two ends of the wire, Padmaja weaves a tale of choices, of the need to think outside the box, of the capacity of humans as well as animals to be different and dare to live a new life. Perhaps reminiscent of her new life in Oman, Padmaja's painting points to the way in which local realities could point to larger, more philosophical issues. The artist herself explains her vocation in the following interview:

> Right from the day I started living in Muscat, I haven't spent a single day without painting! It is a great opportunity for any artist to get out of their home country to experience new culture, new landscapes and new stories of the local people. In fact, as far as my art is concerned, I

haven't missed India because I am all excited to try out new themes that reflect Oman in some way right from the exotic sea scapes to the people and the architecture and want to make the most of what this beautiful country can offer me as an artist, to bring out paintings that would make my memories of Oman fresh and alive all my life. (Padmaja Manju 2013).

Conclusion

The often invoked image of Janus looking at two opposite directions at the same time remains a relevant trope to discuss the predicament of the Indian diaspora, particularly in the Middle East. While the established narrative of the working class, which is struggling away from home, hoping for an early return, is a significant aspect of the immigrant story in the Arabian Gulf, so is the more celebratory angle that posits the creative possibilities of diaspora and the consequent energies it releases. Increasingly, artists and writers have begun to find their voices and created platforms through which the unique nature of their specific experience could be expressed. The narrative of the Indian experience in the Gulf, while still struggling to be recognized in its historical and social complexity, has succeeded in transforming itself into a vocal and expressive group, turning the tale of migration and pain into one of possibilities and hope.

References

Ahluwalia, Sunaina Serna. *A Safe Harbour*. New Delhi: Indialog Publications, 2008.

Ahluwalia, Sunaina Serna. *Point of No Return*. New Delhi: Indialog Publications, 2010.

Allen, Calvin H., Jr. 'The Indian Merchant Community of Masqat'. *Bulletin of The School of Oriental and African Studies*, 44, 1 (1981): 39–53.

Bosworth, Clifford Edmund. *Historic Cities of the Islamic World*. Leiden: Koninklijke Brill NV, 2007.

Das, Tridwik K. 'Spectator of Life', 16 September (2009). Message posted on http://ashaiyerkumar.blogspot.com/2009/09/write-up-in-the-week-oman.html

Deffner, Veronika and Pfaffenbach, Carmella. 'Zones of Contact and Spaces of Negotiation: The Indian Diaspora in Muscat'. Proceedings of Conference The Struggle to belong: Dealing with diversity in 21st Century Urban Settings. Amsterdam, 2011.

Goswami, C. *The Call of the Sea: Kachchhi Traders in Muscat and Zanzibar*. New Delhi: Orient Blackswan, 2011.

Karayil, Sajitha Beevi. 'Does Migration Matter in Trade? A Study of India's Exports to the GCC Countries'. *South Asia Economic Journal*, 8, 1 (2007): 1–20.

Kumar, Asha, Iyer. *Sand Storms, Summer Rains*. Mumbai: Frog Books, 2009.

Nicolini, Beatrice. *Makran, Oman and Zanzibar: A Three Terminal Cultural Corridor in the Western Indian Ocean (1799–1856)* (Penelope Jane Watson, Trans.). Leiden: Koninklijke Brill NV, 2004.

Peterson, J.E. 'Oman's Diverse Society: Northern Oman'. *Middle East Journal*, 58, 1 (2004): 32–51.

Rahman, Anisur. 'The Socio-Cultural Dimensions of Indo-Omani Relations'. *International Politics*, 2, 3 (2009): 100–113.

Risso, Patricia. *Oman & Muscat: An Early Modern History*. Kent: Croom Helm, 1986.

Safran, William. 'Diasporas in Modern Societies: Myths of Homeland and Return'. *Diaspora: A Journal of Transnational Studies*, 1, 1 (1991): 83–94.

Part III

Development and Change

CHAPTER 7

Changing Patterns of Indian Labour Migration to the Gulf

Causes and Effects

Anisur Rahman

The main aim of this chapter is to study the changing patterns of Indian migration in terms of socioeconomic background and origin. What are the effects of labour migration on migrants' families especially on their education? Whether foreign exposure and interaction has brought some positive changes in migrants' attitude towards education? Have they become more skilled while working with more sophisticated technology abroad? How far the remittances have improved the socio-economic conditions of migrants' household? What are the attitudes of family members to education? Besides education, how are they investing Gulf money in order to improve their economic status? All these questions would be examined in the right perspective.

Indian Labour migration to the Gulf, on the large scale, began since the early 1970s on account of oil boom that took place in the Gulf region. As a result, industrialization and other economic activities got momentum, which led to the great demand of manpower in this region. This demand has pulled more than 15 million expatriate workers in this region. Of them, about 6.5 million expatriates are from India at present. Since the beginning, majority of migrants went to the Gulf from the South Indian states, especially Kerala. But now Indian migration is taking place from North India in large numbers. Now Kerala's share has come down to almost one-fifth of the total outflow of labour migration. According to the 2010 Annual Report of the Ministry of Overseas Indian Affairs (MOIA), it is Uttar Pradesh and Bihar from where the maximum migration has taken place to the Gulf countries.

As a result of labour migration, India is benefited enormously in receipt of remittances from abroad. India received more than US $55 billion as remittances in 2010 that rose to US$ 70 billion in 2012. The remittances are increasing every year. The effects of remittances could be observed in terms of human resource development, physical assets, financial investment, and so on. These remittances have positive impact on Indian economy and society. Because of the inflow of the Gulf remittances in migrating villages, enormous change has taken in this area. The Gulf remittances are also playing a major role in the enhancement of education among migrants' families. This is also true that some proportion of remittances is used for unproductive purposes. But as a whole, this labour migration has had positive impact on reducing unemployment and promoting education in migrating places, apart from enriching India's balance of payments, commodity export, business profits and government earnings.

Background

India has had strong relations with the Gulf region, both in terms of trade and the movement of people for a long period. In fact, there are numbers of families of Indian merchants who have, for long, settled in Dubai (Sekhar 1997: 35). Indians acted as intermediaries in great silk route trade between China and the West. The seventh to tenth century are said to be the golden age of Indo-Arab trade (Jain 2010: 178). But it was only towards the latter part of the nineteenth and early twentieth centuries that emigration became significant feature of Indian life. The labour migration from India to the Gulf Cooperation Council (GCC) countries can be traced back to the early oil discovery and exploration days. As a result of steep hike in oil prices, there was a considerable increase in the revenue of oil producing and exporting countries in the region. Many developmental activities such as construction of roads and creation of amenities, such as schools, hospitals, houses, airports, offices and commercial complexes, were taken up in a big way. This created demand for not only highly skilled manpower but also semi-skilled and unskilled manpower. India is not only second most populous country of the world with surplus of labour, but also has a vast reservoir of well trained and educated manpower. Therefore, as soon as opportunities to earn better arose, Indians were the first among the groups of emigrants to flock to the Gulf countries and they were well placed to meet these growing demands. Thus, migration of Indian manpower to the Gulf region offers opportunities for providing gainful employment to these unemployed persons (Rahman 2010: 203).

It is noted that every year large number of Indians migrate to different countries of the world to earn more money in order to raise their standard of living and make their families happier and prosperous. It is a common knowledge that especially after India's independence, Indian workers went mainly to the United States, United Kingdom, Canada and other developed countries during the 1950s and the 1960s. Thereafter, it began to decline for a variety of reasons. The common characteristics of Indian workers who went to developed nations are highly skilled such as the information technology (IT) professionals, whereas those who went to the Gulf regions are unskilled and semiskilled labourers. The other features of Indian labourers in the Gulf region are that the overwhelming majority of them are males. As compared with other migrating countries from South Asia, female migration from India is very less. It is also interesting to note that in the 1970s and the 1980s, migration from India was dominated by Kerala, which sent 50 per cent migrants. At present its composition has declined due to the migration from other Indian states especially from North India. Uttar Pradesh emerged as number one state in terms of labour emigration from India followed by Kerala and Tamil Nadu since 2009. Within the GCC countries, Kingdom of Saudi Arabia (KSA) and United Arab Emirates (UAE) are the major destinations for Indians and together they account for more than 60 per cent of the total deployment of Indian migrant workers.

It is evident that during the mid-seventies the oil boom in the West Asia, especially the Gulf countries, vastly changed the complexion of emigration. The steep hike in oil prices during 1973–1974 and thereafter led to a considerable increase in the revenue of the oil producing and exporting countries in West Asia region. As a result, development programmes including construction of roads and creation of amenities, such as schools, hospitals, houses, airports, office and commercial complexes, were taken up in a big way. This resulted in a spurt in demand for not only highly skilled technical experts but also semi-skilled and unskilled workers. India was well placed to meet these emerging demands (MOIA 2004–2005).

Emerging Trends of Labour Diaspora

It is further noted that there are four major labour importing countries such as Saudi Arabia, the UAE, Kuwait and Oman, which constitute more than four-fifth of the labour flows from India during the 2000–2004. The momentum of labour imports to Saudi Arabia is perhaps due to change in its policy towards India. So far as the case of the UAE and Oman are concerned, India is having very good relations with these countries since long time. Kuwait too has cordial relations with India like other GCC countries. Hence, we can say that this rising trend of emigration from India will continue in future as well.

Table 7.1 *Annual Outflow of Indian Labour to Gulf during 2008–2012*

Country/year	*2008*	*2009*	*2010*	*2011*	*2012*
UAE	3,49,827	1,30,302	1,30,910	1,38,861	1,41,138
Saudi Arabia	2,28,406	2,81,110	2,75,172	2,89,297	3,57,503
Kuwait	35,562	42,091	37,667	45,149	55,868
Oman	89,659	74,963	1,05,807	73,819	84,384
Malaysia	21,123	11,345	20,577	17,947	21,241
Bahrain	31,924	17,541	15,101	14,323	20,150
Qatar	82,937	46,292	45,752	41,710	63,096
Libya	5,040	3,991	5,221	477	01
Other Country	49,318	35,889	36,073	1,92,039	40,482
Total	8,48,601	6,10,272	6,41,356	6,26,565	7,47,041

Source: Government of India, MOIA, Annual Report, 2011–2012.

As the literature show the majority of Indian emigrants go to West Asia, especially the Gulf countries such as Saudi Arabia, the UAE, Oman, Kuwait, Bahrain and Qatar. Out of these, Saudi Arabia, the UAE and Kuwait are the major countries in terms of importing maximum migrants from India. Table 7.1 shows that Saudi Arabia was at the top followed by the UAE till 2002 but Saudi Arabia was replaced by the UAE in 2003. It is also noted that more than 50 per cent Indian migrants were exported to these two countries. We further observe that there are new destinations that have come into picture at the end of the twentieth century. Indians began to migrate to South Asian countries such as Singapore from 1998 and Malaysia from 1999. In 2002, about 35,000 Indians migrated to this region (South East Asia). Singapore and Malaysia combined together imported more than 10 per cent Indians in 2003, which is not shown in the table. Malaysia alone imported 6.06 per cent Indian emigrants in 2004. Hence, it is concluded that the places of destinations for Indian migrants are widening day by day. India must make a policy that promotes manpower expert not only to the Gulf region but also to other countries that need manpower for their growth and development.

Changing Profile of Migrants

It was found that majority of Indian migrants to the Gulf countries were semi-skilled or unskilled (Ecevit and Zackariah 1978: 34). Given the skill composition of migrant workers in the West Asia, the contribution of the different labour-exporting countries to various categories of migrants was different. In case of India and Pakistan, unskilled workers were 65 per cent and 80 per cent respectively. Between the three major labour-exporting countries of South Asia, there had been a remarkable difference between India on the one hand and Pakistan and Bangladesh on the other hand. The proportion of the completely unskilled workers was significantly high in case of migrants from India, while Pakistanis and Bangladeshis had, to some extent, possessed some manual skill (Gulati and Mody 1983: 12). Even the state of Kerala, which has the highest literacy rate in the South Asia, sent more unskilled workers to the West Asia than those of Pakistan and Bangladesh.

It was found that during the mid-1980s unskilled workers comprised about 40 per cent of the total labour outflow from India to the West Asian countries, skilled workers accounted for less than 50 per cent, while white-collar workers and highly skilled workers made up a little less than 5 per cent. The outflow of workers engaged in construction activities, when the skilled and unskilled are taken together, declined not only in absolute terms, but also as a proportion of the total out-migration. The outflow of skilled workers engaged in non-construction activities also declined in absolute terms but increased relatively because of the greater contraction in total outflow.

In contrast, the absolute levels of labour outflow were sustained for white-collar workers as well as for the high-skilled workers and registered an increase among unskilled workers in non-construction activities, so that the share of each of these categories in total out-migration rose. It is observed that large proportion of the out-migration was made up of workers employed in the service sector, so much so that proportion employed in the manufacturing sector was small while that in the agricultural sector was negligible. Since emigration to the West Asian countries is temporary, it would appear to provide an example of international trade in services (Nayyar 1994: 30). Today, the profile of demand for workforce has changed. It is now less for unskilled and semi-skilled and more for skilled and highly qualified professionals. India must prepare accordingly. As we know that there is no dearth of such manpower in India.

Table 7.2 *Major Labour-Sending States of India during 2008–2012*

State	*2008*	*2009*	*2010*	*2011*	*2012*
Andhra Pradesh	97,530	69,233	72,220	71,581	92,803
Bihar	60,642	50,227	60,531	71,438	84,078
Karnataka	22,413	18,565	17,295	15,394	17,960
Kerala	180,703	119,384	1,04,101	86,783	98,178
Maharashtra	24,786	19,128	18,123	16,698	19,259
Punjab	54,469	27,291	30,974	31,866	37,472
Rajasthan	64,601	44,744	47,803	42,239	50,295
Tamil Nadu	1,28,791	78,841	84,510	68,732	78,185
Uttar Pradesh	1,39,254	1,25,783	1,40,826	1,55,301	1,91,341
West Bengal	26,094	21,187	28,900	29,795	36,988
Other States	49,318	35,889	36,073	1,92,039	40,482
Total	8,48,601	6,10,272	6,41,356	6,26,565	7,47,041

Source: Government of India, MOIA, Annual Report, 2011–2012.

New Patterns of Labour Migration

Table 7.2 shows that there are states such as Kerala, Tamil Nadu, Andhra Pradesh, Maharashtra, Rajasthan, Punjab, Uttar Pradesh and Bihar that dominate in the race of migration. These are the states that send considerable number of migrants abroad every year. Out of these, Kerala, Tamil Nadu and Andhra Pradesh send more than 50 per cent migrants as shown in Table 7.2. It was found that in the 1970s and 1980s, migration was dominated by Kerala, which sent about 50 per cent migrants alone. At present, its share has declined to less than 14 per cent due to the entry of other Indian states. Tamil Nadu is now at the top in sending maximum migrants abroad followed by Andhra Pradesh and then Kerala. It is observed that South Indian states are still far ahead in terms of sending more migrants outside the country as shown in Table 7.2. It is also observed that significant number of migrants from Northern Indian states such as Punjab, Uttar Pradesh and Bihar are going to this region. Uttar Pradesh and Bihar together send more than 10 per cent of the total Indian emigrants.

Kerala was the top sending state followed by Tamil Nadu and Andhra Pradesh till 2003. But this trend has not been uniform; the number one position of Kerala was replaced by Tamil Nadu, which was followed by Andhra Pradesh in 2004. Kerala regained its top position in 2005 but it was again outnumbered by Tamil Nadu during 2006–2007. In the year of 2008, the top position of labour emigrating state was restored by Kerala again, which was followed by Uttar Pradesh and Tamil Nadu. Here the North Indian state of Uttar Pradesh has entered into top three labour emigration states of India. Yet the relative share of North Indian states is gradually increasing, largely due to rapid rise in unemployment in all states in India (Rahman 2010: 209).

There are about 6 million Indian expatriates in the GCC countries. Indians constitute about one-third of the total expatriate population and 10 per cent of the total GCC population. The largest number of Indians lives in Saudi Arabia followed by the UAE, Oman and Kuwait. There are about 1,00,000 Indians in Yemen who are permanently settled there. Israel has the other permanently settled Indian community in West Asia. Following the creation of Israel in 1948, more than 25,000 Indian Jews migrated to Israel and well settled in their new homeland, Jews of Indian origin today number around 50,000. Keralites constitute the major group followed by Punjab among the Indian immigrants in West Asia. There are about 1.8 million Keralites working in the Gulf countries. The skill composition of the migrant workforce is still dominated by unskilled and semi-skilled workers, followed by administrative staff and skilled workers. Currently, the Gulf migrants are the major source of remittances and foreign exchange to India. This is realized by Indian government and has started giving importance to them. To look after the affairs of Indians abroad, a new ministry, namely the Ministry of Overseas Indian Affairs (MOIA) was created in 2004.

Transfer of Remittances to India

All labour-sending countries are benefited enormously due to the inflow of remittances. India is one of the major countries in the world that receives the highest amount of remittances from abroad (Table 7.3). Today there are more than 25 million Indians living in the diaspora spread all over the world. Similarly, many countries such as

China, Pakistan, Bangladesh and Sri Lanka have realized the significance of their diasporic population. All these countries have their own policy for diaspora. This diasporic community has contributed immensely both to their host country and to their home country, primarily through transfers of money they earn, that is, remittances. These remittances are used for developmental activities in these countries. In many developing countries, remittances are used for eradicating poverty and generating employment. These remittances are found to be rather more stable than foreign direct investment (FDI). It is also evident that the flow of remittances is rising at the global and national level every year.

Table 7.3 *Transfer of Remittances to India*

Year	*In US$ million*
2000–2001	12.8
2001–2002	15.8
2002–2003	17.2
2003–2004	22.2
2004–2005	21.1
2005–2006	25
2006–2007	30.8
2007–2008	43.5
2008–2009	46.9
2009–2010	53.9
2010–2011	55.9
2011–2012	70

Source: MOIA, Annual Reports, Different Years.

In 2010, worldwide remittance flows are estimated to have exceeded US$440 billion. From that amount, developing countries received US$325 billion, which represents an increase of 6 per cent from the remittances received in 2009. The total amount, including unrecorded flows through formal and informal channels, is believed to be significantly larger. Recorded remittances in 2009 were nearly three times the amount of official aid and almost as large as FDI flows to developing countries (Migration and Remittances Factbook 2011). An important aspect of Indian labour migration to the Gulf has been its lion's share in the remittances sent back to India by the Indian diaspora. Remittances were virtually negligible in 1970, rose to US$2.8

billion in 1980. Global remittances to India reached a level of US$2.1 billion in 1990–1991, to US$8.1 billion in 1994–1995, to US$ 12.4 billion in 1999–2000 and eventually to US$22.3 billion in 2003–2004. Since 2003, India has been the world's largest recipient, at least in absolute terms, of remittances, defined as the inflow of private transfers and between 2000–2001 and 2003–2004, remittances almost doubled (Muzaffar Chishti: www.migrationpolicy.org). The remittances through formal channels were pegged at US$55 billion in 2010 (Migration and Remittances Factbook 2011). Also, in relative terms, remittances gained considerable importance since they now make up a larger chunk of India's gross domestic product: 3.3 per cent in 2007 according to the World Bank (WB) versus 0.7 per cent in 1990–1991 according to the Reserve Bank of India (RBI).

Labour diaspora from India is helping to not only reduce the situation of unemployment but also earn foreign exchange. India has been benefited enormously due to labour diaspora abroad. One of the benefits of Indian labour migration to the Gulf has been the inflow of remittances to India. It all began in the mid-1970s. Initially, there was large proportion of remittances coming from the developed countries, but these were gradually overtaken by larger proportions coming from the Gulf region. The amount of remittances was less than US$ 3 billion in 1980. Throughout the eighties it remained so. In the nineties, it increased rapidly from US$ 3.6 billion in 1991–1992 to more than US$ 12 billion in 2001–2002. It is further observed that this remittance rose to US$ 14 billion in 2002–2003, US$18 billion in 2003–2004 and it further increased to US$ 21.7 billion in 2005 (*Hindustan Times*, 18 November 2005). The latest data show that the global remittances to India reached a level of US$ 55 billion in 2010. If we analyse these data in terms of share of GDP at market prices, they constituted 0.7 per cent in 1990–1991 and 3.0 per cent in 1999–2000.

Thus, remittances sent by Indian diaspora have supposedly contributed positively to the Indian economy. In the middle of 1991, India faced a serious balance of payments crisis. Foreign exchange reserves had fallen to a level hardly adequate to meet essential imports for just a few weeks. The Indian migrants in the developed countries withdrew their dollar deposits from Indian banks at an alarming rate. These problems warranted immediate action for India to avoid defaulting on its international obligations or a collapse of its economy for want of critical imports. It was the slowly but steadily growing remittances from the Indian workers in the Gulf, which saved the situation for India. Today India is at the top of the list of countries receiving remittances from its migrants abroad, close to 10 per cent of the worldwide remittances sent home by 191 million migrants.

Diasporic remittance led to the removal of two kinds of poverty in India—the 'poverty of education' and the 'poverty of health'. At the same time, remittances have led to the opening up of a large number of new schools and colleges, on the one hand, and enabling the youth to buy a costly private education on the other hand—both contributing to unemployment among the current generations of Kerala youth who no longer want to work in traditional lines of occupations. Second, an equally important 'adverse' effect has been the emergence of 'replacement migration' of labour into Kerala from the other Indian states. Apart from the fact that wages have gone up in Kerala, which is highest in India due to shortage of unskilled and semi-skilled workers, labourers from other states also accept low wages and poor living conditions to work in Kerala, adding to unemployment of the local generations of youth.

Economic Effects of Migration

Apart from Gulf remittances, various incentive schemes for investment in India by the non-resident Indians (NRIs) and the permission to bring gold while returning to the country are the contributing factors responsible for increase in the amount of remittances. The employment of Indian workers abroad helps to earn foreign exchange and thereby adds to the foreign exchange reserves in India. There has been increase in the remittances resulting in increase in the foreign exchange reserves. While there was increase in the remittance of foreign exchange during the year 1995–1996 and 1996–1997 over the previous years, there has been marginal change in the subsequent years. This increase, has however, resulted mainly because of the remittances from the Gulf countries. Indians living in other parts of the world remit only a tiny proportion of their savings. The Gulf money has also improved the income level of the migrant households considerably. This rising income level has directly affected the consumption, investment and saving patterns in migrating areas. In this situation, the inflow of remittance played a significant role. The benefit of remittance seemed to be distributed in favour of the districts of the state which ranked low with respect to per capita domestic product and the growth of population.

It is also found that migrant workers become more skilled while working abroad. They work there with highly sophisticated machines and instruments. There is no brain drain in case of migration to the Gulf. It may be rather called brain bank because the migrant workers acquire more skills while working in the Gulf. Even after returning from the Gulf, they are the assets to the nation because their services could be utilized for developmental activities in India It cannot, however, be denied that there is an acute shortage of labour at migrating areas due to outflow of labour from there. As a result, agriculture is badly affected. Moreover, it is also observed that there is a price rise due to the inflow of the gold remittance in migrating villages. All people who reside there are adversely affected on account of Gulf money coming into this region. There is a conspicuous consumption among emigrants' families that too has affected adversely the non-migrants' families.

Social Effects of Migration

Gulf migration has also brought social and psychological effects on migrants' families. A visible change may be noticed in their attitude towards education. There is rising demand for educational facilities by the migrants. An increasingly large proportion of children, particularly the girls, are now going to schools and colleges. A large proportion of young men turning up in the training centres for different technical skills. Social mobility has also taken place rapidly. A family which was looked down in the past is now welcomed in social functions. Poverty stricken and desolated villages are suddenly becoming prosperous (Nair 1983). A sizable proportion of houseless population is now having own houses. Demand for more schools, health centres and domestic electrification, sanitation and transport facilities is rising at the places of migrants' origin.

Moreover, changes are taking place in the attitude of the Gulf migrants' families towards their customs, habits and life style as well. The rise in their social and economic status is gradually resulting in the deprivation of the privileges and power of certain sections of the society, which they had been holding in the past for many decades. This is really a positive development towards the balance of power and social justice. On the other hand, social and psychological implications of migration cannot be ignored. The major factors responsible for the social and psychological problems of the migrants are job insecurity, discrimination in wage/salary, isolation from the social function in the countries of employment, lack of opportunities and avenues for entertainment, inabilities on the part of the majority of Indian workers to bring their wives and children to the countries of employment, poor accommodation facilities, unfavourable climatic conditions and restrictions on seeking alternative employment opportunities. It is also said that the new generation of educated Arabs treat the Indians and other Asian migrants with arrogance and contempt. In sum, the problem is the problems of being total outsiders, facing a future full of uncertainties.

Conclusion

We conclude by saying that this migration has also provided additional revenues to provide services through airlines, hotels, travel agencies, banks, medical clinics, recruiting agencies, training institutions, translation, services and telephone services. The development impact of remittances is also observed in terms of physical assets and financial investment, human capital investment. Many studies reveal that a good proportion of remittances are kept in the form of financial assets after spending a major proportion of it in the acquisition and construction of physical assets. Some proportion of remittances is also kept in banks as fixed deposit. It is also found that the expenditure on education and medicines has been increased as a result of the receipt of Gulf remittances. There is, however, no doubt that some proportion of remittances is used for unproductive purposes such as construction of houses and consumption, expenses on marriages and purchases of jewellery and ornaments. Despite all, we can definitely say that the net benefit of Indian migrants in West Asia is positive for India.

References

Chishti, Muzaffar. 'Migration Policy Institute', Washington: www.migrationpolicy.org.

Ecevit, Zafer and K.C. Zackariah. 'International Labour Migration'. *Finance and Development*, 15, 4 (1978): 34.

Gulati, I.S. and Ashok Mody. 'Remittances of Indian Migrants to the Middle East: An Assessment with Special References to Migrants from Kerala State'. Working Paper No. 182, Trivandrum: CDS, 1983.

Jain, Prakash C. 'Indian diaspora in West Asia'. In Rajendra M. Abhyankar (ed.), *West Asia and the Region: Defining India's Role.* New Delhi: Academy Foundation, 2010.

Migration and Remittances Factbook, 2nd Edition. Washington: World Bank, 2011.

Ministry of Overseas Indian Affairs (MOIA). *Annual Report 2004–2005*. Government of India.

Nair, P.R.G. 'Asian Emigration to the Middle East: Emigration from India-Report of the State of the Art'. Trivandrum: Centre for Development Studies, 1983.

Nayyar, Deepak. *Migration, Remittances and Capital Flows: The Indian Experience*. Delhi: Oxford University Press, 1994.

Rahman, Anisur. 'India Manpower in the Gulf: Strategic and Economic Dimensions'. In Rajendra M. Abhyankar (ed.), *West Asia and the Region: Defining India's Role*. New Delhi: Academy Foundation, 2010.

Sekhar, T.V. *Migration and Social Change*. Jaipur: Rawat Publications, 1997.

CHAPTER 8

Gulf Migration, Social Change and Mobility Among Kerala Muslims

Ajmal Khan

The process of migration due to socioeconomic, political, climatic and other reasons have been taking place from the history of humankind. The human beings have migrated in search of new lands and better prospects. This has led to unprecedented changes both in sending and receiving regions and societies. India has a long history of migration, starting from the prehistoric period to the contemporary times. The literature on migration classified as the migration during pre-colonial period and post-colonial period. The most significant phases of migration started after India became independent. There are three patterns of migration observed in this period: emigration of Anglo-Indians to Australia and England, emigration of professionals and semi-professionals to the industrialized advanced countries such as the United States, United Kingdom, Canada and the emigration of both skilled and unskilled labourers to the West Asia countries surrounding the Persian Gulf (Jayaram 2004). The phenomenon of immigration to the West Asia received much attention, especially after the oil boom during the post-1970s. This immigration is unprecedented because of the volume of remittances that were sent back home by the immigrants and also because of the number of immigrants involve in the process of migration compared with previous patterns of migrations. Though the Government of India has a separate ministry called the Ministry of Overseas Affairs, it does not have an exact estimation of how many Indians are currently living outside, particularly in the Gulf countries. The recent estimation suggests that, 19 per cent of all non-resident Indians (NRIs) and persons of Indian origins (PIOs) living outside India are to be located in the Gulf (Khadria 2006). Indian immigrants in the Gulf were gone from all states of India, but migration from South Indian states such as Kerala, Andhra Pradesh, Karnataka and Tamil Nadu comprised more than 50 per cent of the immigration clearance over the past decade (Indian Council of Overseas Employment, ICOE, 2009). There have been unprecedented impacts in economies and societies of these states. The state of Kerala stands for the top remittance receiving state, which sent 20 per cent of the total immigrants from India and received about the same per cent of the total recorded official remittance for the country. The state of Kerala had around 6,41,000 emigrants by 1992–1993 and increased to 21,94,000 according to the estimates of 2008 (Zachariah et al. 1999).

Several studies have pointed out that the dependence of people on remittances is very high in Kerala (for instance, see Kannan and Hari 2002). In absolute terms, the per capita net state domestic product (NSDP) doubled over the period 1988–2008. The per capita remittances increased nearly sixfold during the same period. Comparison of remittances received by Kerala with all of Indian states shows that the growth trend of remittances during the period 1988–2008 registered around 18.2 per cent in Kerala as compared with 15.7 per cent for all of India (United Nations 2011). So it is evident that the remittances by the migrants from the Kerala state have grown to a considerable amount that helps to sustain the economy of the state. Gulf migrations have had tremendous economic and social impacts in the state of Kerala. This is reflected not only in the remittances, but also in the changing housing patterns and consumer cultures, poverty levels, education, employment and day to day life of the people who have not even migrated from the state. I will discuss the impacts of immigration to the Gulf, the flow of remittances to the state of Kerala and how it has impacted the society of Kerala, particularly looking at the Muslim community to understand the impact of the migration.

Migration, Social Change and Social Mobility

There are some key theoretical positions to consider understanding how and why migration takes place. The main controversy from the 1960s to the 1990s was between neoclassical economic theory and historical—institutional theory. The neo-classicist focuses on individual decision to migrate on the basis of level of opportunities at the migration destinations whereas the historical institutionalist emphasize on political economy approach (Stephen 2008). There is consensus in the migration literature that mobility of human beings from one place to another has resulted in changes and transformation in the sending and receiving societies. Many debates on migration and social change have gone much beyond considering the remittance and remittance led changes in sending countries. However, because of the important contribution of remittances to the welfare, it has been argued that remittances are safety nets in relatively poor areas (Jones 1998). The migration to the Gulf has to be seen in the perspective where the migrants were relatively unskilled or under skilled (Zachariah et al. 1999). The migration to the Gulf was indeed a safety net for the families from where the migrants had originated. The studies on Gulf migration was always dominated on the remittances and how the remittances contributed to the stability of the state's economy and led to the overall development of the state. Many of these studies have paid little attention to how these remittances impacted poverty, education, housing, employment, agriculture and economy. It was neglected that the societal changes within social-religious communities did not get enough attention even when community identity is one of the most important determining factor for the migration of an individual from the state.

This chapter tries to examine the social changes and mobilities among the Muslims in Kerala as a result of the remittances received from the Gulf migrants. Social changes as a result of migration are contested. There are two dominant arguments for the social change generated by migration. As argued by Portes (2008), migration to the surface is yielding only marginal modifications of the social order and leaving the deep elements of values and social structure substantially unchanged. However, migration is part of the process of transformation of social structures and institutions. Migration both shapes social transformation and is shaped by such fundamental change (Nicholas 2010). The Gulf migration and the remittances indeed cannot be argued for a structural change in the society of Kerala. However, one can argue that Gulf migration and the remittances led to the marginal changes, though the reflection of it differs for different categories of people in the state. The social mobility should be looked at, as the mobility of the families, that is, the people who are left behind, such as women, children and the second generations of the immigrants and how the process of migration and remittances impacted them.

Muslims of Kerala and Gulf Migration

Muslims of Kerala have an entirely different narrative of history and development than Muslims anywhere else in India. Historians have pointed out that Malabar (North Kerala) had trade contacts with the Arab lands, even before 3000 BC (Pillai 1940). Many Arabs came, settled and married the women of the region and preached the Islam religion in the coastal regions of Malabar. Most of the untouchables were attracted to the religion as there was prevalence of a rampant caste system. This was the beginning of the Muslim society in this part of the country. Though there are different categories of Muslims such as Thangals, Marakkars, Koyas, Labbays and Ossans, it is Mophlas who constitute the majority, they are believed to be the descendents of the early lower castes and untouchables who were generally known as Mappila or Mophla. According to the Census (1999), Muslims in Kerala constitute about a quarter population of the state's total population (24.7%). Unlike the Muslims of other Indian states, Muslims of Kerala have a higher socioeconomic and educational development. This is reflected in various indicators of socioeconomic development of the Muslims in the state. This is also seen in the general human development achievements of the state (Yoginder 2007). However, one must understand that Muslims in Kerala relatively have a better socioeconomic condition in comparison with their other counterparts, but this is not the complete picture. In comparison with the Hindu and Christian populations in Kerala, the Muslims are backward in terms of education levels, literacy and other general development indicators.[1] The Sachar Committee observes that while Muslims constitute 24.7 per cent of the total population, they constitute 30.7 per cent of the total poor (below poverty line—BPL) in Kerala. Their share under the various government programmes ranges between 5 per cent and 18 per cent, except in programmes such as Co-operative Credit (25%), National Tuberculosis Control Programme (28%) and National Programme for Control of Blindness (21%). The share of Muslims is less than 12 per cent in the schemes implemented by Rural Development and Housing Departments.[2] It is evident that the Muslim representation in the BPL percentage is more than the total share of their population in the state. Their representation in the government services is 11.4 per cent, which is less than half of their total population per cent and which is less than the share of states' scheduled caste and scheduled tribe (ST) population representation in the public sector services (Kerala Padanam 2006). This also gives indications to the educational backwardness, which I will discuss in the next section of the chapter. This is the general condition of the Muslims in Kerala who enjoy a relatively better position than their counterparts in different parts of India.

The 1970s saw the beginning of the huge migration from the state and from all different sections of the populations. This has accelerated during the 1980s and to this date the trend even continues. The earlier studies for the migration in general provided some valid reasons for this trend, including the historical connection with the Middle East in trade and commerce, the Islamic connection of Malabar with the Arab lands, and the ethnic connections (Joseph 2001). The attractive wage rates that migrants could get into these countries were an important factor. At the same time, these earlier studies have not taken into cognizance that there has been poverty and rampant unemployment in the region, especially the Malabar region that consist of the seven districts of present day Kerala. The earlier studies that came up on the Gulf migration from the state had found some of the primary observations. According to Nair's (1989) study, there is preponderance in the number of Muslims among the return migrants, which can be seen as the reflective fact that they dominate in the number of immigrant workers in the Middle East. At the same time, the general educational level of the immigrants from the Muslim community was low. It was higher for Hindus and the Christians. The same study looked at the proportion of the people who have at least levels of education up to matriculation and higher qualified persons and it showed that about 71 per cent among the Christians, 37 per cent among Hindus and for Muslims it was merely 16 per cent. It is clearly evident that in terms of the number of migrants, Muslims were the highest, and at the same time they were also educationally backward as compared with the Christians and Hindus from Kerala.

Some interesting trends came from the migration surveys and studies conducted by the Centre for Development Studies, Trivandrum, India. I would discuss some of the factors that are important for the Muslim community in the state. The most important factor in determining the Gulf migration includes the religion and region. The proportion of households with EMI (Emigrants), RMI (Return Emigrants) or NRK (Non-Resident Keralites) is highest among the Muslims and the least among the Hindus. For example, the proportion of households with either an emigrant or return emigrant for Muslims is 52.9 per cent (one out of two households) compared with 18 per cent among the Hindus (Zachariah and Rajan 2012). The district of origin is equally a critical variable in determining the proportion of households with an immigrant. In Malappuram district, 36.8 per cent of the households had one or more emigrants. Similarly, in Thrissur district, 26.1 per cent of the households had at least one immigrant. Malappuram district was the origin of the largest number of emigrants in 2008. It also has one of the highest immigration rates. There were 53.4 emigrants corresponding to every 100 households in Malappuram. The impact or the results of migration in the household can be understood in two ways. One is purely in economic terms where the amount of remittances received by the family of migrant and the second is changes in the flow of money made at home. According Zachariah, the most important item of remittance expenditure was household consumption followed by construction and/or repair of buildings, purchase and improvement of land, marriage, purchase of vehicles, investment in businesses, purchase of consumer durables, education of the children and investments in the financial assets (Nair 1989). The district of Malappuram is a Muslim majority constituting around 65 per cent of the total population. The following section will look at how the flow of remittances impacted the poverty level.

Remittances and Poverty

The remittances including the money and materials received by the migrant's family and relatives are one of the most important agents for social change. Since the recipients were the families and households, it is difficult to find the exact amount of financial flows. Similarly, the studies that have conducted on remittances mostly focus on the impact by looking at the volume of remittances (both money and materials) received by the family. In the process, other crucial factors that contributed to the social change were not taken into consideration. According to the CDS first migration survey in Kerala, Muslims received 47 per cent of the total remittances. Ezhavas and Syrian Christians each had received about 13 per cent. Latin Christians received 11 per cent and Nairs about 9 per cent. However, it was not the Muslim households that received the highest emigrant remittances. The study shows that nearly 1.5 million Keralites now live outside India. They sent home more than ₹ 4,000 million a year by way of remittances (Zacharia et al. 1999). They argued this on the basis of the data collected from the state that the Muslims received 47 per cent of the total remittances. An average, Latin Christian emigrant sent back ₹ 33 thousand per year and an average Syrian Christian emigrant sent ₹ 27 thousand. In contrast, the average remittance per Muslim emigrant was ₹ 24 thousand only. This is an important indicator to assess the low level of education, the unskilled nature of the job or the less wage jobs taken by the Muslims migrants.

This variation in remittances is based on the educational level and opportunities to work in relatively high paid jobs. The remittance for an average degree-holding emigrant was ₹ 20 thousand. This was another indicator showing the lack of education and less probability of getting a decent job for Muslims migrant as compared with the migrants from other communities. According to the 2001 census, 56.3 per cent of the Kerala's population is Hindu, 19 per cent Christians and 24.7 per cent is Muslim. However, Muslims constitute 41.1 per cent of the emigrants, followed by 37.7 per cent of Hindus and 21.2 per cent of Christians.

Table 8.1 explains the population per cent of migrants of different religious populations from 1998 to 2008 with per cent distribution of emigrants per household. The major highlights of the table are that Muslims constitute the majority in terms of the number of emigrants. At the same time, it is important to note the volume of remittances received by different households in accordance with their religion.

Table 8.1 *Distribution of Emigrants according to Religion*

Religion	*% of the Total Population*	*% Distribution*			*Emigrants per Households*	
		1998	*2003*	*2008*	*2003*	*2008*
Hindus	56.2	29.5	31.2	37.7	14.6	18.7
Christians	19	19.8	25.1	21.2	31.4	29.9
Muslims	24.7	50.7	43.7	41.1	61.1	56.4

Source: Kerala Migration Survey, Centre for Development Studies, Trivandrum.

It is evident that the Muslim families were the recipients of the highest per cent of total remittances. It is important to understand the correlation in receipts of remittances and Muslim populations that lived below the poverty line. It is interesting to see that migration has contributed to poverty alleviation than any other factors in the state. The remittances sent by the immigrant to the family has double fold impact, it alleviates poverty and improves standard of life. First, the impact of the remittances benefit directly to the family and its members. Second, the spillover impact includes an increase in the demand of consumer durables that leads to increased wages and employment and increase in price of the land. Migration has had a very significant impact on the population who live below the poverty line in Kerala. The total BPL populations of Kerala have declined from 53 per cent in 1977–1978 to 32 per cent in 1987–1988 (Planning Commission 1993). This is the same period of acceleration of the migration and remittances. At the same time, it is crucial to note that the full credit for poverty alleviation could not be given to the Gulf migration and remittances (Prakash 1998).

The decline in poverty was the largest among the Muslims that is about 6 per cent and it was relatively high among the Ezhavas (Zachariah et al. 2000). The Ezhava community is one of the most mobile populations of the state at the same time the poverty levels of the Muslims indeed higher. Broadly, migration to the Gulf has contributed to alleviate poverty and reduce the number of people living below the poverty line. It is interesting to note that during the same period of time, parts of Kerala that have seen considerable decline in the level of poverty level seem to have a large population of Muslim community. The Gulf migration and subsequent inflow of remittances enabled this phenomenon largely. Hence, I would like to emphasize that the migration to the Gulf has directly and indirectly contributed to bringing down the number of people who lived below the poverty line. The Gulf migration played a significant role in bringing changes in the lives of Muslims in Kerala. It is imperative to note all the nuances of the Gulf migration, inflow of remittances in Kerala and its subsequent impacts for the Muslim populations.

Education and the Gulf Migration

Education is one of the most important agents of social mobility in the modern world. One has to go through a long period of education in order to attain a gainful employment either at home or outside. I would discuss the impact of Gulf migration in the educational arena of the state. According to one of the study (Kerala Padanam 2006), the unemployment is highest among the Muslim youth in the state and that has a direct correlation to level of education of the community. It further provides statistics highlighting levels of higher educational attainment of different communities in Kerala. It shows that there is 11.8 and 10.30 per cent of the ST and SC youth population in the colleges in Kerala, whereas Muslims constitute only 8.1 per cent. The percentages for different communities, including upper-caste Hindus and Christians are far higher than those of Muslims. The Muslim youths are undereducated and unemployed in comparison with Hindus and Christians. It is crucial to study the school level enrolments and dropout rates to get a complete picture. So far, there is no religion-wise data highlighting the trend and overall picture of the school-level enrolments and dropout rates for Kerala.

According to the CDS migration survey, migration has made significant changes in the arena of education within the Kerala society. First, it led to a strong sense of preference for English-medium education at the school level among migrant families as compared with the non-migrant families. Second, preference for the English medium at school level subsequently increased the preference to the unaided and private schools. The Gulf migration marked an increased demand and ensured future sustenance of the private English-medium schools in Kerala. At the same time, it cannot be argued that Gulf migration brought education for all or it caused educational upliftment for any community. There was an increased perception among the migrant families that English-medium/private education has to be acquired and children are to be sent for English-medium education. This could have been a realization by the non-English educated migrants and others considering the job market requirements and how their next generation has to be equipped for the same.

The importance of education was highly understood and accepted by the first-generation immigrants and their families and that led them to send their children especially boys for education and for higher and professional education. This was particularly significant as far as the Muslim families were concerned since they constituted one of the most educationally backward sections in Kerala. At the same time, the quality of education generally did not get much importance. Here I argue that the overall economic mobility and the realization of lack of education within the family and community led to increased access to quality and English-medium education for second generation. At the same time, the understanding of quality education largely included private educational institutions and high fees, mostly focusing on technical and professional skills. The realization of modern education was largely facilitated by the Gulf migration among the Muslims.

Gender and the Gulf Migration

Muslim women have one of the lowest work participation levels throughout India as well as in the state of Kerala (Das and Desai 2003). It was a male phenomenon altogether as far as Gulf migration is concerned, especially in the case of Muslims. The sex composition of migrants varied considerably in accordance with their religious affiliation. The proportion of women migrants is higher among Christians and lower among Muslims (Zachariah and Rajan 2012). Zachariah and Rajan describe the married women of the Kerala households whose husbands work and live outside India mostly in Gulf, as 'Gulf Wives'. In 2011, there were about 1.1 million Gulf wives and this was about 1.06 million in 2008. Interestingly, the proportion of the Gulf wives is highest among the Muslims with 24 per cent of the married women and lowest among the Christians with 5 per cent (Zachariah and Rajan 2012). The district of Malappuram constituted the highest number of women who were left at home. The husband of every one in four married women of the district lived in the Gulf. Relatively a huge number of married Muslim women and their families were left at home as the proportions of migrants are highest among Muslims males. This undoubtedly caused loneliness, struggles and hardships for married women. At the same time, it is extremely important to note that the Gulf migration in general was a benefiting factor for the women in the community. Zachariah argued that almost all immigrants (97%) sent home remittances and 80 per cent of them sent it in the name of their wives. Thus the status, authority and managerial role in the absence of male members in the family were shifted to women. It has improved their autonomy, independence and experience in managing their affairs (Zachariah et al. 2000). However, it is important to consider bearing the Indian context in mind that other male members such as father, father-in-law and brother could have taken the upper hand in dealing with the financial matters within the family. Most of the women had direct control over the money, which was sent to the family. At the same time, the expenditure and consumption followed a pattern and direction given by the husbands working in the Gulf. However, women used their own discretion in the matter of daily expenses, personal requirements and child's needs.

This way of life enabled more economic freedom and mobility for married women whose husbands are working in the Gulf. This is one of the ways in which the migration of males has affected women within the family. As far as Muslim families are concerned, women have the lowest voice in the decision making within the family. At the same time in the long run, it helped women develop self-confidence, ability to manage the affairs within the family and community. Here I argue that though Gulf migration has led to hardships, difficulties and problems for the Gulf wives, it certainly helped the Muslim women in terms of autonomy, economic independence and managing the family affairs. This has to be taken as one positive impact that migration to the Gulf by their husbands, fathers and brothers has caused for the women.

New Middle Class and Social Remittances

Migration and remittances have created the emergence of a new middle class in the state of Kerala and the same was also reflected among the Muslims, a class that influenced the community to a great extent in almost all spheres of the collective life. It included very big entrepreneurs in the Gulf—professionals who draw comparatively higher salaries than the usual workers. They are involved in community associations, orphanages, schools, trade organizations and every day politics (Osella 2007). The sense of community and need of its development was realized by them. The realization of educational backwardness of the community as a whole led to increased efforts to start schools and professional colleges for the students of the community. This contributed to the efforts aimed at reformation of the Muslim societies in Kerala. However, it is important to note how far the general poor Muslims benefited out of this emergence of a new middle class.

The private educational institutions under the various trusts demanded for high fees as well as the socioeconomic gap between the migrant and non-migrant Muslim families widened. Social remittances are one of the most neglected areas as far as academia is concerned. Social remittances are immaterial remittances that are brought by the emigrants to their homeland. Peggy Levitt (1998) defined social remittances as the ideas, behaviours, identities and social capital that flow from receiving-to-sending-country communities. In the context of migration, there are huge social remittances, which could be taken as positive aspects were, mostly, led to the understanding and realization about the overall developmental deficit of the Kerala Muslims in general. This was first exposed to the people who migrated to do unskilled and low paid jobs. The new middle class that emerged after the Gulf migration within the community and the social remittances in the community have had positive impacts, with some negative impacts as well. One could argue that these elements as a result of the migration to the Gulf have made positive impacts as far as Muslims in general are concerned.

Conclusion

Migration and remittances have been one of the backbones for the economy and society of Kerala for the last three decades and it still continues. Muslims of Kerala are one of the socioeconomic and educationally backward communities in the state as compared with their other religious counterparts. Migration of the huge labour force of the Muslim community to the Gulf has received much attention in the last three decades. Although it is argued that migration may not have solely contributed to the upward socioeconomic mobility for the Muslims community as a whole, however, migration to the Gulf and remittances have contributed in bringing down the poverty levels of the state where Muslims are one of the most important categories. The Gulf migration led to a crucial realization including bringing to the fore educationally backward of the Muslim community, the need of modern education and the general development deficit of the community as a whole. The impacts of remittances are visible among the women in terms of more economic independence and autonomy. This is reflected among the Muslims of the state as a general and the families of migrants in particular. The Gulf migration is one of the most important factors that have contributed to overall mobility for the Muslim community in general and migrant families in particular for Kerala.

Notes

1. Kerala Padanam (Malayalam titled) and Development reports, including Narendran Commission and Sachar Committee reports also validate this fact.
2. This observation was made after learning the data of 2002–2003, 2003–2004 submitted by the states to the committee from various states.

References

Castles, Stephen. 'Migration and Social Transformation'. Migration Studies Unit Working Paper No. 2008/01, London School of Economics and Political Science, London, 2008.

Das, M.B. and Desai, S. 'Why Are Educated Women Less Likely to Be Employed in India? Testing Competing Hypotheses'. *Social Protection Discussion Paper Series No.* 313. Washington, DC: World Bank, 2003.

ICOE. *Impact Assessment of Global Recession on Indian Migrant Workers in Countries of the Gulf Cooperation Council and Malaysi*a. New Delhi: Indian Council of Overseas Employment, 2009.

Jayaram, N. The *Indian Diaspora: Dynamics of Migration.* New Delhi: Sage Publications, 2004.

Jones, Richard C. 'Introduction: The Renewed Role of Remittances in the New World Order'. *Economic Geography*, 74, 1 (1998): 1–7.

Joseph, K.V. 'Factors and Pattern of Migration, the Kerala Experience'. *Journal of Indian School of Political Economy*, 13 (2001): 55–72.

Levitt, Peggy. 'Social Remittances: Migration Driven Local-Level Forms of Cultural Diffusion'. *International Migration Review*, 32, 4 (1998): 926–948.

Khadria, B. *India: Skilled Migration to Developed Countries, Labour Migration to the Gulf.* Asia Research Institute, National University of Singapore, 2006.

Nair, P.R.G. 'Incidence, Impact and Implications of Migration to the Middle East from Kerala (India)'. pp. 343–364 in R. Amjad (ed.), *To the Gulf and back.* New Delhi: International Labour Organisation, 1989.

Nair, P.R.G. 'The Process of Migration'. pp. 37–38 in B.A. Prakash (ed.), *Indian Migration to the Middle East, Trends, Patterns and Socio-Economic Impacts*, Rohtak: Spellbound Publications, 1998.

Osella, C. 'Muslim Entrepreneurs between India & the Gulf'. *ISIM review,* 19 (Spring 2007).

Padanam, Kerala. 'Malayalam titled (*Kerala Study, how state of Kerala Live and Think)*'. Thiruvananthapuram: Kerala Peoples Sciences Movement, 2006.

Pillai, T.K.V. *Travancore State Manual*, Vol. 11. Trivandrum: State Government Publications, 1940.

Planning Commission. *Annual Report, 1993-1994.* Government of India, 1993. http://planningcommission.nic.in/reports/genrep/arep9099/index.php?repts=ar93-94.htm

Portes, Alejandro. *Migration and Social Change: Some Conceptual Reflections.* Princeton: Princeton University Press, 2008.

Prakash, B.A. 'Gulf Migration and Its Economic Impact: The Kerala Experience'. *Economic and Political Weekly*, 33, 50 (1998): 3209–3213.

United Nations. *Impacts of Remittance on poverty in Developing countries.* Geneva, Switzerland: United Nations, 2011.

van Hear, Nicholas. 'Theories of Migration and Social Change'. *Journal of Ethnic and Migration Studies,* 36, 10 (2010): 1531–1536.

Yoginder, Sikand. 'Muslims in Kerala and Elsewhere: Accounting for the Difference'. *Islamic Voice*, 2007. http://islamicvoice.com/August2007/Kerala ShowstheWay/

Zachariah K.C. and Rajan, S. Irudaya. *Kerala's Gulf Connection, 1998–2011; Economic and Social Impacts of Migration.* Hyderabad: Orient Blackswan, 2012.

Zachariah, K.C. and Rajan, S. Irudaya. *Economic and Social Dynamics of Migration in Kerala, 1999–2004: Analysis of Panel Data.* Thiruvananthapuram: Centre for Development Studies, 2007.

Zachariah, K.C., Mathew, E.T., and Rajan, S. Irudaya. 'Impact of Migration on Kerala's Economy and Society'. Working Paper No. 297. Thiruvananthapuram: Centre for Development Studies, 1999.

Zachariah, K.C., Mathew, E.T. and Rajan, S. Irudaya. 'Socio-economic and Demographic Consequences of Migration in Kerala'. Working Paper No. 303. Thiruvananthapuram: Centre for Development Studies, 2000.

CHAPTER 9

International Migration and Development

A Study of Indians in the Gulf Countries

Naresh Kumar

Emigration from India to the Gulf Cooperation Council (GCC) states such as the Bahrain, Kuwait, Oman, Qatar, Saudi Arabia and the United Arab Emirates is not a new phenomenon, it has a historical background and it increased remarkably since 1970s due to the 'oil boom'. According to the Ministry of Overseas Indian Affairs (MOIA) of the Government of India, currently migrant communities in these six GCC states are 6 million approximately (MOIA 2012). These huge bulks of migrant population are not only playing a very significant role to the host countries, but also have a major developmental contribution to their places of origin. The GCC states encircling the Persian Gulf are endowed with oil and natural gas, which has made these countries one of the emerging economic powers in the modern era. The oil boom of the 1970s has attracted semi-skilled and unskilled labours from various Indian states, especially from the southern Indian states. Most of them migrated to these countries for a short period of time and the main reason of emigration is none other than economic betterment. Migrants economic success encourages other Indian youths for migration and in this way, emigration from India to the Gulf countries has increased over time. Remittances sent by these emigrants to their families not only help them to escape from abject poverty, but also fuel economic growth in the parent states. Though life of these migrants in these countries are not completely hassle free, their contribution in the Indian economy has compelled the researchers, policy makers and academicians to give special emphasis on this issue.

Migration, especially international or cross-border migration, always brings a two-way impact on both the place of origin and the place of destination. Moreover, it often stimulates political as well as diplomatic issues. Therefore, in-depth analysis of the trend and pattern of Indian migration to the GCC states, their contribution in Indian economy and issues related with them have been produced in this chapter. The chapter mainly deals with two objectives: (1) to examine the recent trend and pattern of Indian emigration to the GCC states and (2) to examine the role of migrant workers in the context of development at micro and macro level.

This chapter is mainly based on primary and secondary data collected from various national and international documents such as MOIA, International Labour Organization (ILO), International Organization for Migration (IOM) and United Nations (UN) reports on the workers' rights and so on. All these data have been analysed statistically.

Indian Diaspora in the GCC States

The GCC states are one of the best known migrant corridors in the world. These six countries are attracting not only migrant workers from India but also workers from other South and Southeast Asian countries. Indian diaspora is found significantly among all these migrant communities living in the Gulf countries. Indian population almost spread all over the world and make significant diaspora in the world after China. According to the latest estimation by the MOIA (2012), Indian emigrants (both PIOs and NRIs) constituted about 30 million in 130 countries. Out of 30 million, almost 6 million (see Table 9.1) Indian migrants workers are engaged in various kinds of jobs in these six GCC states (Keshri and Bhuyan 2012). They are mainly getting employment in three kinds of jobs: (1) white-collar jobs (doctors, nurses, engineers, architects, accountants and managers); (2) semi-skilled workers or blue-collar jobs (craftsman, drivers, artisans and other technical workers); and (3) unskilled labourers in construction sites, farmlands, livestock ranches, shops, stores and households maids and domestic works. The first category of workers or skilled labours almost comprises about 30 per cent of the total Indian immigrants in the Gulf countries. Second and third categories comprise almost 70 per cent (Khadria 2010) of the total Indian immigrants. Within the GCC states, Kingdom of Saudi Arabia (KSA) and United Arab Emirates (UAE) are the most popular destinations of Indian immigrants and together they contributed more than 60 per cent of the total deployment of Indian migrant workers.

Table 9.1 *Indian Diaspora in the GCC States*

Name of the Country	*Indian Diaspora Population*
Saudi Arabia	2 million
UAE	1.7 million
Kuwait	0.64 million
Oman	0.7 million
Bahrain	0.35 million
Qatar	050 million
Total	5.94 million

Source: MOIA (2012).

Trend of Indian Emigration to the Gulf

As discussed earlier that Indian emigration to the Gulf countries is not a new phenomenon, it started around 5000 years back. Census of India and any other government agencies do not have systematic records of Indian out-migration into these countries or other countries. Most of the results are based on the sampled and worked done by the different authors in respective countries. Information collection was mainly started in 1983 when the Government of India took initiative for keeping records of Indian emigrants living in other countries. It is now coming under the preview of MOIA. This was mainly attempting to safeguard the interests of Indian nationals working abroad and also to protect them in case of any adverse or unfortunate event occurring in their country of work. Emigration Act of 1983 requires all workers seeking contractual employment abroad to seek emigration clearance from any of the eight offices of the Protectors of Emigrants (POEs). The act also mandates that no agency or establishment can undertake recruitment of Indians for employment abroad without obtaining registration from the Protector General of Emigrants (PGE), under the MOIA. The PGE headquarter is situated in New Delhi. It has eight offices of Protector of Emigrants functioning under the overall control of PGE. Eight offices of the Protectors of Emigrants have been established at Delhi, Mumbai, Kolkata, Chennai, Hyderabad, Chandigarh, Cochin and Thiruvananthapuram. According to MOIA, the process of granting of emigration clearance has been decentralized for the convenience of the applicants. Emigration Act of 1983 keeps record of workers who require emigration check before leaving India. It has divided emigrants' workers, those who required emigration check and those under the Emigration Check Not Required (ECNR). First categories mainly include the semi-skilled and unskilled workers, while the second category comprises the skilled workers, professional and businessman. These categories have been marked on the basis of occupation. As the partial recorded data, government only provides statistics of emigration clearance persons. In the absence of well-regulated rules and procedure for recruitment of workers, the statistics on emigration clearance and employment abroad and the outflow for the period till 1983 is quite unreliable.

The massive migration from India to the Gulf countries started after the oil boom in 1973, with increasing oil revenues and stimulated large-scale economies activities in the GCC states. According Winckler (1997), they used oil revenues money in different purposes such as development of infrastructure, including energy stations as well as administrative and governance apparatus, agriculture sectors and improvement of social services, including health care and education. The enormous flow of oil revenues during the oil boom decade (1973–1982) converted the desert economies into one of the fastest growing regions of the world. After the end of the oil boom decade, a contrary situation emerged; oil prices reduced to one of the lowest levels ever, leading to a severe shortfall in oil revenues; hence, overall economies performance plummeted too from the high level of the earlier decade (Al-Kibsi et al. 2007). On the basis of Emigration Check Require (ECR) statistics data (1990–2011), any citizen who obtained ECR for leaving can work in any country of the world. Between the period 1990 and 2011 (see Figures 9.1 and 9.2), I observed five phases of Indian emigration to the GCC states. *First Phase* (1990–1993): in these three years inclined trend of labourer had been noticed regarding Indian emigrants in the GCC states. The demand for foreign workers for various infrastructural projects, low immigration control policy, during the Gulf War in the late 1990s, most of Indian emigrants came back to their home due to political crisis. *Second Phase* or partial constant trend (1993–1997): between these periods almost consistent trends had been observed regarding

Figure 9.1 *Numbers of Workers Granted Emigration Clearance, India 1990–2011*

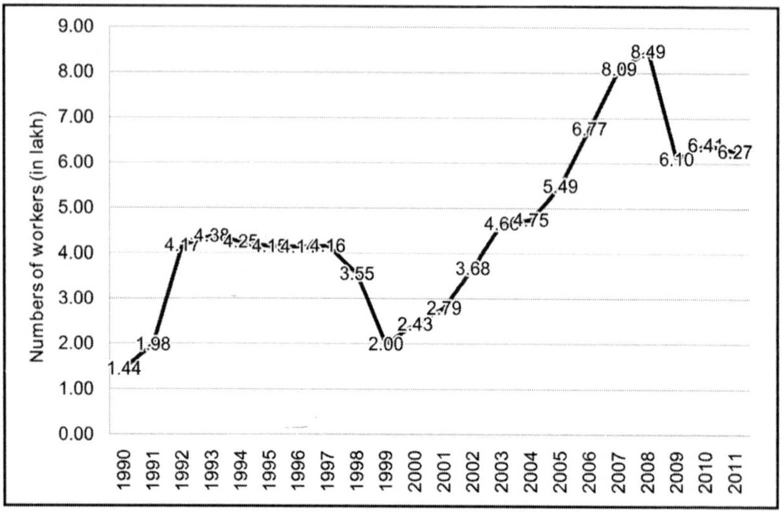

Source: MOIA (2012).

Figure 9.2 *Growth of Indian Emigrants to GCC states 1990–2011*

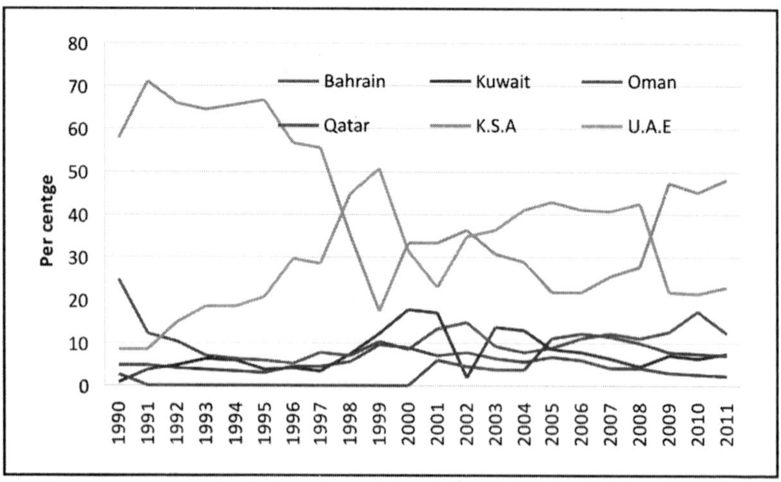

Source: MOIA (2012).

Indian emigrants to the Gulf countries. It is important to note that this is the period of oil boom in the Gulf countries. Oil-generated revenues have been used to create social services (hospitals, educational institutions, services sectors, banking, etc.). An average of 3,84,000 workers annually obtained work permit contract to the Gulf countries. *Third Phase* or declined trend (1997–1999): during this phase, some of the host countries, especially Saudi Arabia and Kuwait, adopted control and restrictive immigration policy for control of non-national or non-Arab population through localization (Kuwaitization, Saudization, Emertization, Qatarization). Between these periods, an average of 3,23,000 workers annually obtained work permit contract especially to the Gulf countries. Moreover, some of the major projects were finished or the labour market reached a saturation point. They recruited the local labour for control outflow of remittances from their countries. *Fourth Phase* again inclined trend (2000–2008): between these phases Middle East counties such as the UAE have taken the positions for the demand of semi-skilled and unskilled workers in their projects and the prices of oil were increased, which generate revenues for further infrastructure projects. Government of India has set up various migration posts for various states in India for promoting of international migration. Between these periods an average of 4,71,000 workers annually obtained work permit contract to the Gulf countries. *Fifth Phase* or declined trend (2009–2011): after 2008 outflow of Indian emigrants to the GCC states has been decreasing, but its absolute forms are still high when compared with previous decades. Between these periods, an average of 6,26,000 workers annually obtained work permit contract to the Gulf countries. Workers getting emigrant clearance towards the Southeast Asian countries such as Malaysia have been increased slightly. These all phases of flows are determined by the demand of particular types of workers in the GCC states from the Asian labour market.

Statewise Variation in Emigration

India has diversity in so many ways such as religion, caste, ethnicity and language. Certain regions are more developed and other regions have partially or less developed in terms of industry and infrastructure. Most of the places in the Indian map have seen the different pattern or level of development, whether it is rural to urban or village to cities. Movement of people from one place to another place is also determined by socioeconomic, demographic, political, cultural and geographical (earthquake, flood, cyclone) factors. With the limitation of data coverage on so many aspect of human life, MOIA collected data on the basis of number of persons who have emigrated from India. On the welfare point of view, MOIA is the apex regulatory body that kept the records of countrywise emigrant persons in the case of unskilled/semi-skilled workers. These workers require emigration clearance before getting employment in the GCC states and other countries. MOIA provides statewise break-up of the numbers of workers granted emigration clearance since 1993. Here we used the statistics to see the trend and pattern of Indian emigrants in 2001–2011. For this we computed statewise percentage on the basis of total numbers of Indian emigration. As earlier discussed in the trend of migrants' workers, Figure 9.2 showed that after year 2000 continuous onwards trend have been recorded in India emigrants workers till 2008. Afterwards, in the year 2008 there has been a declining trend of getting emigration clearance. If we look at the statewise spatial pattern of out-migration, we had noticed that in the year 2001 Kerala stands first position regarding generating of bulk of emigrants (22.09%) followed by Tamil Nadu, Andhra Pradesh, Maharashtra, Rajasthan, Uttar Pradesh, Gujarat, Bihar and Karnataka. These states altogether constituted about 85 per cent of total Indian emigrants (Figure 9.3). These are the major Indian states that contributed large numbers of emigrants into the Gulf countries.

Based on the data of trends and patterns of Indian emigrants who get clearance in year 2011 and compared with 2001, it shows a major statewise shift of Indian emigrant workers. In 2011 statistics, Kerala holds the second rank in terms of absolute numbers of emigrant workers of total emigrants, while Uttar Pradesh has the largest numbers of emigrant constituting around 25 per cent, followed by Kerala (13.8%), Andhra Pradesh, Bihar, Tamil Nadu, Rajasthan, Punjab and West Bengal. Other states individually constituted less than 1 per cent of emigrant workforce. It is interesting to note that between one decade data, earlier those states were shown a predominant positive trend in 2001, but these states have been noticed a negative trend in 2011. These focused states are Kerala, Tamil Nadu, Andhra Pradesh and Maharashtra, while the other northern Indian states such as Uttar Pradesh, Bihar, Punjab and West Bengal show the considerable positive trend of generating emigrant workers. The reasons of shift is

Figure 9.3 *Statewise Pattern of Indian Emigrants (ECR) (2001–2011)*

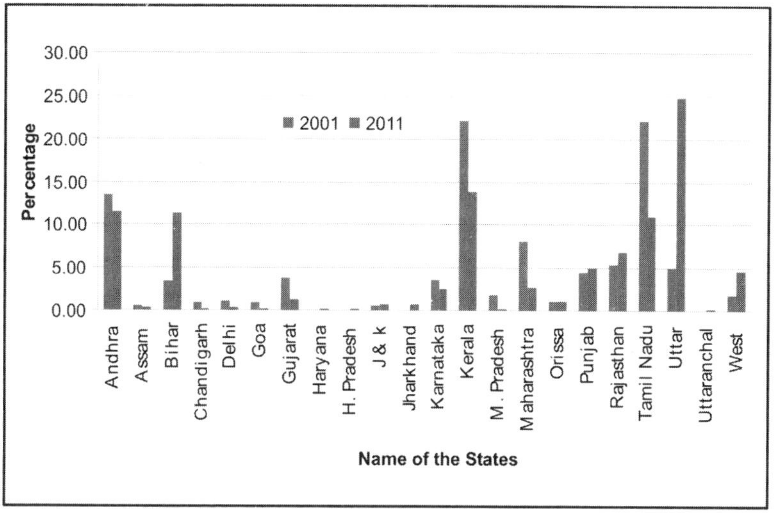

Source: MOIA (2011–2012).

that completion of major projects is controlled by unskilled immigration of the respective countries, given the preference their citizens search other avenues in Southeast Asian countries. The pattern of Indian workers migrating to Gulf countries is the geographical spread. 'Now there are more number of people from the north, north west and west of India coming to Gulf countries, compared to those from south India' (Keshri and Bhuyan 2012).

Migration and Development

Both migration and development are highly interdependent processes. People moving from one geographical or administrative boundary to another not only affects the place of destination, but also affects the place of origin. Development effect can be seen at different levels, at individual, family, village, community and nation. These developments may be in the form of economic, social, demographic, cultural, infrastructural and/or political. On the basis of support of data, we discussed about the Indian migrant workers in the Gulf countries in the context of development. How remittances contributing for the benefit in their family? How often are they invested in such a way to promote sustainable economic development? Is remitted money has an important role in the national economy?

Macro Level Economic Impact

Migrants played quite a significant role in their origin country. This impact can be easily seen not only in the local economy, but also in the national economy. Indian immigrants in Gulf countries remitted huge amount of money back home. As already discussed, most of the Indian migrants in the Gulf are semi-skilled or unskilled (almost 70%) and 30 per cent are skilled persons (Khadria 2010). Most of the Indian migrants in the Gulf are male and young in age group. They remitted money back home in the form of cash and kind. Money remitted by them also varies with characteristics of the family left behind, across the regions, state and with type of migrations. If we look at the global statistics of flow of remittances to the originating country, Indian holds the first position, followed by China, Mexico, Philippines and France. According to the estimation by the World Bank 2012, India received highest remittance from abroad (about US$ 64 billion) and almost contribute 4 per cent of India's national GDP (Migration Fact Book 2011). In 2005, it was (US$ 15 billion) and contributes about 3 per cent of the gross national product (Steve 2005). High-income countries are the main source of remittances (see Figures 9.4 and 9.5). The United States is by far the largest and Saudi Arabia ranks as the second largest, followed by Switzerland and Russia of remittances sending countries.

Here we are only considering the formal channels of remittance by the migrants to their home country. There is also another parallel

Figure 9.4 *World Top Ten Remittances Receiving Countries*

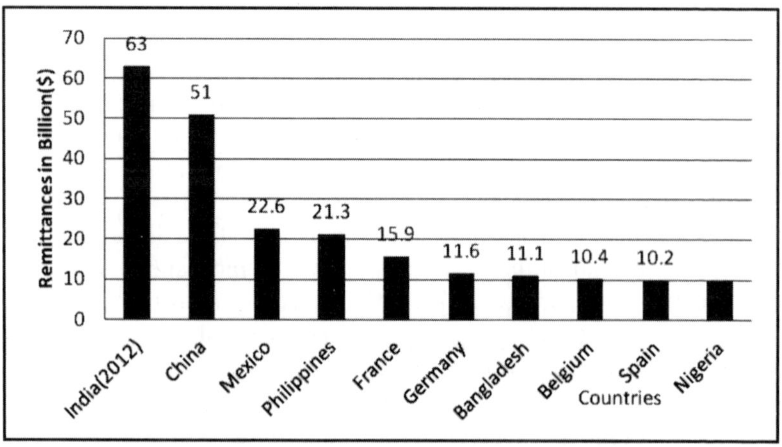

Source: Remittances Data, Development Prospects Group, World Bank (2011).

Figure 9.5 *Share of Remittances in Countrywise GDPs 2009*

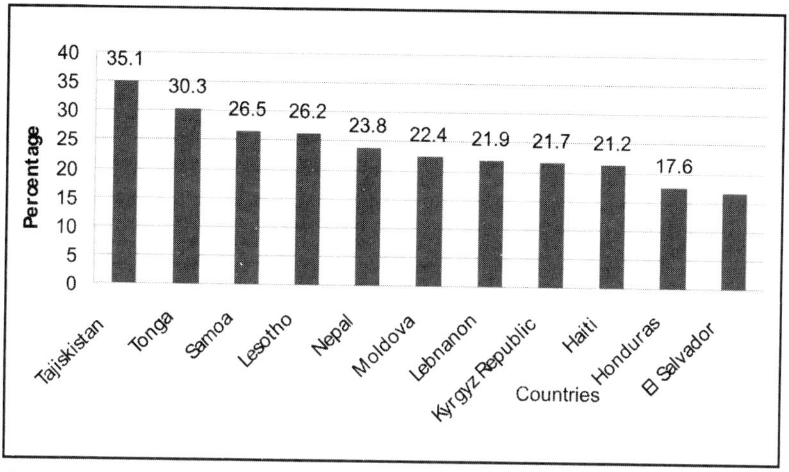

Source: Remittances Data, Development Prospects Group, World Bank (2011).

source of money transfer by the migrants known as informal source or *hawalla.*[1] Indian immigrants in the Middle East countries also used transferring money through *hawalla* to their origin place. We can easily observe the positive impact of remittances in the case of Kerala economy. Compared with Indian economy whose share in remittances from all countries is about 3 per cent of the GDP, the share of Kerala is 22 per cent of NSDP (Zachariah and Rajan 2004). The effect of remittances on Kerala's per capita annual income in 2003 was an increase of ₹ 5,678 (Zachariah and Rajan 2004). The Kerala's per capita income reached 49 per cent above the national level, and reached 49 per cent above average in 1999–2000 (Kannan and Hari 2002). In 1991, when India was facing the serious balance of payments crisis, migrant remittances played a significant role in maintaining foreign reserve of India that helped the India economy. In that year, foreign exchange reserve had fallen to the level barely adequate to meet essential imports for just a few weeks. The Indian migrants in the developed countries withdraw their dollar deposits from Indian banks abruptly (Khadria 2011). These problems needed immediate action for India to avoid defaulting on its international obligations or face a collapse of its economy for want of official imports (Kelegana and Parikh 2003, cited in Khadria 2011). It was slowly but steadily growing remittances from the Indian unskilled workers in the Gulf region, which saved the situation for India.

According to the Reserve Bank of India (RBI) estimates, the Gulf region accounted for an average of 27 per cent of the total remittance inflows to India between 2006–2007 and 2009–2010. In the year of global economic crisis in 2008–2009, the Gulf countries accounted for nearly 31 per cent of the total remittance inflows to India. In 2011–2012, India's trade deficit increased to nearly US$ 170 billion (Keshri and Bhuyan 2012). However, remittances from overseas have been an important source of foreign currency in India and can help in addressing the balance payment issue. Government revenue increase with the outflow of emigrants abroad in various form of visas fees, departure taxes, international telephone calls and so on. All of these facilities had been used by the migrant workers directly or indirectly.

Micro Level Impact

Remittances play very significant role at the micro level, for instance, village or household level. It is quite significant, particularly in the poorer households in Indian society. It plays a crucial role in reducing abject poverty in certain areas. In case of Indian diaspora in the Gulf, most of the migrants are unskilled and semi-skilled. They have no choice or any alternative jobs in the place of origin. They are marginalized in different ways: abject poverty, no frequent job, housing, education, saving, debt, etc. Job opportunity plays very significant role in their life. Once they get the jobs, various positive changes have been seen in their life after migration. All these changes can be easily seen in different ways such as housing, children education, saving, purchasing power, paying debt, transportation, town planning and decision making. When the low skilled or unskilled people migrate, they tend to send more remittances than professionals. According to the Kerala Migration Study conducted by the Centre for Development Studies, Trivandrum, an index of the value of the house of an emigrant shows 7.05 compared with 4.3 of a non-migrant house. At the same time, 87 per cent of migrant houses were found electrified compared with 66 per cent of the non-migrants (Zachariah et al. 2002). The impact of development can be also seen in other aspects such as commercial sector, educational institutions, vocational training institute, created hostel, commercial complex and jewellery outlets. Though the impact of remittances can be quite considerable at family and village level, at the regional or national level (the macro level), their impact is less clear.

Transfer of Labour Force

India has 1.22 billion populations in the world (Census of India 2011). India ranked second in the world in terms of population size after China. At the same time, India is also facing unemployment and underemployment situation. India is one of the developing countries in the world that have the largest (60%) working age group (15–54) population due to high birth rate. The growth of job opportunities and population growth rate has a huge gap. Most of the population in India are engaged in disguised employment. On the other side, the GCC states have shortage of working population for work in their industries and huge demand of foreigners in their various fields. This demographic difference provides opportunity for Indians to work in the Gulf countries.

India has the largest number of expatriates in the Gulf countries among immigrant populations. These six GCC states open the window of opportunity for Indian workers, especially for unskilled and semi-skilled workers. It can be easily said that there is no 'brain drain' in the context of Indian migration to Gulf countries. It is estimated that every year 0.6 million Indians are getting employment in the Gulf region. This considerable number plays a very significant role in the labour market. The Kerala Migration Study of 1998 notes that the unemployment rates in Kerala state have reduced by about 3 per cent as a consequence of Gulf migration (Zachariah et al. 2002). In the case of Indian migration to the Gulf, most of the workers are called incipient diaspora (Jain 2007), the host societies do not allow them to assimilate or bring their families in the case of unskilled labourer, and also they are not engaged in any kind of permanent jobs there.

Other Aspects

The return of migrants—whether permanent and temporary—brings benefit in many ways. In economic terms, returnees bring useful knowledge and contacts from overseas, and can provide an important means for transferring skills. Migration also plays an important role in creating chain migration of their relative/native and village/city within the country with the help of social networking. Whenever they come back after completion of project with earned money or remittances, they used their savings in many ways, such as opening new business/enterprises or create opportunities for others. They play very significant role in the local labour market. There are other dimensions to see the development through the migrant workers, for instance bilateral trade are growing strongly with the UAE, the largest trade partner of India. Expansion in business ties is largely supported by the Indian diaspora in the GCC states and bilateral trade negotiations are growing significantly for Indian workers in white-collar jobs. India has emerged as the second largest trading partner of the GCC states, only slightly behind Japan. Shift of occupational mobility of workers has also been seen in the context of Indian migration to the GCC states.

Conclusions

Migration and development is not a new process, it continued since the ancient times and still continuing. Migration and development can be seen as both positive and negative to the place of origin and destination. In the case of Indian migrants in the GCC states, positive effect has been noticed at the origin places, India. About 70 per cent of Indian workers in the Gulf are from the peripheral regions of India, majority of them are the part of absolute poverty before migration. Multiple changes have been noticed in migrants' life, such as earning money increase at household level/family level, sending their children to school, re-payment of the loan, reducing of the unemployment rate, purchasing houses, increasing saving and increase of commercial sectors.

Globalization along with information and communication technology are playing an important role for further enhancing migration from India into different parts of the worlds. But we cannot ignore the problems faced by the migrants before and after migration at the place of origin and destination countries. Studies show that the living and working environment of Indian migrant workers is harsh in the GCC states. Moreover, violation of human rights against Indians is also noticed in the case of domestic workers. For strengthening Indian migration in a positive way, the Government of India and the GCC states should take immediate action for the welfare of these workers.

Note

1. *Hawalla or Hundi* is an informal value transfer system based on the performance and honour of a huge network of money brokers, which are primarily located in the Middle East, North Africa, the Horn of Africa and the Indian subcontinent.

References

Al-Kibsi, G., Benkert, C. and Schubert, J. 'Getting Labor Policy to Work in the Gulf'. *The McKinsey Quarterly*, 2007. Available at: www.mckinsey quarterly.com/Getting_labor_policy_to_work_in_the_Gulf_1930 (accessed on 20 August 2010).

Binod, Khadria. 'Bridging the Binaries of skilled and Unskilled Migration from India'. pp. 251–285 in S. Irudaya Rajan and Marie Percot (eds), *Dynamics of Indian Migration: Historical and Current Perspectives*. New Delhi: Routledge, 2011.

Binod, Khadria. 'Paradigm Shifts in India's Migration Policy Towards the Gulf'. *Middle East Institute Viewpoints*, 2010. Available at: http://www.mei.edu/content/paradigm-shifts-indias-migration-policy-toward-gulf (accessed on 10 March 2013).

Census of India. *Office of the Registrar General and Census Commissioner, India*. New Delhi: Ministry of Home Affairs, 2011.

Jain, P.C. 'An Incipient Diaspora: Indians in the Gulf Region'. In P.C. Jain (ed.), *Indian Diaspora in West Asia: A Reader*. Delhi: Manohar, 2007.

Kannan, K.P. and Hari, K.S. 'Kerala's Gulf Connections: Emigration Remittances and their Macroeconomic Impact 1972–2000'. Working paper No. 328, Centre for Development Studies, Trivandrum, 2002.

Keshri, Gyanendra Kumar and Bhuyan, Aroonim. 'Gulf Links'. *Pravasi Bharatiya*, 5, 7 (July 2012).

Migration & Remittances Fact Book. *The World Bank*, 2011.

Migration Fact Book. *Migration and Remittances Factbook 2011*. Washington DC: The World Bank, 2011.

Ministry of Overseas Indian Affairs (MOIA). *Annual Report 2011-12*. New Delhi: Government of India, 2012.

Steve, R. 'Dubai's Kerala Connection'. *Yale Global Online*, 2005. http://yaleglobal.yale.edu/content/dubai%E2%80%99s-kerala-conne ction

Winckler, Onn. 'The Immigration Policy of the Gulf Cooperation Council (GCC) States'. *Middle Eastern Studies*, 33, 3 (1997): 480–498.

Zachariah, K.C., Prakash, B.A., and Rajan, S.I. 'Gulf Migration Study: Employment, Wages and Working Conditions of Kerala Emigrants in the United Arab Emirates'. Working Paper No. 326, Centre for Development Studies, Trivandrum, 2002.

Zachariah, K.C. and Rajan, S.I. 'Gulf Revisited: Economic Consequences of Emigration from Kerala'. Working Paper No. 363. Thiruvananthapuram: Centre for Development Studies, 2004.

Part IV
Migration and Distress

CHAPTER 10

Coping and Overcoming

South Asian Domestic Workers in the United Arab Emirates

Habibul Haque Khondker and Mehraj Jahan

The focus of this chapter is on the life of a small number of migrant domestic workers from South Asia in the United Arab Emirates (UAE). In this chapter, we do not deal with all aspects of their everyday life but explore the relationship between the domestic workers and their employers on the one hand and with their families back home on the other hand. This chapter is not a survey of the conditions of the South Asian domestic workers in the UAE. Rather, we argue that the experience of the migrant domestic workers suggest that they do not only remain passive subjects, 'happy slaves' due to their class situation but also exercise a great deal of agency, albeit in a subtle fashion through whatever cultural resources they can muster. They try to make the most of the seemingly worst situation and try to live a full life of work with dignity and often become a source of crucial support for their family back home. As provider for the household, they gain in status and self-worth. This chapter, in other words, sheds light on the coping and

---

An earlier version of the chapter was presented at Inter-Asian Connections, Social Science Research Council Conference, Dubai, UAE Workshop: 'Distant Divides and Intimate Connections: Migrant Domestic Workers in Asia', 21–23 February 2008. We wish to thank Nicole Constable, Director of the workshop and other fellow participants for their comments.

overcoming of adversities by the South Asian domestic workers in the UAE. This study is only explorative, which poses questions and initiates a counter-narrative to the endless tales of victimhood. This chapter is about agency of the subalterns. It explores how domestic workers often use gender and/or religious solidarity with their employers depending on the circumstances. Since most of the domestic workers from Bangladesh are Muslims, they use their common religion as a lever in their relationship with their Emirati employers who are also Muslims. This study may help us reconfigure theoretical discussions on globalization and identity hitherto dominated by discourses of class and rights. Being domestic workers, these women have access to the private domain of the household and have a great deal of knowledge about the domestic sphere in the UAE, one of the opaque sectors of society. Such knowledge and close association with the matriarch often give them a sense of empowerment. This sense of empowerment is also buttressed by their income-earning role and support for their family in their home country. Their economic future also becomes more secure as they buy land, support education of their children and make wiser investments with their savings back home.

Although it is common to see globalization in terms of macro changes, such as the world financial markets, exchanges of commodities on a world scale, production and distribution, telecommunications and Internet, the effects of globalization are felt equally strongly in the private realm. As Giddens points out, globalization is not something that is simply 'out there', operating on a distant plain and not intersecting with individual affairs. Globalization is an 'in here' phenomenon that is affecting our intimate and personal lives in many diverse ways. Inevitably, our personal lives have been altered as globalizing forces enter into our local contexts, our homes and our communities through impersonal sources—such as the media, the Internet and popular culture—as well as through personal contact with individuals from other countries and cultures (Giddens 2002; Rosenberg 2002). Globalization is not limited to mega-structural processes, it also has an everyday dimension (Ray 2007). It is in this light migration, which brings people from different cultures in close proximity, becomes a key feature of globalization (Turner and Khondker 2010). Globalization is about dis-embeddedness, yet it is also about re-embeddedness. Seemingly, the process of globalization isolates individuals from the web of their primordial social network, yet as the lives of the migrant workers reveal, new social relations and networks are formed leading to the reconstruction of social network and social capital that sustain the migrants in new social spaces.

Migration is both a result of global change and a powerful force for further change in both migrant sending and receiving societies. Its immediate impacts are felt on the economic level, but it also affects social relations, culture, national politics and international relations (Castles 2000: 124). The economic impact is registered at both the national level through remittances and the individual level through economic standing (uplift or decline depending on the situation). At the cultural level, migration opens up the possibilities of cosmopolitanism from below, not only triggering new sensibilities in some cases but also solidifying old prejudices in other cases.

Important insights are gleaned from the valuable studies of female domestic workers in Hong Kong (Constable 1997), Malaysia (Chin 1998) and United States (Parrenhas 2001). Few studies are available on the Gulf region and even fewer on the UAE. The studies of Sabban (2002) and Vlieger (2011) are some of the studies on this subject. Migrant domestic workers constitute a significant part of the migrant workers in the Gulf region. The migrant domestic workers in the UAE, as elsewhere in the Gulf region, tell us stories not only of exploitation and subjugation but also of hope and aspirations revealing social and cultural interactions that often remain untold.

Of the UAE's 9.2 million people (according to the World Bank),[1] almost 89 per cent are migrants who fill various professions. Employing live-in domestic workers is common in the UAE. Many families who have the means often employ more than one domestic worker from countries as far as Southeast Asia, South Asia and Africa. There are around 7,50,000 domestic workers in the UAE, making up about 20 per cent of the expatriate workforce. Based on intensive interviews and close observations, this chapter examines the relationship between domestic workers of South Asia and their employers, that is, Emirati women who are in control of the household. The relationship between the female employer and the migrant domestic worker at one level and among the domestic workers themselves leave a significant impact on their identity. Since the same household employs domestic workers from various countries and—sometimes—continents, it presents the domestic workers with an opportunity for intercultural exchanges.

The United Arab Emirates

The UAE is made up of seven Emirates: Abu Dhabi, Dubai, Sharjah, Ajman, Umm al-Quwain, Fujairah and Ras al-Khaimah. The UAE's economy has grown rapidly under a climate of sharp rise of oil price in the international market; internal political stability and a pragmatic public policy framework under the leadership of the late Sheikh Zayed bin Sultan Al-Nahyan. As the UAE took off as an independent nation in 1971, it enjoyed an economic take off with the price increase of oil since 1973. In the last four decades, economic development in the UAE has been spectacular. According to the World Bank (2013), the UAE had a GDP of US$348.6 billion in 2011 and a per capita gross national income (GNI) is US$35,770. The UAE is categorized not only as a high-income economy by the World Bank (2013) but also as a high human development country and was ranked 41 of the 186 countries (UNDP 2013). The UAE also scored the highest rank in governance in the Middle East and North African (MENA) region with a score of 8.1 in a World Bank study on governance. Berlin-based Transparency International also rated the UAE as the least corrupt country in the MENA region and was ranked 26 of 177 countries (Transparency International 2013).

The rapid growth of the UAE economy owes mainly to an abundance of natural resources, mainly oil and natural gas. The UAE has a proved oil reserve of 97.8 billion barrel and natural gas of 45.07 billion cu m (CIA, 2008). Yet to some extent the contribution of a huge number—according to one estimate—2.7 million foreign labourers in the UAE cannot be discounted. In the private sector of the economy, more than 90 per cent workers are overseas contract workers. According to the Tanmia Report, in 2004, the UAE national's share of the labour market stood at 9.3 per cent (Human Resources Report 2005: 17). The percentage of foreign workers varies across the seven Emirates with Dubai as the leader followed by Abu Dhabi. According to a 2005 government report, 97.13 per cent of Dubai's total labour force is foreign (*The Gulf News*, 04/11/2007).

According to the Tanmia Report, the labour force participation rate in the UAE has increased from 49.6 per cent in 1985 to 55.4 per cent in 1995, and 63.2 per cent in 2004. The participation rate of the UAE nationals increased from 20.7 per cent in 1995 to 28 per cent in 2004. The main reason for this rise was an increase in the participation of women in the labour force. Women's participation in the labour force has risen from 4.5 per cent in 1995 to 16.1 per cent in 2004 (Human Resource Report 2005: 19). The increase in women's participation is directly related to the growth in the participation of women in higher education. In 2003–2004, the enrolment at the UAE University, the leading university in the country, shows that female students dominate the higher education by a large margin. Of a total of 14,351 students, there were 11,399 women and 2,952 men (Statistical Yearbook 2004: 371).

As the UAE economy is moving more towards the service sector, a large number of married women with children are either pursuing higher education or are gainfully employed. This has led to an increase in the need for domestic workers. Besides, the UAE culture has a long tradition of employing domestic workers. The traditional Emirati society kept the men's world from the women's world separate. Female domestic workers lived in a women's world. Some of the households employ men servants who have no access to the women's domain and limit their services to the men's section of the household. This gender segregation has opened space for female drivers—mainly, from the Philippines—who chauffer around the female members of the household. Some Emirati families have had foreign housemaids even from pre-oil boom days. We came to know of a Bangladeshi domestic worker who came to work here forty years ago. In her long career as a housemaid she has been able to support her family in Bangladesh. She was also able to get her employer to sponsorship some of her relatives who could come to the UAE in times of economic prosperity and could change their fortunes. However, most of the domestic workers are relatively new in this country and have come here after the oil-price increase in 1973 and the remarkable economic growth in the region since then.

South Asians Domestic Workers in the UAE

The majority of the domestic workers or housemaids in the UAE are from Indonesia, Philippines, India, Sri Lanka, Ethiopia, Bangladesh and Nepal. In the official definition, the domestic worker is defined broadly to include gardeners, family tailors and family drivers in addition to cook and cleaners. There is a hierarchy within the domestic workers at the household level. In households where there are several domestic workers, often Filipinas are placed at the apex while Bangladeshis are placed in charge of cooking and the Ethiopians are in charge of cleaning. Filipinas work as housemaids in rich families since they are quite expensive. The Government of the Philippines has set the minimum monthly salary of US$400 (or 1,469 Dirhams) for the Filipina domestic workers in a bid to protect them from exploitative wages. The Indian government has also set a minimum monthly salary of 1,100 Dirhams. The minimum salary for a Nepalese domestic worker is 900 Dirhams. The majority of the Filipinas work in the service sectors. Filipinas work as nurses, receptionists, security guards, waitresses in restaurants, barbers, secretaries, medical assistants, as well as drivers. The wages remain very low and the savings of the workers come at a very heavy price. One of the maids who work part-time to supplement her income walks to the employer's house and saves the taxi fare that she receives from her employer.

Over the years, Bangladesh has become a major labour-sending country, which has led to the development of social networks that facilitate the movement of the domestic workers. There are about 2.5 million Bangladeshis in the Gulf with more than 1 million living in the UAE. In 2006, Bangladesh received about US$1 billion in remittance from the UAE. In 2007, it was estimated to rise to US$1.2 billion (*Gulf News*, 4 December 2007). By 2013, Bangladesh earned US$1.28 billion in official remittance from the UAE in the period between July and December 2013 (http://www.bangladesh-bank.org/econdata/wagermidtl.php). According to local media estimates, there are estimated 7,00,000 Bangladeshi workers in the UAE. These figures are derived from the Ministry of Manpower in Bangladesh. The officer recognized that although most of these workers are likely to be here, some of them might have taken the necessary papers but did not utilize their papers (which is highly unlikely because in Bangladesh it is quite costly and time consuming to arrange to have such papers). Many of these workers may have become undocumented over the years. Many of the undocumented workers enter the country legally but over time their status becomes irregular as they overstay beyond their contracts or switch jobs unofficially or simply runaway. In 2007, the UAE government declared a general amnesty for the undocumented workers to get repatriated back to their home countries without penalty, it is only after the amnesty period the authorities in the UAE have begun to impose heavy penalty to deter this practice. The new scheme of penalty includes the employers who must pay a fine of AED50,000 for illegal hiring of undocumented workers.

Of the 7,00,000, there are 70,000 female workers from Bangladesh. Of which between 40,000 and 50,000 work as domestic workers (housemaids) or 'Khadamas' or 'Tabbak' (cook) as they are called in Arabic. Other Bangladeshi women work in the cleaning services, and other industries. In the UAE, a domestic worker is also referred to as 'bishkar' (Sabban 2002). In recent years, there has been a huge increase in the number of housemaids in the UAE. Apart from Indian, Bangladeshis and Sri Lankans, there are many Indonesians whose numbers are also increasing. The official data in Bangladesh tend to underreport the extent of female labour migration from Bangladesh. According to Bureau of Manpower, Employment and Training (BMET) in Bangladesh, of a total of 27,54,693 people who have migrated overseas for employment only 17,512 or less than 1 per cent were women (Siddiqui 2005: 10). Blanchet (2002) estimates that about 15 per cent of the Bangladeshi women migrant workers seems to be more realistic. Women, according to United Nations Population Fund (UNFPA), make up nearly half of all international migrants in the world (UNFPA 2006, quoted in Kabeer 2007). In countries such as Sri Lanka, Philippines and Indonesia, women outnumber men by large numbers in overseas migration (Kabeer 2007).

Until recently an employer in the UAE could bring a domestic maid from Bangladesh through the system of sponsorship. Any Emirati citizen could be a sponsor or 'Arbab' in Arabic and sponsor a domestic worker or any other workers. This patronage system, known locally as *Kafeel system*, had its strengths as well as its weaknesses. On the strength side, this informal arrangement as it might have been was very speedy. A migrant worker could come to the UAE on a short notice, thus helping to meet the demands of the labour market with minimum loss of time. As families in the UAE who needed domestic help could get that help on a short notice, and the potential domestic aid from Bangladesh could avoid long-waiting time and bureaucratic hassle. She could also avoid exploitation by unscrupulous manpower agents. However, the system was also susceptible to misuse and exploitation. Many underaged women from Bangladesh were lured to come to the UAE and other Gulf countries with the promise of jobs and many of them fell victims to organized crime without the knowledge of either the Bangladeshi government or the UAE government.

The Official Response and the Institutional Support

The discussion and reporting on the plight of domestic workers have created a certain public awareness of their problems attracting the attention of the government. The UAE government has been particularly sensitive to the criticisms of the plight of the foreign workers in the UAE, especially the domestic workers and has formulated policies and strategies to counteract such trends.[2] According to the 2007 Trafficking in Person Report put out by the State Department of the United States, the UAE presently categorized in the Tier 2 Watch List received mixed evaluation. According to the report:

> The UAE remains a destination country for men and women trafficked for the purpose of involuntary servitude and commercial sexual exploitation. Women from India, Sri Lanka, Bangladesh, Indonesia, Ethiopia, and the Philippines migrate willingly to the UAE to work as domestic servants, but many face conditions of involuntary servitude such as excessive work hours without pay; verbal, mental, physical, and sexual abuse; and restrictions on movement. Similarly, men from India, Sri Lanka, Bangladesh, and Pakistan come to the UAE to work in the construction industry, but are often subjected to involuntary servitude and debt bondage as they work to pay off recruitment costs sometimes exceeding two years' wages. (http://www.migrant-rights.org/research/uae-slavery-report/)

The UAE from April 2007 started enforcing mandatory employment contracts to protect the rights of domestic workers in relation to salary, accommodation, healthcare and working hours. The UAE has pursued active bilateral cooperation with labour-exporting countries by signing at least five MoUs to date (Nepal, India, Pakistan, Bangladesh and Sri Lanka) and encouraging these countries to tackle the problems of illegal recruitment agencies and labour abuse. A wage standard has been introduced by some of these countries including Philippines, Indonesia and Sri Lanka. In order to protect cases of domestic worker abuse, age regulations have also been imposed by two of these countries which the UAE fully supports in its efforts to stop domestic physical or sexual abuse.

On 16 May 2007, Indian minister for women and children, Renuka Chowdhury, announced that India will refuse to grant emigration clearance to women under the age of 30 years who are intending to travel to the Gulf as housemaids. Although the ban covers 17 countries, it is the six oil-rich Gulf states—Oman, Qatar, Saudi Arabia, Kuwait, Bahrain and the UAE—which are believed to be the primary focus of the ban. Reports of physical and sexual abuse of domestic maids at the hands of both employers and people traffickers are common. The UAE government has responded to the needs of the foreign workers by undertaking a wide range of measures including new housing projects.

For example, the Dubai Shelter for Women and Children has been providing victim support and psychological care since 2007. The shelter provides a model for other support centres across the UAE. The Emirate of Abu Dhabi has introduced a comprehensive and compulsory insurance policy for all workers including domestic workers, to be borne at the expense of sponsors. Abu Dhabi has also embarked on a major programme to build model labour accommodation in the UAE.

Focusing on the challenges of domestic labour, a number of measures have been taken to protect the entire labour force. Most recently a proposal from the Ministerial Service Council was to set up a national authority for inspection and occupational health and safety, to implement labour laws and ensure the compliance of companies with occupational health and safety rules. Other measures taken including heavy penalization of companies found to be violating labour laws, an extensive increase in the numbers and training of site inspectors and the introduction of an electronic wage payment system by 2008, which has played a big part in eradicating non-payment or irregular payments of wages.

The above measures demonstrate the UAE's prioritization of labour market regulation and protection as a key national issue. The initiatives undertaken by the UAE to protect domestic workers are in contrast to the assertions in the Human Rights Watch (HRW 2003) report that such laws and mechanisms are not in place in this country. While much remains to be accomplished, the UAE government—working with the private sector and other organizations—is taking significant initiatives to protect human rights and to improve the environments of all workers in the country.

Case Studies[3]

Mr Alam

We start with a Bangladeshi worker, Mr Alam, a male who came to work as a cook at a restaurant with the hope of also working as a part-time cook in local houses. Mr Alam gathered knowledge through his friends and relatives that if he could get a job as a cook in an Emirati household his fortune would change. He took the job of a cook in a small teashop/restaurant as a means to enter in to the country. Such change of job, although not strictly legal, is not too uncommon for many workers. In Bangladesh as well as in India and Pakistan, many households employ men as cooks or servants who work closely with female servants or maids. Each household that can afford employments, various categories of servants and their roles are clearly assigned. Similarly, in the UAE most households employ two or more domestic workers and many households employ part-time domestic workers. In the UAE, many households have male servants who work in the outer houses and do not have access to the inner section of the house. The rule of gender segregation is strictly enforced.

Mr Alam who was sponsored by a small teashop owner was sent a visa since the restaurant had quota for employing workers, especially, the position of a cook. Once he reached Abu Dhabi, he was required to appear for a medical check-up in a clinic at the Abu Dhabi health authorities where he was diagnosed as carrying hepatitis and was disqualified. Medically unfit persons are given a certain amount of time to return to their home countries. In Mr Alam's case an honest medical evaluation by the doctors in Bangladesh would have saved him and his family the huge cost of coming to the UAE. It is quite likely that a middleman or 'dalal' arranged his 'medical certificates', which was obviously fake. Given the prevalence of a culture of corruption in Bangladesh, many would be tempted to prefer a 'less cumbersome' illegal channel than a legal one hoping impunity. He spent a total of 1,00,000 taka or AED5,000 for a future that was never realized. Other workers pay much more. The rates vary according to the nature of work as well as the scruples of the employment agents and their sub-contractors. Mr Alam was in luck to find odd jobs and support from the Bangladeshi community in Abu Dhabi. In Bangladesh upon his return he would work hard to help repay the loans his family incurred to finance his travel to the UAE. While waiting for his return trip to Dhaka, his local sponsor the restaurant owner raised some funds from the customers to help this hapless migrant worker. In the end when his airfare was raised through donations, Mr Alam left and did not get the chance of working part-time as a house cook. His efforts went in vain; his dreams turned into a nightmare.

The problem of such corruption is not limited to Bangladesh. While on a trip to India, I met two returnee foreign-workers on the Delhi-bound plane. Neither was able to fill out the disembarkation forms. As I filled their forms, I gathered from them that one of them was sent to jail for committing some crime and upon release was dispatched off to India. The other person, though he had a 'valid' medical screening report from India, was disqualified after the medical test done in the UAE. Here again corruption in the sending country was the reason for huge financial loss on the part of this poor peasant from the Punjab. In his case too, his family had mobilized the resources for his prospective overseas tour of duty. It is also a story of cooperation and fellowship where community of Bangladeshi workers came to help the victim and raised funds for him so that he could return to his home.

Although the story of Mr Alam does not fit into the theme of women's solidarity and the coping strategies of female domestic workers, it does point to the vulnerability of the overseas workers from South Asia due to a complex set of factors and conditions that cross cut geographical boundaries, national jurisdictions, gender, culture and nationality. It also points to the fact that migrant workers in general remain vulnerable and expose themselves to a host of involuntary risks. The circumstances that exploit and violate the workers are more complex than a binary division between 'us' and 'them' is able to capture. The ubiquity and normalization of local corruption is entangled with the distant structures of domination. Given the failed institutions of the government in the labour-sending countries, a lot depends on the entrepreneurship and judgement of the individual workers where males do not do any better than their female counterparts. For the females, it is often a double trouble, they become the victims of an inept state whose ideology of patriarchy tends to impose moralistic ethos on the mobility of women.

Mrs Nahar

Unlike Mr Alam, Mrs Nahar was lucky. She did not spend anything other than the airfare to come to the UAE. One of her village girls worked with an extended, multi-generational family in the UAE and when she was on a home leave she made special arrangement to get a visa for Mrs Nahar from her employers. Here she used her excellent relationship and trustworthiness as resources to convince her employer to arrange a visa under the 'Kafala' system for her friend. Kafala or Kafeel system has come under a barrage of criticisms. In many cases, the criticisms are not without merits, yet there are cases where domestic workers and others have been benefited by this informal sponsorship system. Had Mrs Nahar gone through the formal system of employment agencies and government bureaucracies, she would still be in Bangladesh. The wholesale demonization of 'Kafala' system needs a careful scrutiny.

Mrs Nahar's story in not too atypical in Bangladesh. She got married at the age of 13. By the time she was 15, she gave birth to her first child, a daughter. She lost her husband when she was 19. Her in-laws were not heartless, they wanted her to remarry and especially, at her sister-in-law's insistence she remarried again. She gave birth to a daughter after a year of her re-marriage. Her second husband had children from a previous marriage. She only spent a few years with her new husband and since her husband's income was not adequate to support a family with five children, she decided to come to the Gulf. Considering the dire economic situation of the family, her husband consented to her overseas venture. She knew from her friends in the village about the job opportunities in Dubai, which was the name of the United Arab Emirates in Bangladesh. Dubai was often viewed as a land of money and opportunities. Whether one comes to Abu Dhabi or Ras al-Khaimah or Fujairah, it is Dubai to the fellow villagers in Bangladesh. They use a simple mental cartography.

At the time of our interview, Mrs Nahar was doing part-time work in three households. Her employer is an expatriate from the Sudan where she works as a live-in maid and her employer allows her to take part-time work in other households. She gets AED600.00 from her employer, who treats her well and allows her to share her room with two other Bangladeshi women who pay rental to the employer. From part-time work in two other households, Mrs Nahar makes AED400.00 and AED500.00, respectively. Her total monthly income is slightly higher than the official salary for domestic workers from the Philippines. It is her entrepreneurship and a will to survive and overcome that rewarded her. She sends money home regularly to her bank account in Bangladesh. So far she has been able to buy a piece of land and her plan is to build a small house, a dwelling for her family. Meanwhile, she is ensuring that her children get a decent education in Bangladesh, which she is supporting financially. Mrs Nahar's own children live with their grandparents. Part of the remittance is spent on the children's education. She wants to live with all her children when she returns to Bangladesh and she wants to ensure that all her children get education and a better life in the future. However, at this moment she is not planning to return home. She is quite happy here. She returned from Bangladesh last year after a month of holiday.

Nahar stressed the fact that she was paid regularly and it is striking that she used the phrase 'Insaf' (justice) to describe the relationship between her and her employer. In the case of Nahar, since she is in a tenuous situation with part-time employment prohibited, it is worth mentioning that without the indulgence (or connivance) of the employer she would not be in a favourable situation. With an increase in income, Nahar is in a position not only to plan her own future but also that of her children. She wants to ensure that her children get the education to overcome poverty. She believes that she can change the fate of her children.

Miss Rangini

Miss Rangini is 33 years old and although she is not a graduate she has finished 9 years of schooling. She wanted to do a degree in hotel management but she could not finish the degree because of poor financial reasons. Miss Rangini was on her own financially since she finished high school at the age of 16. She was supporting her college education by working at a restaurant after school. The money was reasonable but it was too tiring. She could not cope with the demands of the college. Her education remained incomplete and with the help of a cousin who was working as a cleaner at a cleaning company in Abu Dhabi she decided to try her luck in the UAE. She bought a ticket for Abu Dhabi by Etihad, the UAE Airlines.

Miss Rangini is from Sri Lanka she grew up in provincial town and did not even see Colombo, except for the airport, on her way to Abu Dhabi from her small town. She comes from a family of five. Her father worked as a driver for the government and now retired. She came on a visitor's visa and was met at the airport by her cousin. She spent the first two weeks looking for a job and stayed with her cousin and found a job at a cleaning company in Abu Dhabi. In order to change her visa from a visit visa to employment visa, she took a short trip to Doha, Qatar, where at the airport she took a return flight back to Abu Dhabi. She has a monthly salary of AED 700. From her income, she spends 300 on rental which is more than one-third of her monthly income. She shares a room with three other Sri Lankan women. Miss Rangini complained about the rising rental cost in Abu Dhabi. She spends 200–300 Dirhams a month and sends 100 Dirhams to home. She has no savings except her earning from part-time work at two houses. She got the part-time job with the help of an expatriate in an office she cleans. She is now able to spend some money on the extras such as cosmetics, new clothes and so on.

Her part-time employer often provides her food and clothes that help her save money. One of her employers where she works on weekends knows her from work. The employer, an expatriate from South Asia, helped her find a second part-time work. Her present work is very demanding and the income is low. She is determined to change her fortune. Miss Rangini has been engaged for quite some time and her husband-to-be has just found a job in Abu Dhabi and will join her here soon. Even before coming to the UAE, she knew a great deal about this country. Miss Rangini's mother worked in the UAE at a cleaning company who herself did part-time work in local households. Miss Rangini is a second-generation migrant worker.

Mrs Razia

Mrs Razia, a domestic worker from Bangladesh, worked in Lebanon as a domestic worker where her main job was to provide care services to an elderly couple. She was well looked after by her employers. She, a migrant worker, also worked in a family where grown up children were migrants themselves who lived in North America. It was during the war and conflict, Razia was forced to return home. She returned to Abu Dhabi in 2006. She too took enormous risk in making her journey from Bangladesh to the Arab world. She had no idea where Lebanon, or for that matter, where the Middle East was. After the death of her husband, she became a victim of abuse from her in-laws and was desperate to leave the country. Absolute poverty and desperate situation led her to the journey into uncertainty in a foreign land. Being an orphan and after her husband's death, she was left with no other hope. As a widow with two small children and pregnant with the third, a rural woman without education she had no means of supporting her or her children. After the birth of the child, she persuaded her mother-in-law to take care of the children and with the help of a returnee from Beirut in the village she took a leap into the domain of unknown. This returnee worker from her village took pity on her and helped her find domestic work in Beirut, Lebanon. This informal arrangement saved her a lot of hassle and money. She did not have to deal with government bureaucracy or the 'manpower agents'.

By the time she came to the UAE, she had functional knowledge of speaking and understanding Arabic, which she learned in Beirut. Despite her knowledge of Arabic language, her employers in the UAE were not satisfied with her work. They were not kind to her. Razia confessed that sometimes she too can be quite stubborn. Razia was not offended when her female employer would scold her once in a while. However, once her employer slapped her she had had enough of the abuse. Finally, she quit and left the home quietly and found another household job without much difficulty. She worked full-time at a household as a domestic worker without proper visa or papers. Her employer, a kind-hearted woman, took special care of her and would allow her to look for part-time work to enhance her income.

Mrs Razia, like Mrs Nahar, wears the local abaya and covered her face. Although wearing abaya and covering face seemed to be an act in compliance with the local traditions but such a dress code also saved her from detection. She had to cover her since part-time domestic work is not legal any more in the UAE. What is considered a sign of modesty and an age-old tradition was being used strategically by the part-time domestic workers who needed to avoid the gaze of men as well as others who might have questioned their unaccounted for activities.

Living in the shadow between legal and illegal, documented and undocumented statuses, Mrs Razia took a risk that paid her off in the short run. With her earnings, she could bring one of her sons to Abu Dhabi to work. She supported her other son to go to work in Malaysia. She continued to work for another four years before the long arms of the law caught up with her. Arrested by police, she served a term of six months in jail after which she was deported to her homeland. Her tale was that of a personal loss and suffering and gain for her family.

Mrs Nilufer

Mrs Nilufer worked for an Emirati family for 10 years as a cook (Khadama). She had her own room outfitted with a television of her own and her own bathroom. This was in sharp contrast with male workers (in construction) who often had to share a bathroom with dozens of fellow workers. The head of the family passed away several years ago and the lady of the household who Nilufer calls 'mama' (mother) was the matriarch who lived in a large household with two of her divorcee daughters and their children. It was a household full of women.

Nilufer's main work is to cook for the entire family. She cooks excellent Arabic food and all the family members have developed a liking for her cooking. The lady of the house also sends food to some of her neighbours routinely, for which Nilufer was given the responsibility for cooking and delivering the food. That gave her an opportunity to go out of the house and socialize with other Bangladeshi families who lived in the same neighbourhood. There was a Filipina domestic worker in that household as well who often covered for Nilufer when she was on her prowl in the neighbourhood-visiting neighbours.

Nilufer used to get a salary of AED 700 much of which she could save since she got food, clothing and lodging from her employer. Over the years, Nilufer had been given more and more responsibility and she accompanied the daughters of the house for grocery shopping. Nilufer was used to familial responsibility, a role she was comfortable with since she was the eldest child in her own family and grew up looking after her younger siblings.

Nilufer was from a village named, Chalak Char in Narsingdi, a district town in Bangladesh. She was married at the age of 12 and became a mother of a daughter at the age of 14. Soon after her marriage and especially after the daughter was born, she came under routine abuse from her husband and her in-laws. They started mistreating her for not bringing the promised dowry. Her husband abandoned her and took the daughter away. Several years later, she learned that her little daughter drowned in a pond near her husband's family house. Nilufer did not recover from this loss. Even at the time of interview, she felt sad. After the loss of her daughter, she left the village and went to work in Dhaka as a garment worker in the flourishing garment industry. While working as a factory worker in Dhaka, she decided to try her luck in the Gulf. Being the eldest child in the family, she filled the role of the 'eldest son' and helped her father repay his debts.

At that point, she finally decided to take up a job in the Gulf. Through her contacts in the extended family while working at the garment factory she found out about possibilities of going to 'Dubai'—the United Arab Emirates—and took the plunge. With the help of a cousin brother, a veteran of Dubai she came to work as a domestic worker in Sharjah. She was able to save some money from her six years of factory job and she promised to pay the rest from her maid's salary. As Nilufer found her employer in Sharjah to be unreasonable and unkind she ran way and found a good Emirati employer in Abu Dhabi who helped her regularize her papers for which she had to make a short trip to Bangladesh. She has been working there for the past 10 years. Not only she could save money for her future life in Bangladesh, she helped her younger brother and two sisters to get sponsorship from her employer. In fact, now she was satisfied having been able to help her siblings found work in the UAE.

She was very protective of her younger brother who was sponsored by her 'mama' and lived with her. One of her two sisters returned to Bangladesh since then and at the time of this interview was planning to return to Abu Dhabi. She kept saying: 'if three of us work, we will be able to save enough money and we won't have any problem. My 'headache' (the Bengali expression for burden) will be gone. I will build two additional rooms for myself and my sister in Bangladesh'. Nilufer thought of her family as the family that included her parents, brothers and sisters. She was always concerned with the well-being of her family of orientation. She plans to return to Bangladesh after a few years and plan to live off the income from her land, which she would lease out. She has chalked out her future plans and would execute them without fail.

Conclusions

Based on the interview of a small number of housemaids it is evident that they prefer to work in the UAE than to return to Bangladesh. In Abu Dhabi many well-to-do Emiratis employ more than one housemaid, a condition that make the work specialized and less strenuous for the specialized housemaid. Some of the domestic workers or housemaids, as they are known locally, have had experience of working elsewhere before they came to the UAE. With few exceptions, the domestic workers had positive views about their employers and working condition in Abu Dhabi. For them cash, in the final analysis, became the most important vector of social attainment. Given their background of no formal education, they would not have the opportunity to earn the money they earn in the UAE. Earning money gives them a sense of self-worth, which they lacked when they were in Bangladesh. It is the migration experience and life situation that helped them realize their true potential. They were subjects but not subjugated. Their exercise of agency was subtle, not absent.

An evidence of the empowerment of the women in our study is found in the change of perceptions about them. In answer to our question: 'when you first left the village for the Gulf to work as a domestic worker, how did the fellow-villagers look at you? And now when you return on holidays how do they see and treat you?' Initially, when they left their village and came to work as domestic workers in a foreign, people looked down upon them. That situation changed over time. Their answers indicated that they had attained a higher social status and there had been a change of perceptions of them. Economic power gave them social status, recognition and social power in their own village society.

Their female employers protected all the women we interviewed. The relationship they have developed with the employers gives them a sense of belonging. They do not feel a sense of isolation and detachment. The relationship is renewed during the month of Ramadan, which is a very important event in the UAE as in the other Islamic societies. The Bangladeshi domestic workers play an active role in preparing special food for the 'Suhoor', the food consumed at the dawn. They distribute food for breakfast in the evening to the households of the friends of their employers. Exchanging cooked food during the month for evening breakfast is a common practice in Abu Dhabi. The sharing of a common religious rite strengthened the bonding between the employer and her employee, the domestic worker.

One of the Bangladeshi domestic workers was routinely given the responsibility of looking after the entire household when her employer travelled overseas for medical treatment. Such practices, probably, were not very common but it did signify a familial relationship that cannot be simply captured by the industrial model of worker/employer relationship.

The relationship of the domestic workers with other members (some of them professional) of the Bangladeshi community often provides a strong support system for the domestic workers. They tend to help each other in times of need. Recently, Nilufer needed 5000 Dirhams to give to a local 'Arbab' (sponsor) for the visa of her sister. She considered this to be an investment which though entails some risk, it was a risk 'worth taking', according to her. For this she borrowed money from a relatively well-off member of the Bangladeshi community who gave her the loan based on trust alone. This was a trust she earned through her periodic socialization and with a simple promise of repaying by work, if not by cash. The recent policy shift that makes private sponsorship unacceptable and that every domestic worker must come through an employment agent may not be to the advantage of the domestic workers. Although the intention of the new policy is to ensure the welfare of the domestic worker, the consequence could be opposite. The intention of the new policy, protection of foreign workers, may hurt the interest of the domestic workers who often rely more on their agencies than the institutional means of their own countries.

Most of the studies on the female domestic workers have brought to light the mechanism of exploitation and the vulnerability of the South Asian women. However, what those studies overlooked was the agencies of the domestic workers themselves. The role the domestic workers seemed to play the role of victims. The relationship between the domestic workers from South Asia and their employers, mostly female in the context of the UAE, asymmetric as it was, allowed them to mobilize resources such as religion and feminist solidarity to their advantage. This aspect of the everyday life of the domestic workers must not be overlooked in the emphasis on other facets of their experience. There may be some silver lining even in a dismal situation.

Notes

1. According to Census Report of 2005, the population is estimated at 4.1 million. However, the 2013 World Bank source puts the figure at 9.2 million. The remarkable increase in population has given rise to some debates compounded by the existence of undocumented population.
2. In late January 2008, the UAE government co-hosted with ILO and IOM the Abu Dhabi Dialogue on foreign labour representing 11 labour sending and 11 labour receiving countries. Discussion on a variety of issues including workers' rights and vulnerabilities were discussed openly and frankly.
3. Names have been changed to protect their identities.

References

Blanchet, T. *Beyond Boundaries: A Critical Look at Women Labour Migration and Trafficking Within* (Mimeo). A Study presented to USAID, Dhaka, 2002.

Castles, S. *Ethnicity and Globalization: from Migrant Worker to Transnational Citizen*. London: Sage, 2000.

Central Intelligence Agency (CIA). Washington, D.C. *World Fact Book*, 2008.

Chin, Christine B.N. *In Service and Servitude*. New York: Columbia University Press, 1998.

Constable, N. *Maid to Order in Hong Kong*. Ithaca: Cornell University Press, 1997.

Giddens, A. *Runaway World*. London: Profile Books, 2002.

Gulfnews.com. 'Domestic Workers get more protection from exploitation' by Samir Salama. 30 January (2014).

Human Rights Watch (HRW). *Swept Under the Rug*. New York, 2003.

Kabeer, Naila. "Footloose' Female Labour: Transnational Migration, Social Protection and Citizenship in the Asia Region'. IDRC Working Papers on Women's Rights and Citizenship, 2007. http://www.idrc.ca/EN/Documents/WRC-WP1-Kabeer-Migration.pdf

Parrenhas, Rhacel Salazar. *Servants of Globalization*. Stanford: Stanford University Press, 2001.

Ray, Larry. *Globalization and Everyday Life*. London: Routledge, 2007.

Rosenberg, J. *The Follies of Globalisation Theory*. London: Verso Books, 2002.

Sabban, R. 'United Arab Emirates: Migrant Women in the UAE: The Case of Female Domestic Workers'. Working Paper No. 10, International Labour Office, Geneva, 2002.

Siddiqui, Tasneem. 'International Labour Migration from Bangladesh: A Decent Work Perspective'. ILO Working Paper No. 66, 2005.

Statistical Yearbook of UAE. Abu Dhabi: UAE Government Publication, 2004.

Tanmia Report. *United Arab Emirates Human Resources Report.* Dubai, 2005.

Transparency International. *Berlin: Corruption Perception Index*, 2013. cpi.transparency.org/cpi2013/results.

Turner, B. and Khondker, H.H. *Globalization: East and West.* London: Sage, 2010.

UNDP. *Human Development Report.* New York, 2013.

Vlieger, Antoinette. *Domestic Workers in Saudi Arabia and the Emirates: A Socio-legal Study on Conflicts.* PhD dissertation, University of Amsterdam, 2011.

World Bank. http://data.worldbank.org/country/united-arab-emirates, 2013 (accessed on 1 February 2014).

CHAPTER 11

Development and Distress

A Study of Gulf Returnees in Andhra Pradesh

Ajaya Kumar Sahoo and Trilok Chandan Goud

India has exported large numbers of migrants to different parts of the world under different circumstances. Indian migration, mostly as contract labour, to the Gulf countries is a recent phenomenon. The Gulf countries imported a large number of foreign labourers mostly from South Asian countries to work either in the oil companies or in the construction-related jobs in the early 1970s and 1980s by providing travel expenses. However, in recent time the situation has changed because of huge competition among foreign labours in the Gulf and also because of the Gulf economic crisis, as a result India has witnessed significant return migrations from the Gulf. This chapter examines the socioeconomic life of Gulf returns in the state of Andhra Pradesh, India. It is divided into three sections: after a brief introduction on the patterns of Indian emigration, the second section focuses on the Indian emigration to the Gulf countries and the final section focuses on the issues of return and its socioeconomic impact on families in Andhra Pradesh. The chapter argues that although the return is the necessary outcome of Gulf migration, it has mixed results for returnees. While for some the journey is highly successful, for others it is a failure, the latter being the common feature of the majority of respondents in this study. Because of the failure of jobs in the Gulf countries, the returnees were now called 'Gulf victims' in the villages.

Indian Emigration to the Gulf Countries

Although Indian migration to the Persian Gulf started as early as the 1930s after oil was discovered in the region (Khadria 2006; Pradhan 2010), it was in the early 1970s that the large-scale migration took place as a result of the price hike of oil. The consequent earnings of large revenues accelerated the process of industrialization and social change in the GCC states characterized by massive investment in social and economic infrastructure necessitating the service of a large number of foreign workers.[1] As Gardner (2011: 6) rightly points out:

> Each of the states configured modernization and economic diversification plans to make use of this wealth, and those plans required heavy infrastructural development: cities would grow; highways would be constructed; electricity would be produced; new industries would prosper; universities, mosques, stadiums, hospitals, and federal buildings would be constructed and staffed.

For a brief period during the 1990–1991 Gulf War 'the number of low-skilled Indian workers in the Gulf declined due to Indian government restrictions' (Khadria 2010: 67), however, it again picked up afterwards when the demand for labour in the GCC states increased and diversified across many sectors from construction, services, oil and manufacturing (Breeding 2011). In order to avail the opportunities, Indian workers began to migrate to the Gulf countries.

Migration of Indians to the Gulf is totally different from migrating to other developed countries such as the United States, United Kingdom and Canada. Migrants are recruited purely on contract basis as the 'Gulf oil countries do not allow family reunion and settlement' (Castles 2000: 277). Migration to the Gulf countries started with a few thousand per year during the middle of 1970s and assumed large proportions during the 1980s and 1990s. Although it is difficult to know the exact size of the migrant workers in the GCC countries, available information suggests that it was about 12.5 million in 2002; of this total, there were 3.5 million non-Gulf Arabs, 3.6 million Indians, 1.7 million Pakistanis, almost 1 million Bangladeshis, more than 7,00,000 Filipinos and more than 7,00,000 Sri Lankan (Rahman 2010). According to Ministry of Overseas Indian Affairs (MOIA 2007: 3) 'Indian technicians, nurses, teachers and other professionals handle almost the entire services sector in the Gulf. Around 70 per cent are engaged in semi-skilled and unskilled work; while 20–30 per cent comprises professionals and other white collared workers'. Migration from Kerala accounts for more than 50 per cent of the total stock of Indian migrants in the Gulf, with Tamil Nadu ranking second, followed by Andhra Pradesh, Karnataka, Uttar Pradesh and Punjab (Prakash 1998; Zachariah et al. 2002).

Pradhan (2010: 95) categorized the Indian expatriate community in the GCC states into four broad groups: (a) unskilled workers, employed in construction companies, municipalities, agricultural farms and as domestic workers; (b) skilled and semi-skilled workers; (c) professionals, such as doctors, engineers, accountants, employed in government and private sectors; and (d) businessmen. The respondents covered in the present study belonged to the category of semiskilled and unskilled workers, out of which many are even illiterate. Because of the lack of education, these migrants face various problems in their migration process, in the host country itself and then also after return to the homeland. This study explores the internal dynamics of this migration process and its effects on migrants and their families.

The Context

The fieldwork for this study was carried out among the returnees[2] from the Gulf in four districts of Andhra Pradesh—Karimnagar and Nizamabad districts from Telangana region, East Godavari from Costal Andhra region and Cuddapah (Kadapa) from Rayalaseema region—from where migration to Gulf countries has been considerably in the recent past.[3] One of the main factors for migration in these districts is landlessness. For example, the majority of respondents covered in this study opined that they do not have sufficient agricultural land and some of them are even landless. Even those having agricultural land are unable to cultivate and seek profits due to droughts and low irrigation facilities. Apart from this, natural calamities such as famines and floods, shrinking of the cottage industry and lack of employment opportunities forced many of them to migrate to urban areas and also to the Gulf countries (Bhat and Sahoo 2005).

Migration from Andhra Pradesh started with internal migration especially 'from the rural areas of Telangana districts to the coal fields of Godavarikhani, textile centres of Gujarat and Maharashtra' (Sampath 2006: 6). Male migrants used to migrate to Bombay (present day Mumbai) to work in industrial and construction sites and from there they used to gather information about the opportunities available in the Gulf countries. This trend was noticed mainly during the 1980s and 1990s (Azeez and Begum 2009). Once these migrants had reached the Gulf, they would send information to their children, relatives and neighbours about the opportunities available there. Such migrant 'networks' would facilitate further migration (Gold 2005). As Gardner (2011: 9) mentioned, 'chain migration through personal contacts, often arranged by other family members or acquaintances already in the Gulf, remains a significant force in the Gulf'. Several scholars have discussed the role of personal networks in migration. Vertovec (2002: 3), for instance, pointed out that 'for migrants social networks are crucial for finding jobs and accommodation, circulating goods and services, as well as psychological support and continuous social and economic information'.

Methodology

The study is based on data collected from both primary and secondary sources. Primary data were collected from respondents in four districts of Andhra Pradesh. Through a snowball technique, 198 respondents were selected for this study. For collecting information from respondents, a structured interview schedule was used consisting of nine pages in which questions were arranged sequentially. The interview schedule was divided into three parts—personal information, migration and living conditions in the Gulf and coping after return. Besides primary data, we also gathered relevant information from the Non-Resident Indian (NRI) Cell in Karimnagar district and the Overseas Manpower Company of Andhra Pradesh (OMCAP) Limited in Hyderabad. These two organizations conduct various programmes for migrants in Andhra Pradesh. For secondary sources, we relied on the published literature in various journals, books, reports, national and local (Telugu) newspapers and the Internet.

Out of the total respondents selected for this study, 81 per cent were males and 19 per cent females. During the course of this study, we did not find many female respondents. It might be the reason that, and as the literature shows, female migration from India to the Gulf countries is mostly from the state of Kerala (Percot and Rajan 2007) and to a lesser extent from the state of Andhra Pradesh and Goa. Jain (2007) pointed out that 'females are less comparable to male and they have less job opportunities unlike as nurses, teachers, and domestic servants'.[4] Getting work and work permits as a domestic labourer[5] depends on the networks; hence, most migrants prefer their own family members or relatives to refer to such work.

Age is an important determining factor in Gulf migration as most of the migrants engage in construction and service sectors. Since these jobs are risky, only physically fit candidates are preferred and for that reason mostly young people migrate to Gulf countries. Out of the total respondents in the present study 68 per cent belonged to the age group of 18–40 years and the rest (32%) were above the age of 41 years. Zachariah and Rajan's (2012) study showed that 90 per cent of the male and 66 per cent of female migrants belong to the age group of 19–39 years. Another study by Jain (2007) noticed that 84 per cent of migrants were under 35 years of age and in that 50 per cent were unmarried. Thus, it is clear that age is still considered to be the dominant criteria for the Gulf migration at the present time.

Migration of Indians to Gulf countries is not only influenced by economic factors but also by many other factors such as caste, religion and geographical location. The lower castes and tribes have a greater propensity to migrate, and many of them migrate for a short-term; they are low skilled and low paid workers with the highest levels of vulnerability and the lowest level of social protection. Migration offers schedule castes (SCs) and schedule tribes (STs) an escape from the traditional structures of caste-based oppression in villages and gives them some bargaining power vis-à-vis their traditional employers (see Deshingkar and Start 2003). Among the total respondents included in the present study, 25 per cent belonged to general castes, 22 per cent belonged to SCs and 53 per cent belonged to backward castes (BCs). The BCs were having majority in the study areas compared with other caste groups. Nambiar's (1995) study in Kerala found that only 7 respondents were from forward castes (upper castes) and 90 respondents were from backward castes among Hindu religion. Another study by Prakash (2000) in Kerala found that 31 per cent were from upper castes, 59 per cent were from backward castes and 10 per cent were SCs and STs. As a result of shrinking of cottage industries and traditional caste occupations, many backward caste communities (especially the youth) lost their livelihood and this has compelled them to search for new occupations. The alternative was to move to different cities within the country and also migrate to Gulf countries, through personal networks.

Life in the Gulf

Working and living conditions of migrants completely depend on the host society. Immigrants in the Gulf countries face discrimination in getting salaries and sometimes are ill-treated by their owners (Frontpage 2012). Hence, the process of recruitment, wages, terms and conditions of work were the critical factors that affect the living conditions of migrants in the Gulf countries (see Jureidini 2003). For instance, salaries paid to Arab migrants and non-Arab migrants differ (Kapiszewski 2006). Migrants have to live in labourer camps, which are in some cases located near to the work itself and in other cases located in isolated areas far away. Majority of respondents in this study said that the camps were mostly temporary in nature and that the living conditions were unhygienic with no proper sanitation being maintained.[6] In a single room, more than 10 people used to live together. If a migrant decided to live outside the camp he would have to bear the extra cost, unthinkable for an unskilled and daily wage labourer.

Although some companies provide medical and housing facilities to the workers, it again depends on the rules of the company. Some small companies wanted to recruit workers illegally because they could not afford to pay for medical facilities and accommodation for legal migrants. Some of the respondents said that they were 'illegal' (*kalli valli*[7]) in the host country because they had entered the country on tourist visas. Tourist visas create the problem that migrants have to live illegally in the host country after the visa terms get over, which results in severe punishments, deportation or being sent to jail. In 2007, it was reported that there were around 70,000 migrants who have returned from the UAE alone and most of these migrants were illegal because they had overstayed beyond the term of their visa (*Indian News*, 5 November 2007).[8] Many respondents in this study revealed that there were instances that they could recall where Indians were sent to jail. Here the role of recruiting agents (RAs) cannot be ignored as they play an important role in the migration process. As Rajan et al. (2011: 88) found in their study:

> Since most RAs from sending countries like India collect huge amounts of money from the aspirants, they very often fail to ensure that the workers have the necessary skill levels. This results in workers being brought in en masse, and a consequent reduction in salary and depletion in living standards. All these factors can result in workers becoming illegal immigrants in the destination country.

The present study found that the construction and services sectors are the main employers of migrants in the Gulf. As Nambiar (1995) showed, 'migrant workers employed in the Middle East countries ... range from poorly educated ABCD workers (Ayahs, Bearers, Cooks, Drivers) to highly educated professionals. However, by and large a majority belongs to the category of less educated workers engaged in manual jobs'. Working hours in unskilled professions make matters even more complex. For example, most of the respondents (77%) opined that they worked more than 10 hours a day while very less respondents (23%) said that they worked less than eight hours a day. Gardner (2011: 10) pointed out that 'migrants are often forced to work longer hours than those indicated in the contract they signed in the sending country, and many report not receiving additional wages for these additional (overtime) hours'. Working hours vary from company to company; sometimes migrants do not have any time limit and they have to work until the work is completed on the particular day.

The Issues of Return

Return to the homeland is compulsory as they were recruited on a contract basis. Migrants cannot get permanent citizenship or own property even if they stay for more than 10 years.[9] Return is mostly predetermined by the objective they had set out to achieve at the time of migration. Migrants always think that they will earn good money and become successful if they migrate to another country. However, in this study we found a failure to be more often than success among the respondents. Several respondents opined that they have returned back because of different reasons such as expiry of contract (44%), visa problem (22%), less wages and harsh working conditions (17%), health problems (11%) and job loss (6%). In recent times, it was also observed that because of the increasing number of foreign workers in the Gulf, the recruiting companies in collaboration with the government have reduced the salaries and wages for semiskilled and unskilled workers. As Rajan and Narayana (2011) argued, 'the global crisis has affected the GCC economies through falling oil prices, depressed property and equity prices, low investor confidence, and reversal of capital flows. As the GDP growth in the GCC economies spawns large population growth, especially large influx of migrant labourers from South Asia, recession affects the flow of migrants and remittances'.[10] Several respondents reiterated that they wanted to return back to India even a little earlier (as they faced difficulties in accommodation and food due to financial problems) but they could not afford the airfare as they did not have any savings. In August 2008, the Indian consulate in Dubai, for instance, has arranged for the return of large numbers of impoverished workers through a special scheme. More recently, 35 illegal immigrants from Andhra Pradesh were provided free air tickets by the Gulf Telangana Welfare and Cultural Association (GTWCA) and extended amnesty by the government to return to India. They 'did not carry the authorised travel documents and the legal residency permits. They were poor and could not afford the air tickets' (*The Hindu*, 25 January 2013).

As was discussed earlier, the main reason for migration to Gulf countries is unemployment at home and related economic factors. This situation continued for much of the respondents after return even after having gained important work experience in the Gulf. Before migration, these migrants were already in a weak position, then the economic downturn hit them in the Gulf itself and as a result they were forced to return to India. But they returned to a situation that had not improved much, probably got worse, exacerbated by now mounting visa-related debts.[11] Majority of respondents felt that they were not satisfied with their present life as they are still under debts—the money they borrowed at the time of their migration to the Gulf migration has not yet been cleared. Migrants depended on money-lenders and friends as a source for money for visa and travel expenses. And during their stay in the Gulf countries, they worked as a daily wage labourers for less salary and hence they could not save enough money to clear their debts.

The study found that 67 per cent of the respondents were engaged in some work related to their skills after return, while 33 per cent were not at all working. Since the majority of returnees were socially and economically backward at the time of their migration, their status had not changed even after spending several years working in the Gulf. Among those respondents who had found employment after return, several were working as agricultural labourers (54%), daily wage labourer (29%)—which was also their occupation prior to migration, and the remaining were in petty business (17%). Among those respondents who have not found any form of employment, the majority said that they were planning for re-emigration to the Gulf. The question arises why they want to re-migrate to the Gulf when their previous migration was not successful and satisfactory. Many of the respondents felt that they cannot repay the debt if they engage in agricultural work in the village while others opined that they would like to re-migrate because of problems such as reintegration and social factors.[12] Reintegration is another problem for the Gulf returnees; Gulf beneficiaries generally do not have any problem with reintegration, but the problem is for the so-called 'Gulf victims'. Gulf beneficiaries here are those who worked in the Gulf and earned enough money that could be saved and sent back to their families as remittances, while Gulf victims are those who could not benefit (economically) with the Gulf migration at all but ended with the additional burden of clearing their previous debt. Gulf victims have a lot of problems in reintegration because they have to cope with debt issues. Sometimes they plan to re-emigrate only to avoid the pressure from the moneylenders. Some of the respondents (name changed) detailed their visit to the Gulf and shared the experience of their return.

Jalender, aged 37, male from Karimnagar district, said:

> Poor economic condition of my family was the major reason for migrating to the Gulf. In Dubai I got less wages for work compared with what the agent assured me before. Moreover, I also faced problems in food and accommodation. I spent ₹ 1,00,000 for visa which was having three years of validity but I was sent back home after two years of work by paying less wages. When I contacted the agent—who helped me to get the visa—he said that he is only responsible for sending the person to Gulf countries and not responsible for anything after that. After returning from the Gulf we sold our land to partially repay our debt, and the debt is still continuing. We request the Government to support us financially by giving loans to start a new business, so that we can clear our debt in the future.[13]

Jyothi, aged 35, female from East Godavari district, revealed:

> I migrated to Kuwait. The agent helped me in getting the passport and visa. After I reached in Kuwait I worked in Arabs house but I did not like the work in the house and hence I left the job. I was working on another house but meanwhile the first owner gave complain against me and I was sent to jail and later returned to India with Out-Pass given by the Indian embassy. Now I am waiting to clear the Gulf debt.

Katakam Ravi, aged 29, male from Karimnagar district, mentioned:

> I went to Qatar for the purpose of a driver but there they made me as a shepherd in the desert. I had worked 20 hours a day and there was

> no time to eat and take rest properly. My salary was 300 DH with irregular payment but, I spent ₹ 1,20,000 for the visa. There was no electricity in the room where I lived. They did not allow me to come back to India, my passport was with them. I was sent to jail for two months because I came out from my owners without intimation. After coming from jail my friends gave me money for my return ticket, my visa debt is still there to be paid. I will not go to gulf again; we are being cheated by agents and they are charging huge money for visas. After returning from Qatar I am working as a taxi driver and I am getting ₹ 200–300 per day.

Eighty-four per cent of respondents in this study said that they were now the 'Gulf victims' as they were burdened with huge debts. One of the consequences was that it forced many of them to commit suicide. An article in an Internet blog revealed that 'within the state of Andhra Pradesh, Karimnagar district has recorded the highest number of suicides, with 1,363 persons ending their lives in 2008, and 840 till September 2009 ... the problem that the Gulf migrants face could account for the large number of suicides in Karimnagar' (Reddy 2009).

Conclusion

The return is compulsory for all Gulf migrants. Policies of Gulf countries do not allow migrants to become permanent citizens even though they work there for several years. In recent times, Gulf countries have also started restricting the inflows of foreign workers despite the fact that 'foreign workers have helped in the rapid transformation of the infrastructure as well as institutional development in the Gulf' (Shah 2008: 3). This chapter discussed several factors that have resulted in the return migration of Indians from the Gulf. Similarly reintegration for returnees become a serious problem, as they undergo social, economic and psychological pressure when they are burdened with debt. The majority of respondents depended on personal loans with the huge interest amount on it and the amount earned in the Gulf was so meagre that all their savings and remittances were used in order to pay off the interest, leave alone to clear the loan. This study contradicts the study conducted in Kerala where Osella and Osella (2000: 119) found that the 'Gulf migration offers to some the chance of rapid and vast accumulation of wealth ... their newfound wealth and access to consumption may dramatically alter their status and their relationships with others, and offer them the chance to forge new identities'.

It may be concluded that less duration of stay was one of the factors for the failure. Since their stay was cut short, the migrants could not achieve what they had hoped to achieve in terms of financial gains at the beginning of their migration. Another factor was the lack of awareness among migrants. Since many of the migrants were illiterate and less aware of the visa process, they completely depended on the agents. And the agents were more concerned about their commissions—because of competition among the agents—as a result they knowingly cheated the migrants. Because of the failure of jobs in the Gulf countries, the returnees were now called 'Gulf victims' in the villages. Although, in recent time, the Government of Andhra Pradesh started special departments in the district called 'NRI Cell', 'OMCAP' and several other special programmes (see Migrant Forum in Asia 2012) towards orientating the Gulf migrants, but the migrants are less aware of these programmes. Hence, it is suggested that the government should take further necessary steps to popularize these programmes in the districts.

Acknowledgments

We would like to thank the University Grants Commission (UGC), New Delhi, for funding this study under the Major Research Project (2008–2011). We thank all the respondents who have given their valuable time and information without which this study would not have been possible.

Notes

1. According to Leonard (2005), the historical ties between South Asia and some of the Gulf States even go back to eighteenth century.
2. Returnees here mainly imply first-generation migrants. Tsuda (2009: 5) makes the difference between 'return migrants' and 'ethnic return migrants' in the sense that while 'return migrants are going back to their *natal* homeland (i.e. place of birth), ethnic return migrants are later generation diasporic descendants returning to their *ethnic* homeland, where their ethnic group originated'.
3. Andhra Pradesh has three distinct regions known as Telangana, Rayalaseema and Andhra. The Andhra region is also called as Coastal Andhra. Telangana consists of 10 districts, coastal Andhra consists of 9 districts and Rayalaseema consists of 4 districts.
4. Studies have shown that in many cases the female migrants engaged as housemaids, *ayahs* and cleaners were being exploited, cheated and

abused (Jureidini 2003; Human Rights Watch 2010). And because of these reasons most of the countries have restricted the out-migration of women to the Gulf countries (see Ahn 2005). Nevertheless several women have been travelling via other countries illegally, for example, Nepali women travel via India and Indian women via Sri Lanka (Ahmed 2010; Thimothy and Sasikumar 2012).

5. In the context of UAE, Bindulakshmi (2010: 168–169) categorized women domestic workers, based on living arrangements, into two types: live-in and live-out. 'Live-in domestic workers usually stay with the employers whereas live-out workers live outside the employers' households. Even though these are the two large categories, the nature of work of domestic workers depends on the channels through which they migrate to the UAE'.
6. As Bruslé (2009–2010: 154) pointed out, the conditions of labourers' camps 'greatly depend on the willingness of their employer to provide them with proper conditions. If the employer is not a large company, workers share rooms in some derelict buildings in the centre for the town'.
7. An Arabic word commonly used in the Middle East.
8. Shah (2008: 6–7) defined an irregular or illegal migrant in the GCC countries as: (1) a person may enter the country illegally (either without required documents or with fictitious documents), (2) the person may become illegal through overstaying after the contract and the legal residence period has expired and (3) when a migrant worker takes up employment for a person other than the sponsor.
9. Although in many cases it was found that the migrants continue to stay in the Gulf and flourish their families over generations (see Ali 2011; Gardner 2011; Vora 2011).
10. The recent crises in Dubai economy, for instance, affected directly the construction sector. Since most of the construction companies have ceased their work it resulted in the forceful leaving of all temporary workers.
11. India's economy has grown rapidly with a 'growth rate of 7–9 per cent during post-liberalization and post-financial crisis period. Unfortunately, the growth has been uneven during last two decades across states and sectors. It has multiplied incomes but also caused increasing insecurity, particularly, among low income groups and in rural areas' (Sahu 2011).
12. Social factors such as the issue of 'prestige' involved in migrating to a foreign country, this has influenced many migrants from the village to go abroad (see Ali 2007).
13. Interviews were originally conducted in Telugu and latter translated into English.

References

Ahmed, A. 'Migrant Domestic Workers in Kuwait: The Role of State Institutions'. pp. 27–29 in *Viewpoints: Migration and the Gulf*. Washington, DC: The Middle East Institute, 2010.

Ahn, P-S. 'Prospects and Challenges of Out-Migration from South Asia and its Neighbouring Countries'. *Labour & Development*, 11, 1 (2005): 1–33.

Ali, S. "Go West Young Man': The Culture of Migration among Muslims in Hyderabad, India'. *Journal of Ethnic and Migration Studies*, 33, 1 (2007): 37–58.

Ali, S. 'Going and Coming and Going Again: Second-Generation Migrants in Dubai'. *Mobilities*, 6, 4 (2011): 553–568.

Azeez, A. and Begum, M. 'Gulf Migration, Remittances and Economic Impact'. *Journal of Social Sciences*, 20, 1 (2009): 55–60.

Bhat, C. and A.K. Sahoo. 'Transnational Networks of Indian Diasporic Communities: The Case of Telugu Diaspora'. *Man in India*, 85, 1–2 (2005): 61–80.

Bindulakshmi, P. 'Gender Mobility and State Response: Indian Domestic Workers in the UAE'. pp. 163–181 in S.I. Rajan (ed.), *India Migration Report 2010: Governance and Labour Migration*. New Delhi: Routledge, 2010.

Breeding, M. 'India-Gulf Migration: Corruption and Capacity in Regulating Recruitment Agencies'. *Migrant Labour in the Gulf: Working Group Summary Report No. 2*, Center for International and Regional Studies, Georgetown University School of Foreign Service in Qatar, 2011.

Buslé, T. 'Who's in a *Labour Camp*? A Socio-economic Analysis of Nepalese Migrants in Qatar'. *European Bulletin of Himalayan Research*, 35–36 (2009–2010): 154–170.

Castles, S. 'International Migration at the Beginning of the Twenty-First Century: Global Trends and Issues'. *International Social Science Journal*, 165 (2000): 269–281.

Deshingkar, P. and Start, D. 'Seasonal Migration for Livelihoods in India: Coping, Accumulation and Exclusion'. Working Paper 220, Overseas Development Institute, London, 2003.

Frontpage. 'The Exploitation of Immigrant Workers in the Middle East', Interview with Jay Johnson, 2012. Available at http://frontpagemag.com/2012/jamie-glazov/the-exploitation-of-immigrant-workers-in-the-middle-east/(accessed on 15 January 2013).

Gardner, A. 'Gulf Migration and the Family'. *Journal of Arabian Studies: Arabia, the Gulf, and the Red Sea*, 1, 1 (2011): 3–25.

Gold, S.J. 'Migrant Networks: A Summary and Critique of Relational Approaches to International Migration'. pp. 257–285 in M. Romero and E. Margolis (eds), *The Blackwell Companion to Social Inequalities*. London: Blackwell, 2005.

Human Rights Watch. *Slow Reform: Protection of Migrant Domestic Workers in Asia and the Middle East*. New York: Human Rights Watch, 2010.

Jain, P.C. *Indian Diaspora in West Asia: A Reader*. New Delhi: Manohar Publications, 2007.

Jureidini, R. 'Migrant Workers and Xenophobia in the Middle East'. *Identities, Conflict and Cohesion Programme Paper Number 2*, United Nations Research Institute for Social Development, Geneva, 2003.

Kapiszewski, A. *Arab versus Asian Migrant Workers in the GCC Countries.* UN Expert Group Meeting on International Migration and Development in the Arab Region, Beirut, 15–17 May 2006 (UN/POP/EGM/2006/02).

Khadria, B. 'Paradigm Shifts in India's Migration Policy toward the Gulf'. *Middle East Institute Viewpoints*, (February 2010): 67–69.

Khadria, B. *India: Skilled Migration to Developed Countries, Labour Migration to the Gulf.* Asia Research Institute, National University of Singapore, 2006.

Leonard, K. 'South Asians in the Indian Ocean World: Language, Policing, and Gender Practices in Kuwait and the United Arab Emirates'. *Comparative Studies of South Asia, Africa and the Middle East*, 25, 3 (2005): 677–686.

Migrant Forum in Asia. *Programs & Services for Migrant Workers & Members of their Families in 3 Indian States: Kerala, Andhra Pradesh, and Tamil Nadu*. Philippines: Migrant Forum in Asia, 2012. www.mfasia.org.

Ministry of Overseas Indian Affairs (MOIA). *Issues Relating to Overseas Indians: Fourteenth Report Standing Committee on External Affairs*. New Delhi: Lok Sabha Secretariat, 2007.

Nambiar, A.C.K. *The Socio-Economic Conditions of Gulf Migrants.* New Delhi: Commonwealth Publishers, 1995.

Osella, F. and Osella, C. 'Migration, Money and Masculinity in Kerala'. *Journal of Royal Anthropological Institute*, 6 (2000): 117–133.

Percot, M. and Rajan, S.I. 'Female Emigration from India: Case Study of Nurses'. *Economic and Political Weekly*, 42, 4 (2007): 318–325.

Pradhan, S. 'India and the Gulf Cooperation Council (GCC): An Economic and Political Perspective'. *Strategic Analysis*, 34, 1 (2010): 93–103.

Prakash, B.A. (ed.). *Indian Migration to the Middle East: Trends, Patterns and Socio-Economic Impacts*. Rohtak: Spellbound Publications, 1998.

Prakash, B.A. 'Exodus of Gulf Emigrants: Return Emigrants of Varkala Town in Kerala'. *Economic and Political Weekly*, 35, 51 (2000): 4534–4540.

Rahman, A. 'Migration and Human Rights in the Gulf'. *Middle East Institute Viewpoints*, (February 2010): 16–18. www.mei.edu.

Rajan, S.I. and D. Narayana. 'The Financial Crisis in the Gulf and Its Impact on South Asian Migrant Workers'. SANEI Working Paper Series No. 11–13, South Asia Network of Economic Research Institutes, Dhaka, 2011.

Rajan, S.I., Varghese, V.J., and Jayakumar, M.S. *Dreaming Mobility and Buying Vulnerability: Overseas Recruitment Practices in India.* New Delhi: Routledge, 2011.

Reddy, S.U. 'In Andhra Pradesh 39 Persons Commit Suicide a Day', 2009. Available at http://udumulasudhakarreddy.blogspot.com/2009/11/in-andhra-pradesh-39-persons-commit.html (accessed 10 August 2011).

Sahu, B.K. 'Growth or Development: Growth Experiences During Post-Reform Period in India'. *The Indian Economy Review*, 2011. Available at http://theindiaeconomyreview.org/Article.aspx?aid=89&mid=5 (accessed 25 January 2013).

Sampath, R.P. *Impact of Migration on Rural Power Structure: A Case Study of Karimnagar District in Andhra Pradesh, South India*. Unpublished PhD Thesis, Jawaharlal Nehru University, New Delhi, 2006.

Shah, N.M. 'Recent Labour Immigration Policies in the Oil-Rich Gulf: How Effective Are They Likely To Be?' International Publications Paper 52. Cornell University ILR School, 2008. http://digitalcommons.ilr.cornell.edu/intl/52.

Thimothy, R. and Sasikumar, S.K. *Migration of Women Workers from South Asia to the Gulf*. Noida: V.V. Giri National Labour Institute, 2012.

Tsuda, T. (ed.), *Diasporic Homecoming: Ethnic Return Migration in Comparative Perspective*. Stanford: Stanford University Press, 2009.

Vertovec, S. 'Transnational Networks and Skilled Labour Migration'. Working Paper 02, Transnational Communities Programme, Oxford University, 2002.

Vora, N. 'From Golden Frontier to Global City: Shifting Forms of Belonging, 'Freedom', and Governance among Indian Businessmen in Dubai'. *American Anthropologist*, 113, 2 (2011): 306–318.

Zachariah K.C., and Rajan, I.S. *Kerala's Gulf Connection, 1998–2011: Economic and Social Impact of Migration*. Hyderabad: Orient Blackswan, 2012.

Zachariah, K.C., Prakash, B.A., and Rajan, S.I. 'Gulf Migration Study: Employment, Wages and Working Conditions of Kerala Emigrants in the United Arab Emirates'. Working Paper No. 326, Centre for Development Studies, Trivandrum, 2002.

CHAPTER 12

Voluntary Migration and Involuntary Servitude

The Plight of Indian Workers in the Persian Gulf

Chitra Natrajan

Gulf countries are major attraction for Indian migrant workers who are dominantly unskilled or semi-skilled deployed on a contractual basis, resulting in a cycle of migration in construction and other related sectors. As a result of the oil boom during 1970s, the economy of these countries turned towards the petrodollar and invested in infrastructure development and alternate post oil economy. With the completion of infrastructure projects in the 1990s, there was a structural shift in the market with the demand towards the operation and maintenance, which increased the demand for service providers (Zachariah et al. 2002). As the native population were not able to meet the labour demand, these countries had to rely on the foreign workers to fill the gap. This huge demand for labour, low availability of local labour force and higher income compared with local labour market and need for unskilled and semi-skilled labours were the driving pull factors and provided immense opportunities for the Indian migrant workers towards the Gulf for better employment and higher wages, compared with the local domestic labour market where there is huge amount of structured poverty, unemployment and lesser wages (Sasikumar and Hussain 2008).

Gulf migration from India is mainly male dominated until 1990s where there was increasing demand for jobs in domestic work and other service oriented jobs, including caregivers for elder and in-house nurses, which is dominated by female migration. Although the majority of temporary labour migrants are generally men, the number of women migrants has been increasing in the past decade. A large number of women migrants remain statistically invisible as some countries do not publish sex-disaggregated data of migrant outflows (Rajan 2012: 33). Female migrants were mainly deployed in domestic work and caregivers and are thus made to stay along with the employers' residence. Sasikumar and Hussain (2008) in their working paper on *Managing international labour migration from India* state that in 2005, female migrants constituted about half of the total migrant stock (49.6%) of all international migrants, up from about 47 per cent in 1960. However, in developing countries, and especially in the GCC countries, they are particularly underrepresented. In fact, recent estimates reveal that females constitute barely 29 per cent of the total migrant stock in the GCC countries (Sasikumar and Hussain 2008: 3).

The major reasons are both on the demand and supply side. There is increasing demand for female-dominated jobs such as domestic work, caregivers, nannies and health care worker from the GCC countries. On the other hand, increased unemployment of men in many countries of origin combined with job opportunities for women abroad motivated many women to migrate. Research has also shown that women more than men opt for migration to escape from unwanted marriages, abusive relationships or rigid social systems. Break-up of families is sometimes not the consequence, but can result in migration (Rajan 2012: 34).

Thus, migration of Indian labours to the GCC countries is predominantly voluntary migration by the pull factors in the destination apart from the push factors from the country of origin. The migration network established by the recruiting agents operating in the destination countries and in the origin country along with those migrants who are already employed in Gulf acts as a facilitator in aiding the Indians to seek employment in Gulf. Those who are migrating to the ECR[1] countries has to get emigration clearance from the Office of the Protector General of Emigrants, Ministry of Overseas Indian Affairs, Government of India, before migrating. Section 22 of the Emigration Act, 1983, provides that no citizen shall emigrate unless he/she obtains clearance from the protector of emigrants.[2] For female migrants who migrate to ECR countries should have attained the age of 30 years to get the clearance from the Office of Protector of Emigrants and compulsory attestation of employment document is mandatory. These measures are taken by the Government of India to protect the migrants where the labour laws of the destination countries do not protect the foreign workers.

Human Trafficking in the Persian Gulf Region

Most of the Arab countries, including the GCC[3]—Gulf Cooperation Council countries—are infamous for violation of Human Rights and Trafficking in persons. Trafficking in persons is considered to be the fastest growing and third largest criminal industry in the world, after drugs and arms trafficking. The Middle East accounts for more than 10 per cent of the world's total migrants and the oil-rich countries of the Arab Gulf host the highest concentration of migrant workers in the world (Giuseppe 2005: 268). The International Organization for Migration (IOM) estimates that 14 million international migrants and 6 million refugees are currently in the Gulf region, and the Kingdom of Saudi Arabia hosts the largest foreign population in the region, an estimated 6.2 million people.

Although the Gulf states have the highest population of migrant workers in the world, certainly not all of them are victims of human trafficking. Migrants who come through unregistered recruiting agents and illegal means fall prey to the traffickers. Not all migrants coming for jobs are being trafficked, those who come for domestic work, camel shepherd and caregivers are more vulnerable for being trafficked. One of the main forces contributing to the growth of human trafficking in the Middle East is foreign migration (Doe 2008: 3). The most common problem related to migrant workers in the Middle East is the abuse of domestic workers engaged in menial work (Doe 2008: 4)

With respect to India, though the migration is voluntary towards Gulf region, the condition of work in the destination is very harsh and they were put into involuntary servitude leaving them behind with no option but to succumb to it. Currently, labour exploitation is the largest human trafficking concern in the Gulf region, but trafficking for the purpose of the domestic work and sex trade is a phenomenon that has grown in the last decades. Traffickers often lure young women with promises of better paying jobs or higher education in the destination country. There are some young impoverished women who are attracted to the sex industry because it appears to offer quick and easy money. However, they soon find themselves in slave-like situations (Doe 2008: 5).

Human Trafficking

Though the term 'trafficking' was used as early at the end of the nineteenth century, since then there has been persistent confusion about the exact meaning of trafficking, that is, which practices should be defined as trafficking or which has to be combated. This lack of clarity has been reflected in various, sometimes contradictory concepts and definitions, which have been used in national legislation and international instruments. The different elements of human rights violations that occur during the process of trafficking are addressed in numerous international treaties. Particularly relevant are the International Covenant on Civil and Political Rights (ICCPR, 1966), the International Covenant on Economic, Social and Cultural Rights (ICESCR, 1966), the Slavery Convention (1926), the Supplementary Convention on the Abolition of Slavery, the Slave Trade, and Institutions and Practices Similar to Slavery (1956), the ILO Forced Labour Conventions 29 and 105, the Convention on the Protection of All Migrant Workers and their Families and the Convention on the Elimination of All Forms of Discrimination Against Women (1979).

The most recent and comprehensive international treaty that focuses specifically on trafficking is the United Nations Protocol to Prevent, Suppress and Punish Trafficking in Persons, Especially Women and Children,[4] supplementing the United Nations Convention against Transnational Organized Crime (2000). The 'Trafficking Protocol' (or 'Palermo Protocol') is one of the two protocols attached to the organized crime convention. The other focuses on smuggling in persons. Separating these two protocols is important because it reflects the difference between smuggling and trafficking. Article 3 of the above-mentioned Palermo Protocol defines trafficking in persons as follows:

- 'Trafficking in persons' shall mean the recruitment, transportation, transfer, harbouring or receipt of persons, by means of the threat or use of force or other forms of coercion, of abduction, of fraud, of deception, of the abuse of power or of a position of vulnerability or of the giving or receiving of payments or benefits to achieve the consent of a person having control over another person, for the purpose of exploitation. Exploitation shall include, at a minimum, the exploitation of the prostitution of others or other forms of sexual exploitation, forced labour or services, slavery or practices similar to slavery, servitude or the removal of organs;

- The consent of a victim of trafficking in persons to the intended exploitation set forth in subparagraph (a) of this practice shall be irrelevant where any of the means set forth in subparagraph (a) have been used;
- The recruitment, transportation, transfer, harbouring or receipt of a child for the purpose of exploitation shall be considered 'trafficking in persons' even if this does not involve any of the means set forth in subparagraph (a) of this article;
- 'Child' shall mean any person less than 18 years of age.

The League of Nations and the United Nations have made a distinction between slavery and forced or compulsory labour, and the International Labour Organization (ILO) was given principal responsibility for the abolition of the latter (Weissbrodt and Anti-Slavery International 2002). The ILO Forced Labour Convention No. 29 (1930) defines forced labour as 'all work or service, which is extracted from any person under the menace of any penalty and for which the said person has not offered himself voluntarily'. The existence of an element of coercion is a useful indicator of forced labour. The following list of indicators can be used for identifying forced labour:[5]

- Threats or actual physical harm to the worker.
- Restriction of movement and confinement to the workplace or to a limited area.
- Debt bondage: where the person works to pay off a debt or loan, and is not paid for his or her services. The employer may provide food and accommodation at such inflated prices that the worker cannot escape the debt.
- Withholding of wages or excessive wage reductions that violate previously made agreements.
- Retention of passports and identity documents, so that the worker cannot leave or prove his/her identity and/or status.
- Threat of denunciation to the authorities where the worker has an irregular immigration status.

These practices impose a degree of restriction on an individual's freedom, which is often achieved through violent means.

Forms of Human Trafficking in the Gulf

Forms of human trafficking in the Gulf countries mainly include domestic servitude, slavery and forced labour, child trafficking for camel jockeys and sex trafficking and *Misyar*[6] marriages. The tragic phenomena of forced labour and working for very low wages in poor working and living conditions are widely prevalent in the GCC countries among the migrant workers. Most of the Gulf country's laws and cultures do not recognize certain forms of human trafficking as being, in fact, trafficking, as slavery and *Misyar* marriages are legal in *Sharia* laws. Because of this victims of trafficking are often not protected or brought in to media instead, victims of human trafficking are often punished because they are viewed as illegal immigrants. First, documentation and passports are stripped from them before they enter a debt bondage supposedly incurred from transportation fees. Then, women are forced to 'repay' their loans through prostitution. Once trafficked into the sex industry, they are controlled by traffickers through physical and psychological means (Doe 2008). The most seriously affected among them are three categories: female domestic workers and entertainers, trafficked persons and irregular migrant workers. These categories may not be always mutually exclusive since some of the first two may also be in irregular status (Wickramasekera 2002: 17).

> The isolation of domestic workers, most of them women, who are as a rule excluded from national labour laws, is conducive to serious violations of human rights. The conditions of domestic workers often can be comparable to slavery: unduly long working hours, poor remuneration, no access to social security, inadequate food and isolation because they are afraid of the authorities and often do not speak the local language. As with trafficking, they are lured by the empty promises of agencies that are well organized and operate worldwide. (CHR [UN Commission on Human Rights] 2000)

There is increased trafficking of women and children across borders, often for commercial sex and other exploitative and abusive purposes. Organized gangs worldwide are believed to traffic an estimated 4 million people every year as 'human cargo', yielding around US$5 billion to US$7 billion in annual earnings (Wickramasekera 2002: 18).

Because of the seemingly voluntary nature of migrant labour, it is an unfortunate reality that many of these women effectively enslave themselves abroad in hopes of improving their economic situation at home. Once the choice has been made and the contract signed, and leave the country to the destination, all future choices are restricted or non-existent. This deception, combined with the contract system, limits the mobility of the migrant domestic worker and leaves her at the mercy of employers who may also beat or sexually assault her. Because many of these migrants incur substantial debts to emigrate, it is common for women to return to the Gulf or stay back in Gulf after their contract expires, thus continuing the sequence of exploitations and contract slavery. In comparison with other forms of human trafficking, the involuntary servitude of migrant domestic workers is difficult to eradicate because it is so deeply embedded in the global markets of the labour-sending and labour-receiving countries. The women who migrate to the UAE and Saudi Arabia do so voluntarily, submitting themselves to their sponsors with the hope of bettering both themselves and their families.

The Vulnerability of Female Migrants

Gulf is one of the major regions that attract female migrant workers from India. Compared with the 1990s, more Indian women are now migrating to the Gulf countries looking for better work opportunities and monetary benefits. A majority of the unskilled women domestic workers from India to abroad are from Andhra Pradesh, Kerala, Tamil Nadu and Maharashtra. The main reasons for migration of women in general are lack of viable opportunities in the home country, widespread poverty, desire for a better future and a high remuneration in the destination country. At the same time, factors such as the harsh realities of family life, alcoholism of the male members of the family and oppressive social systems seem to play a crucial role in influencing women's decision to migrate. There is demand for Indian workers of various skill sets such as housemaids and home nurses abroad, including in the Gulf countries, Malaysia, Singapore and some European nations.

Women enter domestic jobs because of a combination of push and pull factors either in their own countries or abroad. Rural poverty, devastation of the agricultural sector and economic crises have pushed many women and girls into the domestic labour market (HRW 2006: 16). With few formal jobs available, and facing gender discrimination, often coupled with discrimination based on caste or class, race or ethnicity, their options for decent work are few. And, as most are from poor households, they generally have low levels of education and few marketable skills, other than their skills in keeping house and caring for others (Machado 2003: 3). Domestic work is therefore one of the few employment opportunities open to poor women.

Affordable, low paid domestic work frees up local women to work and fills the gaps in care facilities. Similarly the demand for domestic workers is strong in North America, wealthier Asian countries such as Hong Kong, Japan, Malaysia, Singapore and South Korea, and in many Arab states including the GCC countries (UNPF 2006). For the protection of women domestic workers, on the recommendations of the National Commission for Women, a ban was imposed on the grant of emigration clearance to women below the age of 30 years for all kinds of employment in any ECR country. Therefore, the Indian government has laid down a minimum age restriction of 30 years for eligibility to migrate and made it mandatory for the employment contract to be pre-attested by the Indian Mission. The employer is also required to provide a prepaid mobile phone and make a security deposit of US$2,500 with the Indian Mission. The Indian government has signed memorandum of understanding of labour with seven countries, including Jordan, the United Arab Emirates, Kuwait, Qatar, Oman, Bahrain and Malaysia, to lay down the framework for bilateral cooperation for the protection and welfare of workers.

Millions of migrant domestic workers are employed in the Gulf countries every year due to the increasing need of the demand in the households. For example, in Saudi Arabia, there are approximately 1.5 million domestic workers, primarily from Indonesia, the Philippines and Sri Lanka (HRW 2008: 2) and also a large number of domestic workers from the southern states of India mainly from Kerala, Andhra Pradesh and Tamil Nadu. Female migrants from Hyderabad to Gulf countries is very popular as most of them were Muslims and were wanted in large numbers in Saudi Arabia, Kuwait and Qatar where they were also wanted for marriages by the Arabs.

> Being heavily dependent on the services of recruitment brokers and agencies, indebtedness due to agency fees and other migration costs, a lack of information or misleading information on the working conditions in the country of employment, and immigration arrangements that bind the workers to a specific employer, all contribute to placing migrant domestic workers in situations of vulnerability to exploitation and abuse. (Martin Oelz)[7]

Despite the increasing presence of women in migration flows, especially as workers, the migration policies in both the sending and receiving countries in the South Asia—Gulf migration corridor tend to be gender stereotypical. Migration policies in the regions are often formulated placing women at the margins and reproducing existing gender stereotypes—women as victims of all sorts of violations and incapable of deciding on cross-border migration. It is recognized that domestic work remains invisible and excluded from the scope of labour legislation since it is done in the houses (not considered workplaces) of private persons (not considered employers). In consequence, migrant domestic helpers are not normally considered employees themselves and their work are undervalued. In a number of Gulf countries labour codes do not cover domestic work. In other countries, household helpers are not considered workers, and they are also not protected under any other national legislation. Ironically, it is precisely because domestic workers are employed within the 'private sphere' that there is resistance to recognizing and regulating the domestic work relationship.

Vulnerable Working and Living Conditions of Indian Migrant Domestic Workers

Unfortunately, migrant domestic women workers from India to Gulf countries encounter wide range of human right abuses in the workplace, including extremely long hours of work without overtime pay; no rest days; incomplete and irregular payment of wages; psychological, physical and sexual abuse; poor living conditions; restrictions on their freedom of movement and ability to practice their religion; and, in some cases, trafficking into situations of forced labour and even death while trying to escape. Those who do manage to escape had no access to legal services and redress; many become irregular and face deportation when they refuse to go back to their employers, as per the sponsorship system. The total number of Indian emigrant workers is estimated as more than 6 million (42%) of the Asian emigrant workers in the Gulf. Of the Indian workers, 1.22 lakh (21%) were female workers, which is quite a large number.

Long Working Hours

Lacking documentation and in a foreign country, migrant domestic workers find themselves under the charge of their female employer. Because Middle Eastern households often consist of extended families,

work can be arduous. It frequently includes tasks such as cleaning, washing, cooking, tailoring and taking care of children and the aged. Working hours are long, between 11 and 20 hours a day, with the maid subject to work both day and night at the whim of her employers. Many domestic workers toil between 14 and 18 hours a day with rare moments of rest. In addition to the long hours worked by domestic workers during the day, many are 'on-call' around the clock, for example, to feed or care for infants who wake up during the night.

Wage Exploitation

As the domestic workers are at the mercy of their employers, their wage and other remunerations are also at the disposal of the employer. As the employer pays a huge amount for recruiting domestic workers to the recruiting agent and other fees required, including the visa fee and airfare, they generally charge this amount from the domestic workers itself. So for more than 4 to 5 months they are literally not paid and kept in captivity as there is a clause to keep them till 3 months to ensure they are fit to take up the job or else they can be fired. Domestic workers are typically grossly underpaid for the long hours they work, often making far below the minimum wage. One of the most common complaints by domestic workers across countries is about unpaid wages. In some countries, employers commonly withhold wages from domestic workers before religious feasts or annual leave to ensure that they will return.

Physical and Psychological Abuse

Physical violence against domestic workers ranges from slapping to severe beatings, using implements such as shoes, belts, sticks, electrical cords or household tools; knocking heads against walls and burning skin with irons or chemicals and scalding. In some cases, physical abuse is so severe that it has led to paralysis, blindness and death. Many domestic workers face physical violence by their employer in response to requests for salaries or for mistakes, minor accidents and minor infractions such as responding slowly to an order. Verbal abuse—including harsh insults, threats and belittlement—is most common. Workers report that their employees use derogatory names, shout at them, threaten to withhold pay, send the worker back home or report the worker to labour agents, the police or immigration officials. Such treatment reinforces the employer's domination and

control over domestic workers, making them less likely to resist or seek redress for abusive employment conditions.

Sexual Abuse

Isolation and lack of privacy place make domestic workers at risk of sexual harassment and assault, including propositions, groping, threats of rape, rape and repeated rape. In most cases, the victims endured the abuse because they felt unable to escape, felt financial pressure to remain in their jobs or were under threat of greater harm if they did report. Workers who denounced their victimizers were often disbelieved or blamed for the abuse, and often fired from their jobs. In countries such as Saudi Arabia and Kuwait, domestic workers were frightened to report sexual violence because of the risk that they may be prosecuted and convicted for adultery and fornication. It is the male employers who abuses the domestic workers in the wee hours and threaten them not to disclose to the female head. But since the wives could not do anything about the behaviour of their husbands, they ill-treat and beat the maids.

Living Conditions and Food Deprivation

Many domestic workers are provided substandard, unhealthy and unsafe sleeping quarters with no regard for their dignity, privacy or personal security. Domestic workers are being forced to sleep in store-rooms; laundry rooms; closets and common living areas such as the living room, kitchen, hallways and staircases. The safety of domestic workers is often put at risk because they do not have a lock on their door, must share a room with adult males or are forced to sleep in open living areas, leaving them vulnerable to sexual harassment and assault. A common form of mistreatment that serves to reinforce the inferiority of domestic workers' status in the household is the withholding of food or providing poor quality or rotten food. In some cases, domestic workers are literally starved and forced to steal food, or rely on neighbours or others for sustenance. Some domestic workers who were interviewed were only given rice or bread to eat, and lost significant amounts of weight while working as domestic workers.

Forced Labour

In some cases, the circumstances of domestic workers constitute forced labour, with migrant workers and child domestic workers at

particular risk of becoming trapped in forced labour. Migrant domestic workers, who had been locked in their employer's house or ordered not to leave, are stripped of their passports and work permits, denied their full wages and confronted with inflated agency fees for transferring employment. Some were under direct or indirect threat from employers or labour agents of being trafficked into forced prostitution, charged substantial fines if they did not finish their contracts or being abandoned far from their homes. Some workers who migrate abroad for domestic work find that deduction of 90–100 per cent of their salary are withheld to cover recruitment and placement fees.

Depending on the country, migrant domestic workers may work for 3–10 months without ever receiving the wage. Workers who are unable to pay such large fees upfront often have no choice but to turn over their first several months of pay to cover the debt. Illegal labour recruiters may also extort large sums of money from prospective workers in addition to salary deductions. Some agencies subject women and girls to months of pre-departure abuses in overcrowded training centres. Women are told they will undergo training for a month or two, but instead, spend months in prison-like conditions, with inadequate food and water, and verbal and physical abuse.

Kafala or Sponsorship System

In all the GCC countries, migrant domestic workers must obtain an *iqama*, a residency permit that allows them to work, through a legal resident or national of the Gulf country, who then becomes their *kafeel*, or sponsor. The *kafala* or sponsorship system is the legal foundation that binds a migrant domestic worker to one *kafeel*. The *kafeel* has the power to alter the terms of the employment contract; transfer the *kafala* to another employer without the worker's consent; repatriate the worker without prior notice; and ban the worker from re-entering the country, among other things. Gulf nationals can also make a living out of trading *kafalas*, or the workers' legal right to work. Some do so by transferring *kafalas* to eligible buyers at a profit of US$ 800–1900. Others make use of legally registered, non-existent businesses to sponsor large numbers of migrant domestic workers. The latter are then allowed to work for an employer of their choice—as drivers, gardeners or cooks—as long as they pay their *kafeel* an agreed upon monthly fee. Ironically, this empowers the workers by increasing their negotiating power with their future employers, who in turn save money by not paying the cost of the *kafala* and related fees (Bsheer 2010).

Misyar Marriage

A form of trafficking particular to the Gulf countries is temporary marriage, also known as *misyar* in Sunni Islam and *mut'ah* in Shi'a Islam. *Mut'ah* marriages are contracted for a specified period of time, ranging anywhere from a few hours to a few months. *Misyar* marriages are not considered Islamic if they are temporary, but most of them end in divorces after the husbands' holidays end. According to media investigations, wealthy Gulf nationals (particularly those from Saudi Arabia) often marry young women from poorer Islamic countries such as Egypt or Islamic societies in Asian countries such as India. A dowry is paid to the family and broker, which serves as the payment for the young woman. Whether practiced under Sunni or Shiite law, non-binding marriages take advantage of women's economic vulnerability. After finding themselves quickly divorced, the disgraced women are forced into menial unpaid jobs, married to someone else by proxy or cycled back into prostitution (Doe 2008: 5).

Legislative Framework: Combating Human Trafficking

Human trafficking is a crime against humanity. Because of the globalization and its spill over of transborder migration, the cases filed under trafficking—sexual exploitation and forced labour—are ever increasing. The international organizations and countries of origin, transit and destination had promulgated many acts and regulations to put stricter rules on emigration policies and immigration policies and other amendments in the labour laws, the menace of trafficking is on the high rise without any check. In fact, in some cases the strict immigration policy is also the main cause for illegal recruitment and deportation of workers to fall into the human trafficking chain.

Initiative by Indian Government to Combat Human Trafficking

In 2004, the Indian government created a new ministry to manage India—Gulf migration, the Ministry of Overseas Indian Affairs (MOIA). As there exists a substantial body of research, which assess India—Gulf migration, there has been very little research to trace the processes of recruitment and the steps involved in migrating from India to the Gulf.

The Indian government has signed memorandum of understandings (MoUs) with all the GCC countries, including Saudi Arabia on the protection and welfare of migrants. Still the number of complaints registered against the employees in the Gulf seems raising. According to the human rights, the abuse of migrant workers in the Gulf, where millions are trapped in 'modern-day slavery' in construction or domestic work, needs the global attention.

A 24×7 Overseas Workers Resource Centre (OWRC) helpline has been set up. Indian Community Welfare Fund (ICWF) has been established in 42 countries, including all ECR countries for the on-site welfare of emigrants. For recruitment of 'unskilled workers' and 'housemaids' for all 17 ECR countries, compulsory attestation of employment documents by the Indian Mission is required—for all categories of workers in Yemen, Lebanon, Libya, Jordan, Sudan and Kuwait. Web-based Attestation Procedure for Overseas Indian Workers, the 6th Head of Missions Conference, envisaged the new initiatives in the emigration policy being framed by the ministry, review of various welfare measures at the mission level, strengthening grievance redressal mechanism at the mission level and follow-up on the joint working group meetings.

The age restriction for all women emigrating on ECR with overseas passports is 30 years. A comprehensive insurance scheme, namely Pravasi Bharatiya Bima Yojana (PBBY) 2006, is in place, which was further upgraded with effect from 1 April 2008. Also there is a vigorous campaign in the print and electronic media to educate potential emigrants. Indian Missions also recommend the inclusion of foreign employer in the Prior Approval Category (Black list) based on the merits of the cases. On the basis of such recommendations, the ministry places the concerned foreign employers in the Prior Approval Category. A contributory pension and life insurance fund (PLIF) needs to be set up.

Table 12.1 *Number of Complaints Relating to Female Workers Received by Indian Missions in Gulf Countries, 2007*

Name of Indian Mission	*Year (2007)*
UAE	514
Bahrain	143
Saudi Arabia	128
Qatar	206
Kuwait	764
Oman	110

Source: Rajya Sabha, Unstarred Question No. 1095, 29 November 2007.

As given in Table 12.1, Kuwait had received more complaints in relation to female workers from India with a huge number of 764, followed by UAE with 514 complaints. Most of the complaints were with regard to ill treatment by the employers and abuse, while few complaints were about non-payment of wages and confiscation of passports and forced labour.

Table 12.2 *Number of Complaints against Registered Recruiting Agents in India, 2006–2011*

Number of Complaints (Exploitation of Indian Workers Abroad) against Registered Recruiting Agents in India (2006 to 2011, up to July)					
Year	*No. of Complaints*	*Show Cause Notices Issued*	*No. of Registration Certificates Suspended/ Cancelled*	*No. of Complaints Dropped/ Resolved*	*Cases Pending and being Followed up*
2006	167	167	80	84	3
2007	98	98	22	76	0
2008	118	118	29	89	0
2009	158	158	53	63	42
2010	145	145	32	53	60
2011 (Up to July, 2011)	117	117	26	14	77

Source: Lok Sabha Starred Question No. 69, dated on 22 October 2008,
Lok Sabha Unstarred Question No. 456, dated on 28 July 2010,
Lok Sabha Unstarred Question No. 3166, dated on 29 November 2010 and
Rajya Sabha Unstarred Question No. 1309, dated on 11 August 2011.

In Table 12.2, the number of complaints against registered recruiting agents went down in the subsequent years from 167 in 2006 to 145 in 2010. Though the number of certificates suspended or cancelled is significant, the number of cases dropped is more than the cases that were resolved. This proves that though the victim support system is in action, it is very difficult to assess the penalizing of the offenders. In Table 12.3, the nature of complaints is more for cheating or forgery where women too were victims. In Table 12.4 and Table 2.5, one can notice that the number of complaints against registered agents was more than the unregistered agents in the year 2008. Also it took an opposite direction where the complaints against unregistered agents went up against the registered agents showing the dominance of illegal recruiters on raise leading to illegal recruitment and thus falling into the vicious cycle of illegal migration and human trafficking.

Table 12.3 *Complaints Received in MOIA from Indian Mission from the Gulf*

Number of Complaints Received in Ministry of Overseas Indian Affairs from Indian Missions/Workers from Gulf Countries—2007

Nature of Complaints	*No. of Complaints in 2007*
Cheating/Forgery (Illegal Recruitment/Sending for work on Visit Visa/Forged/Fake Documents/Overcharging)	16 (Women Related—1)
Job related (Non-providing of Job/Change of Nature of Job/Change of Destination)	5 (Women Related—2)
Salary Related (Non-payment of Salary/Less Salary)	8
Ill-Treatment (Ill-Treatment/Harassment/Residence Visa Problem/Repatriation)	13
Total	42

Source: Compiled from the statistics released by Rajya Sabha Unstarred Question No. 1095, dated on 29 November 2007.

Selected Statewise Number of Complaints Filed with State Police Authority Against Illegal/Unregistered Recruiting Agents in India (2002–2004)

State	*2002*	*2003*	*2004*
Mumbai	16	7	8
Gujarat	—	—	1
Goa	—	3	—
Kerala	9	11	6
Andhra Pradesh	11	1	2
Tamil Nadu	5	4	7
Chandigarh	1	—	—
Punjab	2	—	2
Haryana	1	—	3
Jammu & Kashmir	—	—	1
West Bengal	2	1	4
India	47	27	34

Source: Rajya Sabha Unstarred Question No. 4577, dated on 5 May 2005.

Year: Period of fiscal year in India is April to March, for example, year shown as 1990–1991 relates to April 1990–March 1991.

The process of recruitment as outlined by the Ministry of Overseas Indian Affairs is that an Indian citizen has to go through a recruitment agent to work in the Gulf. Recruitment agents are brokers mostly residing in India, who conduct the process of emigration from India to the Gulf. By law, they are required to be registered with the ministry. Employers based in the Gulf develop working relationships with recruitment agencies in India, and the agencies provide qualified job candidates to the employers. When Gulf employers need labour, they first send an official letter to the recruitment agency then they work with them to hire Indian workers. The recruitment agent finds qualified candidates to meet employers' demands. The agent helps candidates in obtaining approval from the Indian government for the candidate to migrate. Indian government itself inhibits women younger than 30 years to leave the country in search of domestic labour, but this move has actually increased the number of women going abroad illegally. These agents actually work in collaboration with the Government of India. But there are many illegal agents who are not registered. They actually misguide the people, especially women. This leads to their victimization in the Gulf. There are no labour laws for the domestic workers in the Gulf. 'Implementation of minimum wages for Indian workers is not going to happen any time soon as it requires the agreement of all parties involved, said Minister of Overseas Indian Affairs'. The Government of India has to intervene in this situation so as to minimize the exploitation and abuse of women in the Gulf. There should be regular check on the recruitment agents in India every year to avoid this corruption. The Government of India should provide strict laws on the emigration and try to restrict women migration for domestic labour in the Gulf.

Table 12.4 *Complaints against Registered and Unregistered Recruiting Agents*

Year	*No. of Complaints*	*Show Cause Notice*	*No. of Registration Certificate suspended/cancelled*	*No. of Complaints/Dropped/Resolved*	*Cases Pending and Followed Up*
2008	118	118	29	89	0
2009	158	158	51	33	74
2010 (up to) 30.9.10)	78	78	18	6	54

Source: Rajya Sabha, Unstarred Question No. 393, 11 November 2010, Annexure I.

Table 12.5 *Complaints Received against Unregistered Recruiting Agents and Action Taken Thereof*

Year	No. of Complaints	Prosecution Sanction Issued	Case Referred to State Government/POE for Action
2008	93	56	37
2009	136	14	136
2010	166	10	166

Source: Rajya Sabha, Unstarred Question No. 393 11 November 2010, Annexure I, and Lok Sabha, Unstarred Question, NO.459, 23 February 2011.

Initiatives by the Gulf Countries to Combat Human Trafficking

The initiatives taken by the GCC countries to combat human trafficking in recent decades are inadequate in many ways. The Saudi Arabian government in July 2008 announced that it was considering an end to the *kafala* sponsorship system, which requires migrant workers to have a local sponsor to obtain a work permit. Migrants must obtain the employer's permission to change jobs or leave the country. Under one proposal, the Saudi government will establish agencies to recruit and manage foreign workers. But the issue of the exit visa provided by the employer, which is mandatory to leave the country, puts those who escape from the clutches of erring employers and traffickers in a difficult situation. In an attempt to curb criticism, Saudi Arabia campaigned successfully to join the UN Commission on Human Rights in May 2000. In the same year, it also highly publicized its signatory status to the Convention on the Elimination of All Forms of Discrimination against Women (CEDAW). Upon signing CEDAW, however, it placed significant reservations on the convention by appealing to respect Islamic law. It stated, 'In case of contradiction between any term of the Convention and the norms of Islamic law, the Kingdom is not under obligation to observe the contradictory terms of the Convention'.

By asserting that Islamic norms could override CEDAW, the Saudis showed that the ratification was merely ceremonial. That same year, Saudi Arabia sought membership in the World Trade Organization (WTO). By signing CEDAW, it attempted to pose as a legitimate international player.

Kuwait's Labour Ministry announced that it was also considering an end to the sponsorship system. The Kuwaiti government sets a minimum wage of 40 dinars ($150) a month for migrants who clean offices, schools and hospitals. The Kuwait government said it may introduce a 40 dinars ($150) monthly minimum wage, at least for workers employed by government agencies, and stop recruiting low-skill workers from countries such as India, where they are subject to excessive fees.

Bahrain, which has 51 per cent citizens and 49 per cent foreigners among its 1million residents, provides migrant workers with more labour rights than most other Gulf states. The 5,00,000 foreigners include 3,00,000 Indians. Bahrain is considering extending labour rights to domestic helpers, which would make it the first Gulf country to explicitly guarantee their rights. Families seeking foreign domestic helpers must pay a fee of BD30 for a 2-year permit, but once the foreigner arrives, she is considered part of the family where she works and is not covered by labour laws. Advocates want domestic helpers included under labour laws.

In November 2006, the UAE government adopted a new Federal Law 51 providing strict enforcement provisions and penalties for convicted traffickers. The following year, the UAE National Committee to Combat Human Trafficking was formed. The committee coordinates antitrafficking efforts at all levels in the seven Emirates of the federation. At a United Nations forum, then US Ambassador Mark Lagon noted that the UAE is 'the first government in the Gulf to enact a comprehensive anti-trafficking law'. The UAE's commitments are in accordance with the International Convention on the Elimination of all Forms of Racial Discrimination, the Convention on the Elimination of All Forms of Discrimination against Women and the Convention on the Rights of the Child. In addition, the UAE ratified the UN Protocol to Prevent, Suppress and Punish Trafficking in Persons, especially Women and Children, in 2008.

The UAE is working to increase law enforcement capacity and awareness. Steps include training and workshops for police officers and public prosecutors and developing mechanisms to monitor and track human rights abuses. In addition, the UAE has held several training sessions with various law enforcement departments and ministries, focusing on the prevention of human trafficking, security and the enforcement of laws. Twenty human-trafficking-related cases were registered in 2008, which was double the number from the previous year. Simultaneously, the number of prosecutions and the severity of punishments prescribed by the UAE courts also increased significantly. There were six convictions in 2008, compared with five in

2007. In 2007, jail terms for those convictions ranged from 3 to 10 years, while in 2008 two people received life sentence for their crimes. In addition, a new visa regime aimed at curbing illegal recruitments came into effect in July 2008.

Human trafficking has its point of origin in the home countries of guest workers, and the UAE has signed agreements with several labour-exporting countries to regulate the flow of the workforce. In order to deny unscrupulous private recruitment agencies from cheating and trafficking workers, all labour contract transactions will be processed by labour ministries or offices in the supplying countries. The UAE, India and the Philippines are collaborating on a pilot project to survey and document best practices in the management of the temporary contractual employment cycle. The project will receive expert input from the Arab Labour Organization, the International Labour Organization and the International Organization on Migration. A range of other international collaborations include a UN partnership to recreate the UAE police administration into a 'centre of excellence', exchanges with nongovernmental organizations to build knowledge and expertise, and outreach to foreign embassies in the UAE.

In March 2007, the UAE made a significant multi-year commitment to the United Nations for the establishment of the unprecedented Global Initiative to Fight Human Trafficking (UNGIFT). This forum unites many countries, multiple UN agencies, intergovernmental entities and the NGO sector under a single banner and has facilitated unprecedented cooperation by the international community in 2008. The UAE has established stringent contract standards for domestic workers, which became effective in April 2007. These standards govern working conditions, vacation, air tickets, medical care and salary, ensuring that the labour rights of domestic workers are standardized and protected across the UAE. Government agencies are required to enforce the new contract when issuing new work visas, ensuring that the standards are upheld in all individual agreements.

In January 2008, the UAE hosted a forum with Asian labour-exporting countries to address concerns surrounding overseas employment, including domestic work. This ministerial consultation was part of the Colombo Process, a regional consultation on overseas employment, and was the first meeting to be hosted by a country of destination. The 'Abu Dhabi Dialogue' included the Colombo Process countries and other GCC states, as well as an observer from Human

Rights Watch. In November 2009, Peter Sutherland, Special Representative of the UN Secretary-General on International Migration and Development, noted, 'What the UAE is doing to improve living conditions for expatriate workers is impressive'.

Initiative by International Organizations to Combat Human Trafficking

The United Nations General Assembly adopted the Protocol to Prevent, Suppress and Punish Trafficking in Persons, Especially Women and Children marked a significant milestone in international efforts to stop the trade in people. United Nations Office on Drugs and Crimes (UNODC) is the custodian of the protocol and by January 2008, 117 countries signed the protocol and 116 countries had ratified (UNODC 2000: 2). The prohibition is normally linked to the prohibition of slave trade, which is forbidden independently by the means of conveyance. The 1956 Supplementary Convention on the Abolition of Slavery (hereinafter Supplementary Convention) adds the criminalization of the act of enslaving another person or of inducing another person to give himself or a person dependent upon him into slavery or other servile status. Consequently, there is no consensual slavery under international law. There is an evident overlap between slavery and the notion of forced labour, infra, though the first notion is characterized by the concept of condition or status. Another overlap exists with the Palermo Trafficking Protocol, which encompasses trafficking for slavery purposes, as already mentioned.

Finally, the ILO Convention on the Worst Forms of Child Labour forbids child slavery. In addition to slavery, the Supplementary Convention forbids further practices similar to slavery. Forced labour is also forbidden by human rights law, and it does neither mean only low wages nor poor working conditions, nor cover situations of pure economic necessity (ILO 2003). It comprises two elements: the work or service, exacted under the menace of a penalty that is undertaken involuntarily. The penalty does not need to be a criminal sanction. The most extreme form involves physical violence or restraint, or even death threats addressed to the victim or relatives. Subtler forms can be psychological menaces, including threats to denounce the person to the police or immigration authorities, if the employment status is not legal, or denunciation to village elders, if girls are forced to prostitute themselves in distant cities. Penalties can also be financial, such as those linked to a debt, non-payment of wages, loss of wages accompanied by threats of dismissal, if workers refuse to do overtime beyond their contracts or in breach of legislation. Moreover, from the ILO perspective, an activity does not need to be recognized officially as an economic activity to fall within the ambit of forced labour. Forced labour is included among the worst forms of child labour, as defined in the ILO's Worst Forms of Child Labour Convention, 1999 (No. 182). The notion of 'position of vulnerability' in the Palermo Trafficking Protocol could provide for some guidance to assess situations deserving protection.

Conclusions

India is both labour-sending and labour-receiving country, in the context of human trafficking it falls under country of origin-transit and destination. As a labour-sending country, protection of migrant works before their departure from the home country is of more significance. Migrant working women constitute quite a large number in the Gulf, especially in the UAE, Saudi Arabia and Kuwait. Females are employed at very low wages and in the pathetic conditions. Lack of proper labour laws is basically one of the most important factors for the women's victimization. It is the prime concern for everyone, especially the Government of India to take necessary steps for their protection in the Gulf. It is also likely that women migrants will continue to encounter discrimination and exploitation at different phases of the migration cycle, in both sending and receiving countries. It is also critical to provide a provision that made it mandatory for female emigrants from India to have completed matriculation or be of 30 years of age. Though it was initiated with the objective to protect the rights of workers, anecdotal evidence indicates that the provision not only restricts the rights of women to work, but also promotes unregulated migration, where female workers end up in more vulnerable situations. Insufficient pre-departure orientation makes single women migrant workers vulnerable to exploitation and human rights abuse, as they are often duped by agents or employers. Migrants who come through unregistered recruiting agents and illegal means fall prey to the traffickers. Stringent measures are to be taken to regulate the recruiting agents and the international criminal network to be scrutinized to stop illiterate and unskilled labours falling into prey for the perpetrators. In spite of various mechanisms and convention to support the protection and safeguard of migrant labourers, migrant workers' rights are increasingly being flouted. In spite of enacting more and more new laws, with the available standards, the government must now be led to ratify them and most importantly of all they must be enforced to curb all forms of trafficking in human.

Notes

1. ECR—Emigration Check Required—countries include 18 countries listed by Indian Government to which the migration of men and women whose education is below 10th standard are required to get clearance from the Office of the Protector of Emigrants.
2. Such clearance is granted only after the Protector of Emigrants verifies the relevant employment contracts.
3. GCC—Gulf Cooperation Council—countries include Saudi Arabia, United Arab Emirates, Bahrain, Kuwait, Qatar and Oman joined together for several purposes in an association.
4. See full text of the Protocol at: http://www.unodc.org/unodc/en/human-trafficking/index.html?ref=menuside and UNGIFT: http://www.ungift.org/knowledgehub/en/about/human-trafficking.html
5. See the Special Action Programme to Combat Forced Labour, Human Trafficking and Forced Labour Exploitation—Guidance to Legislation and Law Enforcement, ILO, Geneva, 2005.
6. A form of temporary marriage, also known as *Misyar* in Sunni Islam and *mut'ah* in Shi'a Islam, contracted for a specified period of time widely practiced in Saudi Arabia and rest other GCC countries.
7. Martin Oelz, International Labour Organization's legal specialist in the Conditions of Work and Employment Programme.

References

Bsheer, Rosie. 'Kafala Politics and Domestic Labour in Saudi Arabia'. *Migrants Rights,* 22 September 2010. http://www.jadaliyya.com/pages/index/153/kafala-politics-and-domestic-labor-in-saudi-arabia (accessed on 11 January 2013).

CHR (UN Commission on Human Rights). 'Fifty-sixth session Item 14 (a) of the provisional agenda, Specific Groups and Individuals, Migrant Workers, Human rights of migrants'. Report of the Special Rapporteur, Ms. Gabriela Rodríguez Pizarro, submitted pursuant to Commission on Human Rights resolution 1999/44, E/CN.4/2000/82, 6 January (2000).

Doe, Stephanie. 'Misyar Marriage as Human Trafficking in Saudi Arabia'. *Global Tides*, 2, 1 (2008). Available at http://digitalcommons. pepperdine.edu/globaltides/vol2/iss1/1/

Giuseppe, Calundruccio. 'A Review of Recent Research on Human Trafficking in the Middle East'. *International Migration,* 43, 1–2 (2005): 268.

Human Rights Watch. *As If I Am Not Human: Abuses against Asian Domestic Workers in Saudi Arabia,* 2008. http://hrw.org/reports/2008/saudiarabia0708/

Human Rights Watch. *Swept Under the Rug: Abuses against Domestic Workers Around the World*, 2006. http://hrw.org/campaigns/women/2006/domestic_workers/index.htm

ILO. *Fundamental Rights at Work and International Labour Standards.* Geneva, (2003): 36–38.

ILO. *Special Action Programme to Combat Forced Labour, Human Trafficking and Forced Labour Exploitation—Guidance to Legislation and Law Enforcement*. Geneva, 2005.

Machado, Jose Maria Ramirez. *Domestic Work, Conditions of Work and Employment: A Legal Perspective.* ILO, Geneva, 2003. www.ilo.org/public/english/protection/condtrav/publ/7cwe.htm

Rajan, Irudaya (ed.), *Global Financial Crisis, Migration and Remittances.* New Delhi: Routledge, 2012.

Sasikumar, S.K. and Zakir Hussain. 'Managing International Labour Migration from India: Policies and Perspectives'. ILO Asia-Pacific Working Paper Series, New Delhi, 2008.

UNGIFT: http://www.ungift.org/knowledgehub/en/about/human-trafficking.html

United Nations Population Fund (UNPF). 'State of the World Population 2006, Domestic Workers Far From Home'. http://www.unfpa.org/swp/2006/moving_young_eng/introduction.html

UNODC. *United Nations Protocol to Prevent, Suppress and Punish Trafficking in Persons, Especially Women and Children*, 2000. http://www.uncjin.org/Documents/Conventions/dcatoc/final_documents_2/convention_%20traff_eng.pdf

Weissbrodt, D. and Anti-Slavery International. 'Abolishing Slavery and Its Contemporary Forms'. Working paper, Office of the United Nations High Commissioner for Human Rights, New York, 2002.

Wickramasekera, Piyasiri. 'Asian Labour migration: Issues and Challenges in an Era of Globalization'. International Migration Programme Paper No. 57, ILO, Geneva, 2002.

Zachariah, K. C, Kannan, K. P, and Rajan, S. Irudaya (eds), *Kerala's Gulf Connections: CDS Studies on International Labour Migration from Kerala State in India.* Thiruvananthapuram: Centre for Development Studies, 2002.

Index

Rajeshwar